Understanding Addiction Behaviours

Theoretical and Clinical Practice in Health and Social Care

G. Hussein Rassool

First published 2011 by
PALGRAVE MACMILLAN

Palgrave Macmillan in the UK is an imprint of Macmillan Publishers Limited, registered in England, company number 785998, of Houndmills, Basingstoke, Hampshire RG21 6XS.

Palgrave Macmillan in the US is a division of St Martin's Press LLC, 175 Fifth Avenue, New York, NY 10010.

Palgrave Macmillan is the global academic imprint of the above companies and has companies and representatives throughout the world.

Palgrave® and Macmillan® are registered trademarks in the United States, the United Kingdom, Europe and other countries.

ISBN   978–0–230–24019–3

This book is printed on paper suitable for recycling and made from fully managed and sustained forest sources. Logging, pulping and manufacturing processes are expected to conform to the environmental regulations of the country of origin.

A catalogue record for this book is available from the British Library.

A catalog record for this book is available from the Library of Congress.

10   9   8   7   6   5   4   3   2   1
20   19   18   17   16   15   14   13   12   11

Printed and bound in Great Britain by
CPI Antony Rowe , Chippenham and Eastbourne

Contents

List of Figures and Tables

Figure

Tables

Acknowledgements

I would like to thank Lynda Thompson and Kate Llewellyn at Palgrave Macmillan for their support throughout the process of writing and publication of this book.

I am also particularly grateful to Professor James P. Smith, Professor John Strang, Professor A. Hamid Ghodse, Dr. Nek Oyefeso and the Florence Nightingale Research Foundation for their guidance in my professional development. To Professor Margarita Villar-Luis, Escola De Enfermagem de Ribeirao Preto, Universidade de Sao Paulo, Brazil for our collaboration and development in publishing, teaching and research activities in addiction and mental health. I am beholden to my patients and students for teaching me about the practice of addictive behaviours. To all the brothers and sisters at Les Guibies for their friendship and support.

I would like to acknowledge the contributions my teachers who enabled me, through my own reflective practices, to follow the path.

I am thankful to my beloved parents who taught me the value of education. My special thanks also to Mariam for her unconditional support and encouragement to pursue my interests. Special thanks are due to my children Yasmin, Adam and Reshad – without their love and support I am sure that I would not have been able to achieve so much.

The author and publishers are grateful to the following publishers and organizations for granting permission to reproduce copyright material in the main body of this book: The National Center on Addiction and Substance Abuse at Columbia University (CASA) for Table 11.4, originally from Wiseman, C., Sunday, S., Halligan, P. Korn, S., Broan, C., and Halmi, K. (2003) *Food For Thought: Substance Abuse and Eating Disorders* (New York: The National Center on Addiction and Substance Abuse at Columbia University) (see: www .casacolumbia.org); The Royal College of Psychiatrists for Activity 15.1, originally from Banerjee, S., Clancy, C. and Crome, I. (2002) *Co-existing Problems of Mental Disorder and Substance Misuse (Dual Diagnosis)* (London: Royal College of Psychiatrists' Research Unit); Taylor and Francis for Table 16.1, originally from G. Hussein Rassool, *Alcohol and Drug Misuse* (Oxford: Routledge, 2009).

Every effort has been made to trace and contact all the copyright holders but if any have been inadvertently overlooked, the publishers will be pleased to make the necessary arrangements at the first opportunity.

PART
1

Addiction and Society

Introduction 1

Reflective activity 1.1

Much of our understanding of addiction and addictive behaviours is tied up in belief systems. This reflective activity focuses on the myths of addiction.

Before reading the chapter, state whether you think each statement is fact or fiction, and why.

Statements	True	False
Addiction is a disease.		
Addiction cannot be treated.		
Addicts have a personality flaw.		
Addiction to drugs can damage brain cells.		
Anyone who uses drugs or alcohol or the Internet too much or too often will become addicted.		
Alcohol and drugs cause addiction.		
Addicts who continue with their addictive activities after treatment are hopeless.		
Addicts need to reach rock bottom before they can accept help.		
It is possible to overdose on LSD or cannabis.		
It is not possible to overdose on caffeine.		
You can overdose on alcohol.		
Addiction to the Internet is not a problem.		
Treatment for addictive behaviours does not work.		
There is a high rate of relapse among addicts in treatment.		
Addiction is treated by cognitive behavioural therapy, so it must be a behavioural problem.		

We now live in an 'addictive society'; that is, most of us are exposed to a range of addictive behaviours that have an impact on individuals, families, and communities. Addiction is a universal phenomenon that extends across socio-economic, cultural, religious and ethnic boundaries. Not only have we all been exposed to an addictive society but we have also been trained into an addictive process. This addictive process is not a normal state for the human organism as it is something that we have learned (Schaef, 1989). Our constant exposure to, and the accessibility of, both addictive substances and addictive activities have created new social and cultural norms that have influenced and made people more susceptible to addictions. In a way, these addictive behaviours have enabled us to escape from reality and from the stress and strains of developed societies.

In contemporary society, the range of addictive behaviours include both pharmacological and non-pharmacological addictions or activities leading to excessive behavioural patterns. Addictive behaviour may be defined 'as any behavioural activity, substance, object or thing that has taken control of a individual's lifestyle that is causing harm to the individual and family. Individuals who have problems with excessive behaviours such as eating, drinking, drug use, gambling and sexuality present similar descriptions of the phenomenology of their disorders (Cummings et al., 1980; Orford, 1985; Marks, 1990; Ghodse, 2010).

The argument for raising the profile of addictive behaviours is challenging in the light of the fact that addiction is more likely to be the norm rather than the exception among the population. Given the extent and nature of the normalization of addictive behaviours in our society, only a minority of those addicted to pharmacological substances and activities are likely to come into contact with specialist agencies. Most of them will invariably have first come into contact with primary care services, medical and psychiatric services, social services and voluntary agencies and the criminal justice system. The need for the management and treatment of those with addictive behaviours is no longer confined to the specialist services.

Health and social care professionals may be reluctant to respond appropriately due to a lack of adequate preparation and negative attitudes towards those who have addictive problems. Various attitudinal studies have shown that many health and social care professionals have negative views towards substance misusers and are reluctant to work with them. Negative attitudes have been identified among general practitioners (Roche, Guary and Saunders, 1991); psychiatrists (Tantam et al., 1993) and nurses (Rassool, 1998a; Selleck and Redding, 1998). However, the attitudes of nurses towards substance misusers may be changing. The findings of a study by Rassool (2006, 2007) showed that undergraduate nursing students generally held positive attitudes towards those with a pharmacological addiction. There is also evidence to suggest that substance abusers are reluctant to utilize health services for drug-related or other health problems due to the negative attitudes and behaviour of staff (McLaughlin et al., 2000).

Studies support the idea that the development of a more positive and non-judgmental attitude, confidence and skills in identifying and working with substance misuse and related problems, may be partly related to the provision of education and training (Rassool, 2009). It is clear that unless health and social care education addresses the attitudes that underpin the stigmatization of addicted patients, and supports the acquisition of the necessary skills and knowledge, a significant proportion of patients will be denied appropriate response and intervention.

The need for health and social care professionals to develop their knowledge and clinical expertise in relation to addictive behaviours is beyond dispute. However, education and training in dealing with addictive behaviours has been largely patchy and limited; and has lagged behind the growth in service provision (Rassool, 2009). Despite the few 'centres of excellence' that have provided undergraduate and postgraduate courses in addictive behaviours, the overall emphasis among various levels of training remains disproportionately low compared with other chronic medical disorders (Isaacson et al., 2000; Prochaska et al., 2006). Rassool and Rawaf's (2008a) study aims to evaluate the impact of an educational programme on alcohol and drug knowledge acquisition, changes in attitude and intervention confidence skills of undergraduate nursing students. The study provides some evidence that a short intensive educational programme on alcohol and drugs can be effective in improving educational outcomes. In addition, the findings of another study (Rassool and Rawaf, 2008b), showed an improvement in the level of intervention confidence skills of undergraduate nursing students. A summary of the research studies on the educational programme showed that the duration of the educational programme ranged from two hours to five weeks. Most studies showed that educational interventions were influential in knowledge acquisition, attitude changes in the area of treatment optimism and in improving nurses' confidence skills (Rassool, 2009). There is evidence to suggest that the development of a more positive and non-judgmental attitude along with confidence and skills in identifying and working with substance misuse and related problems, may be partly related to the provision of education and training (Rassool, 2009).

The integration of addictive behaviour components in the undergraduate and postgraduate health care sciences curriculum should not be ad hoc but based upon systematic planning. The content of addictive behaviour components should be based on the local needs of the population and should be service-driven. For those developing training in educational programmes relating to addiction at a local level for continuing professional development, a training needs analysis is of paramount importance and should be part of a coherent strategy. The targeted audience for training should, in effect, be all those who come in contact with service users, including generic and specialist staff, in both hospital and community settings.

The principles of good practice in education and training and the design and delivery of training require the setting of clear aims, learning outcomes, content, teaching methodologies and evaluation (Rassool, 2009). The challenge for educators and trainers in professional education is to move away from a traditional method of course development by adopting a framework based on the learning/occupational needs and curriculum model (Rassool, 2009).

Addiction is not the sole property of one particular discipline. It is everybody's business.

In fact, these are all potential definitions of a drug. There are various essential elements of what constitutes a drug (food or chocolate is considered a drug) as the concept is heavily influenced by the socio-cultural context and purpose of its use. The therapeutic use of a drug means a pharmacological preparation used in the prevention, diagnosis and treatment of an abnormal or pathological condition whereas the non-therapeutic use of drugs commonly refers to the use of illegal or socially disapproved substances (Rassool, 1998b). A drug, in the broadest sense, is a chemical substance that has an effect on bodily systems and behaviour.

Reflective activity 1.2

For this activity, you will be required to consider your own addictive behaviour. Are you addicted to a substance or activity? The substance could be your own use of tea, coffee, chocolate, alcohol or drugs. An addictive activity might include exercise, dieting, internet addiction or gambling. In order to understand the nature and reasons behind the addictive behaviour you will need first to understand your own 'addiction'.

Tasks to do

1 List your addictions/dependencies
   (a) Substances
   (b) Activities
   (c) People/Things
2 (a) What are the reasons why you think you may be addicted?
   (b) Why do you need them?
   (c) What do they do for you?
3 (a) How would you feel if you had to give up your preferred choice of dependence?
   (b) Would it be easy or difficult?
   (c) Would you have physical or psychological withdrawal symptoms or both?

Reflective activity 1.3

What is a drug?

By ticking Yes or No, state what you think is/are the definition(s) of a drug:

Definitions	Yes	No
A substance other than food intended to affect the structure or function of the body.[1]		
A substance intended for use in the diagnosis, cure, mitigation, treatment, or prevention of disease.[1]		
A substance used as a medication or in the preparation of medication.[1]		
A substance recognized in an official pharmacopoeia or formulary.[1]		
A substance intended for use as a component of a medicine but not a device or a component, part or accessory of a device.[1]		
A substance used in dyeing or chemical operations.[1]		
A commodity that is not saleable or for which there is no demand.[1]		
Something, often an illegal substance, that causes addiction, habituation or a marked change in consciousness.[1]		
Any substance or chemical that alters the structure or functioning of a living being.[2]		
A psychoactive substance that affects the central nervous system and alters mood, perception and behaviour.[2]		

Source: 1. Encyclopædia Britannica (2007). 2. World Health Organization (1981).

This includes a wide range of prescribed drugs, illegal and socially accepted substances. However, a drug can be either therapeutic or non-therapeutic or both.

Substance use and misuse

Substance use is referred to as the ingestion of a substance that is used for therapeutic purposes or as prescribed by medical practitioners. The term 'substance misuse' may be seen as the use of a drug in a socially unacceptable way that is harmful or hazardous to the individual or others (Royal College of Psychiatrists and Royal College of Physicians, 2000). Substance misuse is the result of a psychoactive substance being consumed in a way that it was not intended for and which causes physical, social and psychological harm. It may take the form of physical or psychological dependence or be part of a wider spectrum of problematic or harmful behaviour. The generic term 'substance misuse' is often used to denote the misuse of alcohol or drugs. The World Health Organization recommends the use of the following terms:

- Unsanctioned use: A drug that is not approved by society.
- Hazardous use: A drug leading to harm or dysfunction.
- Dysfunctional use: A drug leading to impaired psychological or social functioning.
- Harmful use: A drug that is known to have caused tissue damage or psychiatric disorders.

Tolerance

Tolerance refers to the way the body usually adapts to the repeated presence of a substance. Higher quantities or doses of the psychoactive substance are required to reproduce the desired or similar behavioural effects. The drug must be taken on a regular basis and in adequate quantities for tolerance to occur. For example, amphetamines can produce considerable tolerance and strong psychological dependence with little or no physical dependence, and cocaine can produce psychological dependence without tolerance or physical dependence. Tolerance may develop rapidly in the case of LSD or slowly in the case of alcohol or opiates.

Psychological dependence

Psychological dependence can be described as a compulsion or a craving to continue to take the substance because of the need for stimulation, or because it relieves anxiety or depression. Psychological dependence is recognized as the most widespread and the most important form of dependence. This kind of dependence is not only attributed to the use of psychoactive drugs but also to food, sex, gambling, relationships or physical activities.

Physical dependence

Physical dependence is characterized by the need to take a psychoactive substance to avoid physical disturbances or withdrawal symptoms following cessation of use. The withdrawal symptoms depend on the type or category of drugs. For example, for nicotine, the physiological withdrawal symptoms may be relatively slight. In other dependence-inducing psychoactive substances such as opiates and depressants, the withdrawal experience can range from mild to severe. The withdrawal from alcohol for instance can cause hallucinations or epileptic fits and may be life-threatening. Physical withdrawal syndromes are not, however, the essence of dependence. It is possible to have dependence without withdrawal and withdrawal without dependence (Royal College of Psychiatrists, 1987).

The dependence syndrome

The original framework of the dependence syndrome referred specifically to alcohol dependence but this has been expanded to include other psychoactive substances. The dependence syndrome, derived from the disease, biological and behavioural models, has provided a common language for academics and clinicians to talk about the same phenomena. According to Edwards and Gross (1976), there are seven components of the syndrome:

- Increased tolerance to the drug.
- Repeated withdrawal symptoms.
- Compulsion to use the drug (a psychological state known as craving).
- Salience of drug-seeking behaviour (obtaining and using the drug becomes more important in the person's life).
- Relief or avoidance of withdrawal symptoms (the regular use of the drug to relieve withdrawal symptoms).
- Narrowing of the repertoire of drug taking (pattern of drinking may become an everyday activity).
- Rapid reinstatement after abstinence.

Aims and structure of the book

This book offers a basic understanding of addiction behaviour for health and social care professionals. The theme of the book, which is interwoven in all the chapters, is the multi-professional nature of the work with those with addictive

---

Reflective activity 1.4

Reflect on what you have read and test your understanding:

- What is substance use and misuse?
- What is meant by tolerance?
- What is meant by physical and psychological dependence?
- List the criteria for the dependence syndrome.

problems. The content includes a rich array of addictions and encompasses both the current theory and research which is of interest to students, and an awareness of the practice implications for professionals. This concise volume on addictive behaviours acts as an excellent resource for those who are unfamiliar with the addiction field and goes into detail about the addictive behaviours, their effects, and the assessment and intervention strategies available. The book is a synthesis of the body of knowledge, research and clinical practice within the framework of dealing with addictive behaviours.

The aims of the book are to: provide knowledge and understanding of addiction in contemporary society; provide a framework of skills-oriented approaches to assist students and practitioners in dealing with addiction; provide accessible literature on clinical issues and practice, interventions, management, education and evidence-based practice; and, encourage practitioners to reflect critically on what they have read and to consider the implications for practice.

In addition, it aims to provide a framework for health and social care professionals in dealing with difficult contemporary issues in working with those with special needs and diversity. It is of relevance to students in medicine, nursing, psychology, social work and the criminal justice system and those attending postgraduate courses in addiction and mental health studies. It is also intended as a valuable resource for generic and other specialist health care professionals who are unfamiliar with this area of work and are likely to encounter individuals with addictive behaviours as part of their daily clinical practice.

The book is presented in three parts. Part One provides an introduction to addiction behaviours by focusing on the themes of addiction and society and the perspectives and theories of addiction. Part Two presents pharmacological and non-pharmacological addictions covering the areas of alcohol, opiates, psychostimulants, cannabis, hallucinogens, synthetic drugs, eating disorders, gambling, and internet and sexual addiction. The chapters also focus on the explanation of the addictive substance or activity, indicators of signs and symptoms, the adverse consequences and assessment and intervention strategies. Part Three examines addiction in the context of dual diagnosis, harm reduction, issues and interventions relating to special needs and diversity and service provision.

The book is practice-oriented and each chapter contains reflective activities related to the theme of the chapter. In addition, relevant chapters are supplemented by case studies.

References

Cummings, C., Gordon, J.R. and Marlatt, G.A. (1980) 'Relapse: Prevention and Prediction', in Miller, W.R. (ed.), *The Addictive Behaviours: Treatment of Alcoholism, Drug Abuse, Smoking and Obesity* (New York: Pergamon Press).

Ghodse, A.H. (2010) *Ghodse's Drugs and Addictive Behaviour: A Guide to Treatment*, 4th edn (Cambridge: Cambrige University Press).

Isaacson, J.H., Fleming, M., Kraus, M., Kahn, R. and Mundt, M. (2000) 'A National Survey of Training in Substance Use Disorders in Residency Programs', *Journal of the Study on Alcohol*, 61, 6, 912–15.

Marks, I. (1990) 'Behavioural (non-chemical) Addictions', *British Journal of Addiction*, 85, 1389–94.

McLoughlin, D. and Long, A. (1996) 'An Extended Literature Review of Health Professionals' Perceptions of Illicit Drugs and Their Clients Who Use Them', *Journal of Psychiatric and Mental Health Nursing*, 3, 5, 283–88.

Orford, J. (1985) *Excessive Appetites: A Psychological View of Addictions* (Chichester: John Wiley and Sons).

Prochaska, J.J., Fromont, S.C., Louie, A.K., Jacobs, M.H. and Hall, S.M. (2006) 'Training in Tobacco Treatments in Psychiatry: a National Survey of Psychiatry Residency Training Directors', *Academic Psychiatry*, 30, 5, 372–78.

Rassool, G.H. (1998a) 'Contemporary Issues in Addiction Nursing', in Rassool, G.H. (ed.), *Substance Use and Misuse: Nature, Context and Clinical Interventions* (Oxford: Blackwell Science).

Rassool, G.H. (1998b) *Substance Use and Misuse: Nature, Context and Clinical Interventions* (Oxford: Blackwell Science).

Rassool, G.H. (2006) 'Nursing Students' Perception of Substance Use and Misuse', *Nursing Times* 102, 44, 33–34.

Rassool, G.H. (2007) 'Some Considerations on Attitude to Addictions: Waiting for the Tide to Change', *Journal of Addictions Nursing*, 18, 2, 61–63.

Rassool, G.H. and Rawaf, S. (2008a) 'Predictors of Educational Outcomes of Undergraduate Nursing Students in Alcohol and Drug Education', *Nurse Education Today*, 28, 6, 691–701.

Rassool, G.H. and Rawaf, S. (2008b) 'Educational Intervention of Undergraduate Nursing Students' Intervention Confidence Skills with Alcohol and Drug Misusers', *Nurse Education Today*, 28, 3, 284–92.

Rassool, G.H. (2009) 'Competence in Professional Development', in Rassool, G.H., *Alcohol and Drug Misuse, A Handbook for Student and Health Professionals* (Oxford: Routledge).

Roche, A.M., Guray, C. and Saunders, J.B. (1991) 'General Practitioners' Experiences of Patients with Drug and Alcohol Problems', *British Journal of Addiction*, 86, 263–75.

Royal College of Psychiatrists (1987) *Drug Scenes. A Report on Drugs and Drug Dependence* (London: Gaskell).

Schaef, A.W. (1989) *Escape from Intimacy: the Pseudo-Relationship Addictions – Untangling the 'Love' Addictions, Sex, Romance, Relationships* (New York: Harper and Row).

Selleck, C.S. and Redding, B.A. (1998) 'Knowledge and Attitudes of Registered Nurses Towards Perinatal Substance Abuse', *Journal of Obstetric, Gynaecologic and Neonatal Nursing*, 27, 1, 70–78.

Tantam, D., Donmall, M., Webster, A. and Strang, J. (1993) 'Do General Practitioners and General Psychiatrists Want to Look After Drug Misusers? Evaluation of a Non-specialist Treatment Policy', *British Journal of General Practice*, 43, 376, 470–74.

Addiction and Society 2

Introduction

Our society has an appetite for the use and misuse of psychoactive substances and other addictive behaviours. Our addictive behaviours include the use of alcohol, drugs and chocolate, texting on mobile phones, jogging, watching soap operas on TV, gambling and internet addiction. Most of us have some addictive behaviour patterns but most of the time these do not cause us any physical or psychological harms or both. The danger arises when we have the uncontrolled, compulsive use of a substance or activity despite the physical, psychological and social harm. The use of psychoactive substances such as drugs and alcohol continues to be a major concern for society, and alcohol and drug addiction are now regarded as a public health problem. The consequences of drug and alcohol addiction do not only affect the individual user but also their families, communities and the entire society and economy. The public health problem related to alcohol and drug misuse is not confined to illicit drugs but to prescriptions of painkillers and a new class of 'happy and magic pills' that doctors are prescribing or that can be bought on the Internet.

Addictive behaviours are no longer confined to the 'stereotyped addict' but affect all level of strata within society. Addiction to drugs arises from unsuspected sources from legally prescribed medications and over-the-counter drugs to illicit drugs. Prescription drugs account for the second most commonly misused category of drugs, behind cannabis and ahead of cocaine, heroin, methamphetamine, and other drugs. Antidepressants, painkillers and sleeping tablets are medications that are regularly prescribed by General Practitioners for a wide variety of reasons and quite frequently, greatly increase the chances that they will be misused. This has a significant influence on the prevalence of iatrogenic addiction (drug addiction or abuse during medical treatment). Iatrogenic disease has become 'one of the most prevalent conditions facing modern health services, occupying countless hospital beds all over the Western world' (Butterfield, 1986).

Many individuals taking prescribed or over-the-counter medications do not know that prescription drugs are addictive and can lead to serious health problems if misused. The illicit sale of prescription drugs has increased enormously in recent years as a result of the sale of prescription drugs over the Internet without any requirement for a prescription. The increased accessibility and availability of over-the-counter drugs and prescribed drugs have significantly increased the number of misusers and addicts. The over-prescription of psychoactive substances poses a unique challenge because of the need to balance prevention, education, and law enforcement, with the need for legitimate access to prescribed controlled drugs.

In most societies, especially in the Northern hemisphere, many individuals will consume 'our favourite drug': alcohol. Others will misuse illicit psychoactive substances such as cannabis, heroin, cocaine and amphetamines. With the socially acceptable nature of alcohol and some 'soft' drugs in our society, the signs are so subtle and easily overlooked that millions of individuals do not even realize the fact that they are on a dangerously slippery slope towards addiction and dependence. Club drugs such as cocaine, ecstasy, GHB, and ketamine have become a permanent fixture in our social network. There is no way, for some individuals, to know when recreational drug and alcohol use will become a 'problem'. The progression of addiction in itself is subtle and grows with each individual's tolerance and continued use of one or multiple psychoactive substances. The nature and extent of the problem will depend upon the individual, the type of psychoactive active substance(s) and the environment. However, the consumption of alcohol or a psychoactive substance may result in the development of dependence and addiction for only a sizeable minority but have other serious consequences for others.

There are also non-pharmacological addictions such as problem or compulsive gambling, eating disorders, sexual addiction and internet addiction. Some of these activities may not be as life-threatening as pharmacological addictions or eating disorders, but they can have profound negative effects on the individual and society. In general, any compulsive behaviour carried out by an individual to the extent that it causes physical, social, or psychological harm to the individual, his/her family, or society would be considered to be an addictive behaviour for that individual.

Addiction is a very serious problem and the most disturbing of all facts associated with addiction is that it has physical, psychological, social, economic and legal consequences. However, despite the efforts in terms of legislative control, prevention, treatment and rehabilitation intervention strategies our society remains disturbingly more focused on the temporary enjoyment of psychoactive substances and other addictive behaviours.

New addictions?

There are new behaviour patterns amongst individuals that may lead to compulsive and problem-behaviours. One of the most serious problems affecting people is the rise of online gambling. Gambling can be seen as a form of escape from stress and the everyday pressures of life. However, this pastime may become an obsession and people may be unable to stop gambling online. This form of addiction can have serious personal consequences resulting in increasing debt and can spiral out of control.

Increased use of the Internet has corresponded with the increasing availability of online pornography and cybersex addiction. Cybersex addiction is a type of sexual addiction where individuals can spend hours on the net in the privacy of their own home, and engage in fantasies. An addict spends a lot of time either engaging in or planning their next cybersex encounter and this may lead to the erosion of genuine intimate relationships. If you persistently act out in ways that go against your underlying values and beliefs, yet you continue to engage in those sexual behaviours anyway, then you are likely to have a problem.

Mobile phones have become a social network tool rather than a business tool. Some people have severe problems with their phone in terms of psychological and financial relationships (James, 2007). Addiction danger signs include running huge mobile phone bills and having irrational reactions to being without a phone.

In the twentieth century, there is no lack of interest in the use of psychoactive substances and plants and new synthetic drugs. In Europe, one of the recent concerns regarding the use of psychoactive herbal mixtures is, for example, the use of 'Spice'. Spice refers to a blend of plant or herbal ingredients, including Indian Warrior and Lion's Tail (EMCDDA, 2009a). Different blends and flavours are marketed under a variety of names including: Spice silver, Spice gold, Spice diamond, Spice tropical synergy and Spice Yucatan fire. Dozens of UK-based websites and shops are still free to market and sell alternatives to illegal drugs and to ship them to any country that doesn't yet prohibit them. The United Kingdom has joined the growing number of European countries that have tackled legal highs over the past several years. One of the drugs now listed under the new legislation is BZP (benzylpiperazine) which has been replacing ecstasy and gamma-butyrolactone (GBL). There has been an increase in the availability and use of mephedrone in some European countries (EMCDDA, 2010). Mephedrone, a group of synthetic cathinone derivates, and mephedrone-containing products have been marketed by online suppliers as a legal alternative to estasy, amphetamines and cocaine (EMCDDA, 2010).

In the United States (US), there is a shift in the drug culture, in which cocaine and ecstasy are being replaced by Vicodin, a potent combination of paracetamol and dihydrocodeine, which is now the most prescribed painkiller in the US. OxyContin, a narcotic pain reliever, is also being misused as it is similar to morphine. The prescription drugs causing most concern are antidepressants

Prozac and the newcomers Efexor and Cymbalta. These are classed as 'selective serotonin and noradrenaline reuptake inhibitors', or SSNRIs. These drugs do not simply increase levels of serotonin, the brain chemical that makes us feel more sociable and relaxed. They also boost adrenaline making us more energetic and sometimes slightly manic.

When these statistics are added to those of the already staggeringly high numbers of cannabis, heroin, cocaine, and methamphetamine misusers in society, we are faced with both pharmacological and non-pharmacological aspects of addictive behaviours.

Culture and addiction

We live in a cultural worldview that promotes addiction, that is, an 'addictogenic' culture (Peele, 1985). Our culture is always seeking the next novel enjoyment and instant gratification. Alcohol and drugs have been the most common intoxicating psychoactive substance in almost all cultures for centuries. In many countries in the Northern hemispheres, alcohol use is widely accepted as a social lubricant for promoting relaxation and sociability and viewed as part of the daily diet. By contrast, in abstinence-based cultures, especially in Islamic countries, alcohol use is viewed as a dangerous and harmful substance and strictly prohibited under any circumstances. The consequences of alcohol use outweigh its benefits.

In many cultures young people are introduced to alcohol early in life as a normal part of daily living. In some cultures, other psychoactive substances are given as part of the rites de passage for young people. However, most cultures impose some informal or legal restrictions on 'underage' drinking. The legal drinking age ranges from 16 (for example, in countries including Italy, France, Belgium and Spain) to 21 (for example, Chile, Egypt, Honduras, Russia and Samoa). The majority of states in the United States (31 out of 50 states) have laws that prohibit or limit the consumption of beverage alcohol for those individuals under 21 (ICAP, 2002). In Canada, where minimum drinking age laws are legislated by each province, three provinces set the consumption age at 18 and the others at 19. Many countries, including Azerbaijan, China, Georgia and Thailand currently have no established legal limits (ICAP, 2002).

Some ethnic communities, including Chinese, Japanese, and Korean communities have a deficiency or absence of the liver enzyme, alcohol dehydrogenase (ALDH). These genetically-determined variations in the body's ability to metabolize and eliminate alcohol affect their consumption rate. The consumption of alcoholic beverages may result in vomiting, flushing, and an increased heart rate. These communities tend to consume less alcohol and are regarded as at a lower risk for alcoholism. In contrast, Native Americans generally don't become intoxicated as quickly as other races and therefore may tend to drink more, resulting in a high incidence of problem alcohol use (Thompson and MacDonald, 1989). The findings of a study of a group of Native Americans about the inherited sensitivity to alcohol found that they were not more sensitive to the effects of alcohol. Rather they were less sensitive and so had to drink more to get drunk (a sign of susceptibility to developing alcoholism) (Garcia-Andrade, Wall, and Ehlers, 1997).

Religious practices and cultural traditions also have a significant influence on drug taking and drinking practices. Many ethnic minorities have adopted the pattern of drug taking behaviours of the host countries. The Judeo-Christian traditions accept alcohol use for social purposes while Islam, Buddhism and Sikhism prohibit its consumption. However, in spite of the religious norms, social stigma and serious cultural reservations, complex patterns of alcohol use already exist within these communities (Subhra and Chauhan, 1999). In Britain, the rate of prevalence of drug misuse within the Black and minority ethnic groups, particularly among South Asians and Black Africans, is lower than that of the white population but with increasing trends (Aust and Smith, 2003). The British Crime Survey 2001/02 (Aust and Smith, 2003) also indicates higher levels of drug use among people defining themselves as mixed background compared to any other ethnic group (including white).

Research results suggest that the concept of addiction is a cultural construction (Room et al., 1996). The cross-cultural applicability of criteria for the diagnosis and assessment of substance use disorders found that the main criteria for the diagnosis of substance use disorders are not applicable to all societies due to different cultural attitudes toward substance use. There is evidence to suggest that perceptions about what behaviour is considered a problem in a particular culture should be considered as a potential indicator of addiction (Room et al., 1996).

Impact of addiction on society

Addiction to alcohol and drugs has a major economic impact on society. The UK has the highest level of dependent drug use and the second highest level of drug-related deaths in Europe. In regard to alcohol-related social harm, the UK and Finland have higher levels than some other European countries (IAS, 2009). The annual economic and social cost of drug addiction has risen to £18.8bn, according to a study by the UK Drug Policy Commission (2009). The figure is three times larger than previous estimates of the annual cost of addiction. Drug misusers cost the NHS, the state benefits system and the criminal justice system around £6.8bn a year. The social costs of drug addiction, mainly the cost to victims of crime, amount to a further £12bn annually. But research into the use of Class A drugs – mainly ecstasy, cocaine and heroin – found that 99 per cent of the costs were racked up by as few as 281,125 'problem drug users'.

More than one million people over the age of 25 and at least 400,000 people under 25 are believed to be using Class A drugs but they are costing society less than £20 a year each on average. The mean alcohol consumption is higher than our European counterparts, costing the nation some £23 billion as the outcome of alcohol harm (SJPG, 2007). In addition, there are costs related to the criminal justice system, alcohol treatment, medical costs from overdoses and alcohol-related injuries and complications, time lost from work and social welfare benefits.

The Department of Transport (2008) estimated that statistics for drink-driving casualties in 2007 show that fatalities numbered 460 in 2007, while serious injuries fell by 11 per cent from 1,970 to 1,760. It is estimated that almost a quarter of all drivers killed in road accidents, and 13 per cent of motorcyclists killed, were over the prescribed limit. About 60 per cent of all those killed in an accident in which at least one person was over the prescribed limit were over that limit themselves. About 90 per cent had a BAC (blood alcohol concentration) over 100 mg/100 ml, and 37 per cent were over 200 mg/100 ml – two and a half times the prescribed limit.

One of the fastest ways to spread the HIV virus and other blood-borne infections is through the sharing of needles and other drug paraphernalia. In this exposure category, there have been differences within the UK. Scotland experienced rapid HIV spread through injecting drug users in the early 1980s, which was not the case in the rest of the United Kingdom (Health Protection Agency, 2008). Localized epidemics on the scale of Scotland have not occurred elsewhere in the UK as a result of the introduction of harm reduction strategies. The latest statistics on AIDS and HIV in the UK (Health Protection Agency, 2009) show that injecting drug use accounts for almost a quarter of all HIV diagnoses ever made in Scotland, but only 4 per cent of those made in England. Most of the diagnoses among Scottish injecting drug users were made in the 1980s.

Gambling addiction in Britain is on the rise, fuelled by an explosion in internet betting (Wardle et al., 2007). The cost of the UK's gambling habit is estimated to be about £10 billion. The losses have been driven by the abolition of betting duty, the emergence of online betting, poker and casino sites, and a steady unwinding of regulatory constraints. But the biggest single drain comes from a new type of slot machine, offering video roulette in betting shops (Bowers, 2007). The prevalence of problem gambling in the population, based on the Diagnostic and Statistical Manual of Mental Disorders, Fourth Edition (hereafter referred to as DSM-IV) was 1.0 per cent for men and 0.2 per cent for women (0.6 per cent overall) (Wardle et al., 2007).

Prevalence and patterns of alcohol and drug misuse

The World Drug Report 2009 (UNDOC, 2009) shows that global markets for cocaine, opiates and cannabis are steady or in decline, while production and use of synthetic drugs is feared to be increasing in the developing world. UNDOC (2009) estimates that between 172 and 250 million persons used illicit drugs at least once in the past year in 2007. Those with problem drug use are estimated to number between 18 and 38 million aged from 15–64 years.

Opium cultivation in Afghanistan, (where 93 per cent of the world's opium is grown), declined in 2008. Colombia, which produces half of the world's cocaine, saw a decline in cultivation and in production. Cannabis remains the most widely cultivated and used drug around the world, although estimates are less precise. Data also shows that it is more harmful than commonly believed. The average THC content (the harmful component) of hydroponic marijuana in North America almost doubled in the past decade. In the developing world, there is concern that amphetamines, methamphetamine and ecstasy production and consumption may be growing, and has become big business. Some countries in the European Union are the main suppliers of ecstasy; Canada has become a major trafficking hub for meth and ecstasy. Use of the amphetamine captagon has sky-rocketed in the Near and Middle East (UNDOC, 2010).

There are variations in different regions in the misuse of psychoactive substances. In Africa and Oceania, more people presented for treatment due to problems with cannabis than any other drug (63 per cent in Africa; 47 per cent in Australia and New Zealand). In contrast, opiates were the primary drug addiction treated in Asia and Europe (65 per cent and 60 per cent, respectively). Cocaine was more prominent in North America (34 per cent) and South America (52 per cent) than in other regions; and amphetamine type substances (ATS) were more prominent in Asia (18 per cent), North America (18 per cent) and Oceania (20 per cent). In relation to treatment, cannabis is playing an increasingly large role in drug treatment in Europe, South America and Oceania and ATS use now comprises a greater share of drug treatment in North and South America than in the past.

It is estimated that between 11 and 21 million people worldwide inject drugs. China, the USA, the Russian Federation and Brazil are estimated to have the largest populations of injecting drug users (IDUs). Injecting drug use is responsible for an increasing proportion of HIV infections in many parts of the world, including countries in Eastern Europe and South America. It is estimated that between 0.8 and 6.6 million people who inject drugs worldwide are infected with HIV. Regions with the largest numbers and highest concentration of HIV-positive IDUs include Eastern Europe, East and South-East

Asia and Latin America. The trend in the incidence of reported HIV infection among injecting drug users appears to have remained low in most countries of the European Union after the year 2007. This may, at least partly, follow from the increased availability of prevention, treatment and harm reduction measures, including substitution treatment and needle and syringe programmes. Viral hepatitis and, in particular, infection caused by the hepatitis C virus (HCV), is more highly prevalent in injecting drug users across Europe.

In Europe, it is estimated that around 22.5 million Europeans (aged 15–64 years) are estimated to have used cannabis in the last year (EMCDDA, 2009). Stimulant drugs such as amphetamines, ecstasy and cocaine are the second most commonly consumed drug types in Europe. Some 13 million adult Europeans have tried cocaine in their lifetime, compared with around 11 million for amphetamines and 10 million for ecstasy. Lifetime prevalence of amphetamines is about 12 million (3.5 per cent of European adults). Opioids remain at the heart of Europe's drug phenomenon with an estimated number of between 1.2 and 1.5 million problem opioid users and account for more than 50 per cent of all treatment demands (EMCDDA, 2009). Drug-induced deaths accounted for 4 per cent of all deaths of Europeans aged 15–39, with opioids being found in around three quarters. In the European Union, about 650,000 opioid users received substitution treatment in 2007.

Alcohol, a favourite drug worldwide, is consumed by approximately 2 billion people and over 76 million people have alcohol-use disorders. Alcohol is the third most significant risk factor for ill health and premature death in the EU, behind tobacco and high blood pressure. Within the WHO European Region, alcohol is responsible for 6.5 per cent of all deaths (11 per cent of male deaths and 1.8 per cent of female deaths) and 11.6 per cent of all the years lost to disability or premature death (disability-adjusted life years, or DALY) (17.3 per cent for men and 4.4 per cent for women) (WHO, 2009). The worrying concerns are that the alcohol industry is rapidly infiltrating the markets of Brazil, India, China, and Russia (The Lancet, 2009).

Historical perspectives

In the 1880s few restrictions were placed on psychoactive substances such as opium, morphine, cannabis, cocaine and heroin, and these drugs were legal and fairly accessible. Patterns of drug use and misuse frequently changes as a result of political and socio-economic conditions and the same 'old' drugs may reappear in different forms or as so-called 'designer drugs'. A brief account of historical perspectives is presented below.

The word 'alcohol' comes from the Arabic language and may be derived from the *al-kuhl*, the name of an early distilled substance. In ancient Egypt, alcohol was used for pleasure, nutrition, medicine, ritual, remuneration and funerary purposes. Alcohol is used for ceremonial drinking and casual drinking and is regarded as the world's favourite social lubricant.

Amphetamine, synthesized in 1887, was marketed in the form of a benzedrine inhaler for use in the treatment of nasal congestion, mild depression, schizophrenia, alcoholism and obesity. More recently, amphetamines have also been used in the treatment of narcolepsy and hyperactivity in children. It was not until the 1960s that amphetamine misuse erupted in the UK among young people and subsequently resulted in an epidemic of injection of methamphetamine. The use of the stimulant is also widespread amongst athletes, and sportsmen and women to enhance their exploits and performances.

Cannabis Sativa (or Indian hemp), more commonly known as cannabis or marijuana was one of the first plants to be cultivated for its non food properties, and was primarily harvested for its fibre. The drug was used for its pharmacological properties in the treatment of physical and psychological problems and for religious functions. However, the widespread use of cannabis or hashish for its psychoactive properties in Europe in the 1960s seemed to occur as a result of the cultural movement of the young generation imported from the United States (Rassool, 2009).

The use of the coca leaf dates back to the Inca civilizations and their descendants and it was used for medicinal purposes, religious significance, rituals and burials and for special occasions. Freud recommended the use of cocaine as a local anaesthetic and as a treatment for drug addiction, alcoholism, depression, various neuroses, indigestion, asthma and syphilis. By the 1880s cocaine was widely available in patent medicines that could be obtained without prescription. These include Mariani's Coca Wine, a bestseller in Europe and Coca-Cola. Cocaine became very popular and was also sold in cigarettes, in nose sprays and in chewing gum (Gossop, 2000). It was not until the 1980s that cocaine became associated with a glamorous image and compounded with the idea of the 'non-addictive' nature of the drug.

Caffeine is the world's favourite and most popular psychoactive substance and was used medicinally and for religious purposes. Coffee is the major source of caffeine and other familiar psychoactive substances such as tea, cocoa and chocolate also contain caffeine. In eighteenth century England, coffee was seen as an alternative to sex and as a cure for alcohol intoxication. The drinking of coffee and the spread of coffee houses shocked public opinion at that time. According to Ghodse (1995, xi), attempts were made in different countries 'to close down the coffee houses which were seen as centres of sedition and dissent and to ban the use of coffee altogether'.

Hallucinogenic drugs were originally called 'phantastica' (Lewin, 1964), and have played an important role in cultural and religious traditions. It was the synthetic hallucinogens such as LSD (lysergic acid diethylamide) that came under scientific and medical scrutiny. Initially, LSD was primarily used as an adjunct to psychotherapy and later in the treatment of alcoholism, drug dependence, sexual problems and psychotic and neurotic disorders. By the early 1960s the drug was used for spiritual enlightenment and for mystical peak experiences. Throughout the 1980s in the UK there was a decline in the use of LSD but the drug resurfaced in the late 1980s together with other hallucinogens in the 'Rave' subculture. Ecstasy (MDMA) appeared on the scene in 1985 and was first used as an appetite suppressant.

Opium is an extract of the exudates derived from seedpods of the opium poppy. The opium plant produces lots of small black seeds called poppy seeds. Arab physicians such as Ibn-Sina (or Avicenna; 980–1037), used opium extensively, writing special treatises on its preparations and recommended the plant especially for diarrhoea and diseases of the eye. In the nineteenth century laudanum, a mixture of alcohol solution and tincture of opium, could be bought over-the-counter at any grocer's shop and for decades it was every family's favourite remedy for minor aches and pains (Royal College of Psychiatrists, 1989). Other substances with opium-based preparations such as Godfrey's Cordial, a soothing syrup of opium tincture, effective against colic; Street's Infants' Quietness; Atkinson's Infants' Preservative; and Mrs Winslow's Soothing Syrup were used for babies and young children for sedation. In effect, opium was used in preference to alcohol and in various forms for endemic conditions such as malaria.

Morphine was first isolated from opium in 1805 by a German pharmacist, Wilhelm Sertürner who named it morphium – after Morpheus, the Greek god of dreams. In the late nineteenth century, morphine became the drug of choice for high society and middle-class professionals and was believed to be effective in treating those with opium dependence. In 1874, English pharmacist C.R. Alder Wright boiled morphine and acetic acid to produce diacetylmorphine (heroin).

Tobacco is a plant that grows natively in North and South America. Tobacco was believed to be a cure-all, and was used to dress wounds, as well as providing a painkiller for toothache. In South and Central America, a complex system of religious and political rites were developed around tobacco use (Imperial Tobacco Canada, 2007). In 1847, the famous British retailer Phillip Morris was established, selling hand rolled Turkish cigarettes. During the Crimean War (1854–1856) and the two World Wars, soldiers were offered cigarettes to overcome the misery of food deprivations and were included in a soldier's rations. During the 1950s, important epidemiological studies provided the first powerful links between smoking and lung cancer. But it was not until 1971 that tobacco manufacturers in the UK voluntarily put health warnings on cigarette packs. During the 80s and 90s, the tobacco industry started marketing heavily in developing countries in Asia and Africa.

Policy initiatives and strategies

The United Kingdom remains at the top of the European ladder with the highest level of problem drug use and recreational drug use in spite of the long-standing political prominence of the problem, coherent strategies and substantial investment (UKDCP, 2007). However, the international evidence suggests that drug policy appears to have a very limited impact on the overall level of drug use as this is more influenced by wider social, economic and cultural factors. The government has successfully increased the number of dependent drug users entering treatment. Research suggests that this will have led to substantial reductions in drug use, crime and health problems at the individual level (UKDCP, 2007).

According to The Joseph Rowntree Foundation (2009), the 'social evil' that poses the greatest threat to British society in the twenty-first century is drug misuse. Drug misuse is seen as 'very damaging' to society because of the connection between drug misuse, antisocial behaviour and crime. However, efforts to tackle the problem through treatment and rehabilitation may be hampered by negative attitudes towards drug users. Drug and alcohol misuse was also described as a consequence of family breakdown, weak communities, child abuse, domestic violence, poverty, stress, unemployment and lack of opportunities or education. Since the 1990s, the UK government has responded to high-profile alcohol and drug problems with a comprehensive demand reduction strategy in dealing with this public health problem. The Government's wider national drugs strategy sets out a harm reduction approach aimed at reducing the number of drug-related deaths and blood-borne virus infections.

The models of care for the treatment of adult drug misusers (MoCDM) (NTA, 2002) sets out a national framework, in England, to meet the needs of diverse local populations and to improve the quality and effectiveness of drug treatment. The Update 2006 (NTA, 2006) incorporates the new strategy to improve the quality and effectiveness of drug treatment. The Model of Care for alcohol misusers (MoCAM) (Department of Health/NTA, 2006) sets out a framework for the development of structured treatment and of integrated care pathways for those who misuse alcohol.

The 2007 Clinical Guidelines (Department of Health, 2007) provide guidance on the treatment of drug misuse in the UK. The guidelines focus on drug treatment effectiveness, principles of clinical governance, essential elements of treatment provision, psychosocial components of treatment, health considerations and specific treatment situations and populations.

A ten year drug strategy (2008–2018) (Home Office, 2008) aims to restrict the supply of illegal drugs and reduce the demand for them. It focuses on protecting families and strengthening communities. The Government's wider national drugs strategy is to reduce drug-related death due to overdose and blood-borne viruses. Blood-borne virus infections can cause chronic poor health and can lead to serious disease and to premature death.

The Alcohol Harm Reduction Strategy for England (Prime Minister's Strategy Unit, 2004) is a coherent strategy that sets out the Government's aims for reducing alcohol-related harm and the costs of alcohol misuse. The strategy recognizes the need to tackle alcohol-related disorder in town and city centres, improve treatment and support for people with alcohol problems, clamp down on irresponsible promotions by the industry and provide better information to consumers about the dangers of alcohol misuse.

Classifications and diagnostic criteria

Addiction is not specially defined by the Diagnostic and Statistical Manual of Mental Disorders, (Fourth Edition) Text Revision (APA, 2000), which is the current official text on which diagnoses are based. Addictive behaviours are dispersed throughout the manual. It would be valuable to have a special category of addictive behaviours not necessarily to draw attention to a real problem which is not being addressed but in terms of the value in defining a group of disorders, thus enabling proper diagnosis and the delivery of intervention strategies. Substance abuse, according to DSM-IV (APA, 2000), is the maladaptive pattern of use not meeting the criteria for dependence that has persisted for at least one month or has occurred repeatedly over a long period of time. Dependence, according to DSM-IV (APA, 2000), requires that three out of seven criteria occur at any time in the same 12 month period.

In 2010 or later, there will be a new release of a major revision of the DSM (i.e. DSM-V). It is proposed that a new diagnostic category will include both substance use disorders and non-pharmacological addictions. Gambling disorders have been moved into this category and there are other addiction-like behavioural disorders such as 'internet addiction' that will be considered as potential additions to this category as research data accumulates. The work group on DSM-V has proposed to tentatively re-title the category, Addiction and Related Disorders. So far, there is the inclusion of a binge eating disorder and the combination of the two categories of substance abuse and dependence.

Conclusions

Society has learned to coexist with drugs and alcohol. However, the strategies of demand and supply reduction have consolidated some gain in the proliferation of psychoactive substances. In 2009, there are signs of overall stability in the production, trafficking or consumption of cocaine, heroin, cannabis and amphetamines. Whether, a 'drug-free world', which the United Nations describes as a realistic goal, is attainable remains to be seen. Addiction to alcohol and drugs is a global public health problem that is associated with health problems, poverty, violence, criminal behaviour and social exclusion.

The UK Drug Policy Commission (2009) stressed the need to focus on drug harms not just drug arrests. The Commission suggested that enforcement agencies have an opportunity to reduce the damage drugs inflict on communities. For instance by: cracking down on particularly harmful behaviours, such as gun violence, sexual exploitation or use of children as lookouts or couriers; 'closing' open (flagrant) markets that can erode community confidence; pushing markets out from particularly damaging places e.g. residential areas; and ensuring addicted users and dealers get treatment and support. It is envisaged that a comprehensive response to addiction would include efforts to stop or reduce production and trafficking of illicit drugs (supply reduction), combined with prevention of drug use and treatment and harm reduction.

Summary of key points

- Our society has an appetite for the use and misuse of psychoactive substances and other addictive behaviours.
- Alcohol and drug misuse remain a global health problem
- The illicit sale of prescription drugs has increased enormously in recent years as a result of the sale of prescription drugs over the Internet without any requirement for a prescription.
- There are new behaviour patterns amongst individuals that may lead to compulsive and problem-behaviours. For example, internet addiction, cybersex, online gambling etc.
- We live in a cultural worldview that promotes addiction – that is, an 'addictogenic' culture.
- Religious practices and cultural traditions also have a significant influence on drug taking and other addictive behaviours.
- The UK has the highest level of dependent drug use and the second highest level of drug-related deaths in Europe.
- Addiction to psychoactive substances is also one of the fastest ways to spread the HIV virus and other blood-borne infections, through the sharing of needles and other drug paraphernalia.
- Gambling addiction in Britain is on the rise, fuelled by an explosion in internet betting.
- The global markets for cocaine, opiates and cannabis are steady or in decline, while production and use of synthetic drugs is feared to be increasing in the developing world.

- The United Kingdom remains at the top of the European ladder with the highest level of problem drug use and recreational drug use.

Reflective activity 2.1

- List the pharmacological and non-pharmacological addictions.
- Briefly discuss the dangers of the over-prescription of antidepressants, painkillers and sleeping tablets.
- What is iatrogenic or therapeutic addiction?
- Briefly discuss how culture has a significant influence on our addictive behaviours.
- What is the impact of addiction on society?

References

American Psychiatric Association (2000) *Diagnostic and Statistical Manual of Mental Disorders,* 4th ed, (DSM-IV) (Washington, DC: American Psychiatric Association).

Aust, R. and Smith, N. (2003) *Ethnicity and Drug Use: Key Findings from the 2001/2002 British Crime Survey* (London: Home Office).

Bowers, S. (2007) 'Cost of UK's Gambling Habit: £10bn', *The Guardian.* 29 September 2007.

Butterfield, Sir J. (1986) 'Foreword', in D'Arcy, P.F. and Griffen, J.P. (eds.), *Iatrogenic Disease,* 3rd edn (Oxford: Oxford University Press).

Department of Health (2007) *Drug Misuse and Dependence: Guidelines on Clinical Management* (London: HMSO).

Department of Transport (2008) *Road Safety Compliance Consultation.* Published on 7 August 2008, available online at http://www.dft.gov.uk/pgr/statistics/datatablespublications/accidents/, date accessed 10 November 2009.

European Monitoring Centre for Drugs and Drug Addiction (EMCDDA 2009): *The State of Drugs Problem in Europe* (Lisbon: EMCDDA) http://www.emcdda.europa.eu/index.cfm, date accessed 15 November 2009.

EMCDDA (2009a) Drugnet Europe, *Newsletter of the European Monitoring Centre for Drugs and Drug Addiction,* January–March 2009, available at www.emcdda.europa.eu.

EMCDDA (2010) Drugnet Europe, *Newsletter of the European Monitoring Centre for Drugs and Drug Addiction,* April–June 2010, available at www.emcdda.europa.eu.

Garcia-Andrade, C., Wall, T.L. and Ehlers, C.L. (1997) 'The Firewater Myth and Response to Alcohol in Mission Indians', *American Journal of Psychiatry* 154, 983–87.

Ghodse, A.H. (1995) *Drugs and Addictive Behaviour. A Guide to Treatment* (Oxford: Blackwell Science).

Gossop, M. (2000) *Living with Drugs* (Aldershot: Wildwood Publications).

Health Protection Agency Centre for Infections and Health Protection Scotland (2009) *Unpublished HIV Diagnoses Surveillance Tables 01:2009* http://www.hpa.org.uk/web/HPAweb&HPAwebStandard/HPAweb_C/1252660002826, date accessed 12 December 2009.

Home Office (2008) *Drugs: Protecting Families and Communities – 2008–2018 Strategy* (London: Home Office) http://drugs.homeoffice.gov.uk/drug-strategy/overview/, date accessed 15 October 2009.

HPA Communicable Disease Surveillance Centre (2008) (HIV and STI Department) and the Scottish Centre for Infection and Environmental Health: http:// www.hpa.org.uk/HPA, date accessed 12 December 2009.

Institute of Alcohol Studies (IAS) (2009) Alcohol Consumption and Harm in the UK and EU (Cambridgeshire: IAS) http://www.ias.org.uk/resources/fact-sheets/harm_ukeu.pdf, date accessed 15 December 2009.

International Center for Alcohol Polices (ICAP) (2002) ICAP Reports 4, *Drinking Age Limits* (Washington: International Center for Alcohol Policies). http:// www.grsproadsafety.org/themes/default/pdfs/Drinking%20Age%20Limits.pdf.

James, D. (2007) *Study Reveals Social Obsession with Mobile Phones.* Queensland University of Technology. http://www.news.qut.edu.au/cgi-bin/WebObjects/News.woa/wa/goNewsPage?newsEventID = 11364, date accessed 5 January 2010.

Joseph Rowntree Foundation (2009) *Contemporary Social Evils* (London: The Policy Press).

Lewin, L. (1964) *Phantastica-narcotic and Stimulating Drugs: Their Use and Abuse* (London: Routledge and Kegan Paul).

National Treatment Agency (NTA) (2002) *Models of Care for Adult Drug Misusers. Parts 1 and 2* (London: NTA Publications).

National Treatment Agency (2003) *Black and Minority Ethnic Communities: A Review of the Literature on Drug Use and Related Service Provision* (London: NTA Publications).

National Treatment Agency (2006) *Models of Care for Adult Drug Misusers Updated* (London: NTA Publications).

National Treatment Agency/Department of Health (2006) *Models of Care for Alcohol Misusers* (London: NTA Publications).

Peele, S. (2005) 'Combating the Addictogenic Culture', in *The Stanton Peele Addiction Website*. http://www.peele.net/lib/combating.html, date accessed 6 January 2010.

Rassool, G.H. (2009) *Alcohol and Drug Misuse. A Handbook for Student and Health Professionals* (London: Routledge).

Room, R., Janca A., Bennett, L.A., Schmidt, L. and Sartoriuos, N. (1996) 'WHO Cross-Cultural Applicability Research on Diagnosis and Assessment of Substance Use Disorders: An Overview of Methods and Selected Results', *Addiction*, 91, 22, 199–230.

Royal College of Psychiatrists (1989) *Drug Scenes. A Report on Drugs and Drug Dependence* (London: Gaskell).

Social Justice Policy Group (SJPG) (2007) *Breakthrough Britain. Ending the Costs of Social Breakdown. Volume 4, Addictions Towards Recovery* (London: SJPG).

Subhra, G. and Chauhan, V. (1999) *Developing Black Services: An Evaluation of the African, Caribbean and Asian Services* (London: Alcohol Concern).

The Lancet (2009) Editorial. *Alcohol Misuse Needs a Global Response*, 373, 9662, 433. doi:10.1016/S0140-6736(09)60146-.

The Prime Minister Strategy Unit (2004) *Alcohol Harm Reduction Strategy for England* (London: Cabinet Office). http://www.cabinetoffice.gov.uk/media/cabinetoffice/strategy/assets/caboffce%20alcoholhar.pdf, date accessed 20 December 2009.

Thompson, P.R. and MacDonald, J.L. (1989) 'Multicultural Health Education: Responding to the Challenge', *Health Promotion*. 8, 11.

UK Drug Policy Commission (2007) *An Analysis of UK Drug Policy* (London: UK Drug Policy Commission) www.ukdpc.org.uk.

UK Drug Policy Commission (2009) *Hidden Cost to Families of Britain's Drug Problem is £1.8 billion*. Press Release 26 November 2009, www.ukdpc.org.uk, date accessed 6 January 2010.

UK Drug Policy Commission (2009) *Focus on Drug Harms Not Just Drug Arrests* (London: UK Drug Policy Commission) www.ukdpc.org.uk.

UNDOC (2009) *World Drug Report 2009*. http://www.unodc.org/, date accessed 20 December 2009.

UNDOC (2010) *World Drug Report 2010*. http://www.unodc.org/documents/wdr/WDR_2010/Executive_summary.pdf, date accessed 31 January 2011.

Wardle, H., Sproston, K., Orford J., Erens, B., Griffiths, M., Constantine, R. and Pigott, S. (2007) *British Gambling Prevalence Survey 2007* (London: National Centre for Social Research).

World Health Organization (WHO) (2009) *Handbook for Action to Reduce Alcohol-related Harm* (Copenhagen: WHO).

Tobacco History (2007), http:// www.imperialtobaccocanada.com/, date accessed 24 November 2009.

Perspectives on Addiction 3

Introduction

This chapter examines the theories of addiction in an attempt to explain the reasons for the initiation into alcohol and drug misuse and the maintenance of the addictive process. The theories include moral theory, genetic theory, neuro-pharmacological theories, psychoanalytic theory, behavioural theories, social learning theory, personality theory, socio-cultural theories, and bio-psychosocial theory. No single theory should be considered to be the definitive account nor is any one theory mutually exclusive of any other. It is acknowledged that a range of physical and psychosocial 'risk factors' has to be considered. However, the reason for the initiation of using drugs may not be the same reason for continuing to misuse psychoactive substances.

Theories of addiction

The theories of addiction include moral theory, disease theory, genetic theory, neuro-pharmacological theory, psychological theory, socio-cultural theory and bio-psychosocial theory. For more comprehensive theories of addiction (see West, 2006). A summary of the theories of addiction is presented in Table 3.1.

The moral theory or model is based on the belief that using alcohol or drugs is a sign of moral weakness, bad character or sinful people. The proponents of this theory refute the biological basis for addiction and suggest that the individual has deviated from the acceptable religious and socio-cultural norms. The focus of intervention under this model is the control of behaviour through social disapproval, spiritual guidance, moral persuasion or imprisonment.

The disease theory of addiction maintains that addiction is a disease that is firmly attributable to the genetic/biological or neurochemical processes, or of some combination of the two. This theory views alcohol and drug misuse as a progressive, irreversible and incurable disorder and its primary symptom is the inability to control consumption. Abstinence is the only option. By defining alcohol or drug addiction as a physical or biological disease, the focus of

Table 3.1 Theories of addiction

Theory	Key elements
Moral	• Sign of moral weakness, bad character or having weak will. • Deviation from the acceptable religious and socio-cultural norms. • Individual is responsible for the initiation and development of addiction-related problems. • There is a biological basis for addiction. • Individual is a 'bad person' where the 'victim-blaming' approach is evident. • The focus of intervention is the control of behaviour through social disapproval, spiritual guidance, moral persuasion or imprisonment.
Disease	• Attributable to genetic/biological make up of the individual or behavioural processes, or some combination of the two. • Adoption of the sick-role. • Alcohol or drug addiction is a unique, irreversible, and progressive disease which cannot be cured. • Due to the inability of the individual to control consumption, abstinence is the only option.
Genetic / Neuro-pharmacological	• Studies on family, adoption and twins have suggested that alcohol or drug addiction is the result of genetic or induced biological abnormality of a physiological or structural nature. • The degree to which genetic factors play a role in addictive behaviour is still unclear and remains to be further investigated. Addiction may be due to increased dopamine transmission in the limbic system by different mechanisms. • The 'endogenous opioid' system is involved in the rewarding effects of other psychoactive substances. • There are other chemicals (neurotransmitters) such as serotonin, norepinephrine and gamma amino butyric acid (GABA) that may be involved in process of addiction to psychoactive substances.
Psychological	• The consumption of alcohol provides relief from the conflict generated by oral fixation, or repressed homosexuality. • The aetiology of alcohol or drug dependence is assumed to develop from sensual satisfaction (avoidance of pain or anxiety).

(Continued)

Table 3.1 Continued

Theory	Key elements
	• In behavioural theories, the use of psychoactive substances is viewed as an acquired behaviour (classical conditioning, operant conditioning) and social learning.
	• The role of positive reinforcement in the use of psychoactive substances can be explained by the fact that drugs can cause pleasurable sensations.
	• The maintenance of drug taking behaviour is the result of past associations with a drug taking environment or situation.
Socio-cultural	• From a sociological perspective, addiction is described as an individual behaviour that has a social effect.
	• The idea of alcoholism as a 'family disease' or 'family disorder'.
	• The greater the availability of alcohol or other psychoactive substances, the greater the prevalence and severity of substance use problems in society.
	• The influence of culture is a strong determinant of whether or not individuals fall prey to certain addictions.
	• Other socio-cultural factors that may have an influence on the choice of drug and alcohol use and misuse include gender, age, occupation, social class, ethno-cultural background, subcultures, alienated groups, family dysfunction and religious affiliation.
Bio-psychosocial	• There are multiple pathways to addiction and the significance of these individual pathways depends on the individual.
	• The focus is on biological and psychological processes, but social factors are also included in this model through learning, perceiving and interpreting the world around us as well as through the person's social relationships and larger cultural environment.
	• Another component may be added to the bio-psychosocial theory; that is the spiritual dimension.

intervention is on health and social care treatment instead of punitive action or imprisonment. The disease concept of addictive behaviour is incorporated in the philosophy underpinning the approaches of 'AA', 'NA' and 'GA' (Alcoholics Anonymous, Narcotics Anonymous and Gamblers Anonymous).

The genetic model puts forward a genetic predisposition to alcohol or drug addiction. Studies on family, adoption and twins have suggested that alcohol or drug addiction is the result of genetic or induced biological abnormality of a physiological or structural nature. Family studies of problem drinkers suggest that such disorders do cluster in families, especially among siblings (Merikangas et al., 1998; Bierut et al., 1998).

The neuropharmacological theories of addiction require an understanding of the pharmacological effects of drugs on the brain. Psychoactive substances have different actions on the brain based on the reward systems. The reason why individuals self-administer psychoactive substances is that these chemicals activate the reinforcement system in the brain. The focus for the neurobiological mechanism for the positive reinforcing effects of drugs of abuse has been the mesocorticolimbic dopamine system and its connections in the basal forebrain (Koob and Moal, 1997). Addictive behaviours are presented as a cycle of spiralling dysregulation of brain reward systems that progressively increases, resulting in compulsive drug use and a loss of control over the addictive behaviours. In relation to psychoactive substances such as cocaine, amphetamine, and nicotine, the facilitation of dopamine neurotransmission in the mesocorticolimbic dopamine system appears to be critical for the acute reinforcing actions of these drugs (Koob and Moal, 1997). Reinforcers have the characteristic of releasing dopamine in the nucleus accumbens. This effect can be produced by addictive drugs such as amphetamine, cocaine, opiates, nicotine, alcohol, PCP, and cannabis as well as natural reinforcers such as food, water and sexual contact (White, 1996; Di Chiara, 1995). There is a theory that the release of dopamine into the forebrain is believed to cause feelings of pleasure. However, this theory has been refuted by Garris et al. (1999). It is now believed that the release of dopamine may not be critical for reinforcement once the task is learned. Garris et al. (1999) suggest that dopamine may be a neural substrate for novelty or reward expectation rather than reward itself.

The psychoanalytic theory of addiction stems from the belief that addiction stems from fixation in relation to psychosexual development or death wishes. Addiction is also seen as stemming from unconscious death wishes as a form of 'slow suicide', the notions of conflict between a repressed idea and the defence against it and a deficient ego (Leeds and Morgenstern, 1996). In behavioural theories, behaviour is learned through the process of classical conditioning and operant conditioning. That is, the desire to use drugs may be the result of specific factors associated with the use of a particular substance. The role of positive reinforcement in the use of psychoactive substances can be explained by the fact that drugs can cause pleasurable sensations. The pleasure or in some cases fear of withdrawal reinforces the continued use of the substance. Cue exposure theory, an element of classical conditioning theory, is based on the notion that cues are important in the development and maintenance of addictive behaviour (Drummond et al., 1995).

The personality theory stresses the importance of personal traits and characteristics in the formation and maintenance of dependence. There is a commonly held misconception about the notion of the addictive personality. Those who support this notion perceive an addictive personality as having a psychological trait that predisposes particular individuals to addictions. There is a general consensus among experts that the predisposition to addiction is more accurately a combination of bio-psychosocial factors However, there is no evidence to suggest the existence of a true addictive personality. But there are a number of personality traits that have been associated with addiction.

Traits such as hyperactivity, sensation-seeking, antisocial behaviour and impulsivity have been found to be associated with substance misuse (Sher et al., 1991). In social learning theory, in order to understand the effects of alcohol or drugs, cognitive processes must be considered in relation to other factors. Addictive behaviours are formed and maintained through the process role modelling and the need to conform. Orford (1985) proposes a theory of 'Excessive Appetites' within the context of a social learning paradigm. He develops a theory of addiction and maintains that the degree of an individual's involvement with 'appetitive activities' include biological, personality, social and ecological determinants.

Socio-cultural theories include a number of sub theories such as systems theory, anomie theory, family interaction theory, anthropological theory, economic theory, gateway theory and availability theory. From a sociological perspective, addiction is described as 'an individual behaviour that has a social effect, it affects other people; it is also an individual behaviour that is controlled at the societal level' (Adrian, 2003, 3). The cultural model recognizes that the influences of cultural and religious attitudes are a defensive shield against alcohol and drug addiction. Both ethnicity and religious values have a strong influence on the nature and pattern of drug taking and drinking behaviour (Oyefeso et al., 2000).

However, other socio-cultural factors that may have an influence on the choice of drug and alcohol use and misuse include gender, age, occupation, social class, ethno-cultural background, subcultures, alienated groups, family dysfunction and religious affiliation. In the bio-psychosocial theory, genetic inheritance, physiological differences, family, community, peer or social pressure are all considered. Kumpfer et al's (1990) bio-psychosocial 'vulnerability model' includes biological factors (genetic inheritance, physiological differences), psychosocial and environmental factors (family, community, peer or social pressure). In addition, another component may be added to the bio-psychosocial theory: that is the spiritual dimension (Hammond and Rassool, 2006).

Addictive Experience: Influencing an individual's decisions

There are interrelated sets of non-pharmacological and pharmacological factors that influence an individual's decision to take a psychoactive substance and elevate the 'drug experience'. These include pharmacological factors, the personality of the individual and the context or setting (Ghodse, 1989). It is stated that 'it is necessary to see the drug-brain interaction not as a simple chemical event but as a matter of considerable complexity involving the drug, the particular person, and the messages and teachings which come from the environment and which powerfully influence the nature and meaning of the drug experience' (Royal College of Psychiatrists, 1987).

The pharmacological factors include the type of addictive substance used, the chemical properties, the drug dosage, the cost of the drug and the route of administration. In addition, the effects or actions of an addictive substance are influenced by the personal characteristics of the drug user. These characteristics include factors such as the person's biological makeup, personality, gender, age and drug tolerance (Rassool, 1998b). Health problems such as cardiovascular disease, hypertension, asthma, epilepsy, diabetes mellitus or liver disease can exacerbate the use of psychoactive substances and make them more unsafe.

The psychological state of the individual has a significant influence on the effects and dangers of alcohol and drug use. In addition, the psychological set of the individual will have an influence on how the desired effect may be experienced. In cases of depression or low mood or other affective disorders, the individuals are more liable to have disturbing experiences when using psychoactive substances. Psychological disorders such as anorexia nervosa or bulimia can also deteriorate as a result of the use of psychoactive substances. The wider social context needs also to be considered and this includes the physical environment where the drug is used, the cultural influences of the community where the drug is consumed, the laws relating to drug use and the context in which a drug is used. The factors that influence an individual's decisions to use an addictive substance and the 'addictive experience' are presented in Table 3.2.

Why do people use addictive substances?

Addictive activities and addictive substances such as cocaine or tobacco smoking cause a series of temporary changes in the nervous system that produce a feeling of 'high' resulting in a rush of euphoria or pleasure. The subjective initial experiences of taking addictive substances or involvement in addictive behaviours or activities are often pleasurable. In relation to psychoactive substances, most individuals start taking drugs not because they have any problems. Furthermore,

Table 3.2   Alcohol and drug experience: factors influencing an
individual's decisions

Pharmacological factors	Personality of the individual	Context and setting
• Type of psychoactive substance. • Chemical properties. • Mode of action. • Quantity of alcohol or drug dosage. • Route of administration. • Cost of substance.	• Person's biological makeup. • Personality. • Gender. • Age. • Drug tolerance (Rassool, 1998). • Psychological state. • Low mood. • Anxious mood. • Physical or psychological health problems. • Interpersonal skills. • Values. • Self-esteem. • Assertiveness or social competence. • Decision-making skills	• Knowledge, attitude and expectations (psychological set). • Social context. • Physical environment. • Cultural influences.

the use of addictive substances for pleasure is readily identifiable throughout history and across most cultures (Siegel, 2005).

According to Weil and Rosen (2004), the basic reason people take an addictive substance is to vary their conscious experience as changing consciousness is something people like to do. Other ways of altering consciousness include listening to music, dancing, exercising, day dreaming, jogging and religious rituals. However, for some it is a means of 'escaping reality' by taking him/her away from any and all problems in their life. Individuals may be attracted to addictive substances or activities as a form of social and recreational lubricant for similar reasons as they are to alcohol.

The environs in which people live can have a major influence on an individual's likelihood of using psychoactive substances. Alcohol and drug misuse thrive in areas of social exclusion and multiple deprivation with high unemployment, low quality housing and a lack of social and community services. In fact, having a less stressful, more privileged environment may provide a degree of protection from addiction or relapse during recovery, according to a review of the role of environment in addiction (Nader and Czoty, 2005). However, substance misuse is certainly not restricted to areas of urban deprivation. Curiosity, subset of youth culture and music, social acceptability, peer pressure, and the media can also promote addiction (Rassool, 2009).

In every culture, people 'learn' how to use drugs and the rules and regulations. That is, we learn what acceptable behaviour is and what is not. These behavioural rules and regulations are learned from our parents, friends, colleagues and the mass media. We are strongly influenced by role models and when the messages we are receiving are credible. In addition, we also learn from our own experiences when using addictive substances or through involvement in addictive activities. However, in some cases, we do not learn all the rules or customs that reduce the harm that is caused by our addiction behaviours.

A list of the reasons why people use addictive substances is presented in Table 3.3.

However, the reason for starting to use addictive substances may not be the same reason why users continue the desired behaviours and activities. Continued alcohol and drug misuse is driven more by physiological and psychological dependence rather than by rational decisions. The continuation of addictive behaviours includes a combination of factors such as dependence, chaotic use, fear of withdrawal symptoms, social exclusions, mental health problems and other psychosocial and environmental conditions. Although the initial decision to take an addictive substance is mostly voluntary, the continuing use may not be under the control of the individual. For example, brain imaging studies from drug-addicted individuals show physical changes in areas of the brain that are critical to judgment, decision-making, learning and memory, and behaviour control (Fowler et al., 2007). What is common to many alcohol and drug misusers is that they may in fact be able to stop for

Table 3.3 Why people use and continue to use addictive substances

Use addictive substances	Continue to use addictive substances
• To enjoy the experience. • To get the same experience as alcohol. • To enjoy the short-term effects. • To feel confident. • To 'break the rules'. • To be part of the subculture. • To be curious about the effects. • The drugs are easily accessible and available. • Their friends use them. • To enhance work performances. • It is part of one's home/social life. • To relieve boredom. • To alleviate pain. • To lose weight.	• To counter the unpleasant effects of prescribed medications. • To continue the habit. • To avoid unpleasant feelings. • To satisfy cravings. • To avoid withdrawal symptoms. • To counter the withdrawal effects of other drugs (use of benzodiazepines after stimulants).

short periods of time without withdrawal but could not remain abstinent. The same characteristics may be applicable to other addictive behaviours.

Patterns of substance use and misuse

The patterns of substance misuse are often described as no use, experimental, recreational and problematic users. The progression of an addiction reflects a broad spectrum and sometimes varies over a period of time. Individuals may move back and forth within this continuum, but generally they advance from no use, to use, misuse and finally to dependence. Key elements of experimental, recreational and dependent use are presented in Table 3.4. Other patterns of substance misuse include binge drinking or drug taking and chaotic use.

Table 3.4 Patterns of substance use and misuse

No Use	• In this stage there is no use of alcohol or other drugs. • People have their own reasons not to be involved, including religious beliefs, their age, criminal justice system etc.
Experimental Users	• Anyone's initial use of a drug, alcohol or tobacco smoking is experimental (Rassool, 1998). • There is no 'pattern' in the use of psychoactive substances. • The choice of the drug misused is indiscriminate. • Choice depends on factors such as availability, social marketing, and reputation of the drug, subculture, fashion and peer-group influence. • Motivating factors include curiosity, desire to share a social experience, anticipation of effects, availability and value for money (cost of drug). • Highest category of risk for infections (if injecting), medical complications or overdose due to the indiscriminate use of adulterated psychoactive substances.
Recreational Users	• The most common drugs that are used by recreational users are alcohol, caffeine, nicotine, cannabis, LSD and ecstasy. • There is a strict adherence to the pattern of use (e.g. the drug is only used at weekends and less likely to be used on consecutive days). • There is usually a preference for a particular drug (drug of choice), where the user has learnt how to use it and appreciates its effects. • Drug or alcohol use is one aspect of the user's life and tends to complement social and recreational activities.

(Continued)

Table 3.4 Continued

Dependent Users	• Problematic use of a psychoactive drug or becoming a poly-drug user (multiple drug use).
	• Tolerance is very high and there is the presence of psychological and\or physical dependence.
	• The pattern of use is more frequent and regular but less controlled.
	• The process in obtaining the drug is more important to the user than the quality of experience.
	• Injecting drugs is common, and the frequent use creates problems of intoxication, infections if sharing a needle and syringe, and other medical complications.

No use, recreational and dependent users

The phase of no use refers to total abstinence. Individuals have their own reasons not to be involved, including cultural factors, religious beliefs, their age, socialization and resilience. Experimental users can be described as those who have used drugs, legal or illicit, on a few occasions. Experimenting with psychoactive substances and other activities are usually part of the desire amongst adolescents to experiment and try new risky experiences and can be seen as a normal developmental pattern. In this phase, there is no 'pattern' in the use of psychoactive substances but the choice of the drug misused is indiscriminate or unplanned. The choice of using a psychoactive substance depends on factors such as availability, social marketing, and reputation of the drug, subculture, fashion and peer-group influence.

The prime movers of using psychoactive substances include curiosity, desire to share a social experience, anticipation of effects, availability and value for money. Experimental users, however, are in the highest category of risk for infections (if injecting), medical complications or overdose due to the indiscriminate use of adulterated psychoactive substances (Rassool, 2009). What is unclear is the likelihood of further engagement with, or disengagement from, further alcohol and drug use. That is, the transition from experimental to dependent use.

The term 'recreational' refers to a form of substance use in which pleasure and relaxation are the prime motivations and include psychoactive substances such as alcohol, caffeine, nicotine, cannabis, LSD and ecstasy. There is usually a drug of choice but there is a strict adherence to the use of drugs on certain occasions such as the weekend and drug use is less likely on consecutive days. Recreational drug use is best understood as a matter of the complex calculation of risks and benefits. Recreational users estimate the main hazards as damage to their health, or legal risks (getting caught), and the main benefits as gaining 'time-out' from stress leading to leisure and relaxation (Parker et al.,

1998). Recreational users are also considered in the highest category of risk for infections as a result of using sexual stimulants which often leads to risky sexual behaviour and increased likelihood of HIV infection.

A dependent user has made the transition from recreational to regular and problematic use of a psychoactive drug or when he or she becomes a multiple drug user. There is a high degree of tolerance and the presence of psychological and/or physical dependence. Injecting drugs is common, and the frequent use creates problems of intoxication, infections if sharing a needle and syringe, and other medical complications. Personal, social, psychological and legal problems may be present with dependent users.

Chaotic use

Chaotic use refers to the use of several psychoactive substances in an intensive way over a prolonged period of time. Chaotic use is referred to when an individual is regarded as taking a drug or drugs in a spontaneous way that tends not to follow any typical drug-using pattern. It is generally associated with problematic bouts of heavy use that may cause the user harm (Drugscope, 2010). The individual's life is circumscribed by their drug use in completely unordered and unpredictable ways. There is usually the use of different opioids as well as cocaine, amphetamines and alcohol. This is combined with other significant health issues such as HIV, liver damage and mental health problems. When drug users are homeless they are likely to increase their drug use and progress to patterns of chaotic drug misuse (Martin, 2007).

Binge drinking

Binge drinking can be regarded as a form of addictive behaviour. Binge drinkers often don't believe that they have a problem with alcohol because they don't drink every day. However, binge drinkers think that they have control over their alcohol consumption. Those who are classified as binge drinkers keep on using alcohol even when it is causing physical, social, legal and psychological problems. They find it difficult to control the alcohol using behaviour. In addition, they have a strong desire or compulsion to use alcohol. These features fit well within the paradigm of addictive behaviours.

'Binge drinking' has gained currency in the United Kingdom amongst young people but it is not restricted to them. Binge drinking is often defined as the consumption of more than a certain number of drinks over a short period of time, a single drinking session, or at least during a single day (Institute of Alcohol Studies, 2007). In the UK, drinking surveys normally define binge drinkers as men consuming at least eight, and women at least six standard units of alcohol in a single day, that is, double the maximum recommended 'safe limit' for men and women respectively. In the United States, binge drinking is defined as a pattern of drinking that brings a person's blood alcohol concentration (BAC) to 0.08 grams per hundred or above. This typically happens when men consume five or more drinks, and when women consume four or more drinks, in about two hours (NIAAA, 2004).

A much simpler definition of binge drinking is drinking too much alcohol over a short period of time and it is usually the type of drinking that leads to drunkenness (Alcohol Concern, 2007). Binge drinking and severe intoxication can cause muscular uncoordination, blurred vision, stupor, hypothermia, convulsions, depressed reflexes, respiratory depression, hypotension and coma. Death can occur from respiratory or circulatory failure or if binge drinkers inhale their own vomit (Institute of Alcohol Studies, 2007). Binge drinkers are at increased risk of accidents, alcohol poisoning, unsafe sex and having poor social behaviour.

How people take drugs – routes of drug administration

In order to understand the nature of addictive behaviours in relation to drug use, it is important to be aware of how people take drugs. The rituals of how the drug is taken also form part of the addictive process. Exposure to the paraphernalia of drugs can act as a cue in increasing the use of a drug in the desired route of administration. For example, paraphernalia includes a hypodermic syringe, needle, metal or plastic (snorting) tube, or other instrument or implement. Cocaine paraphernalia includes mirrors, razor blades and scales whereas cannabis paraphernalia includes rolling papers, clips and pipes.

The absorption of a drug is in part dependent upon its route of administration which influences the speed with which the physical and psychological effects of the drug are felt. People take drugs orally, by smoking, by inhalation and by injection. Oral administration of a drug, in either liquid or tablet form is the most common route of administration. However, when a drug is required to act more rapidly, the preferred route of administration is by injection.

Certain psychoactive substances are smoked, for example cannabis, crack cocaine and heroin. Some psychoactive drugs, for example cocaine and amphetamine, are also taken by the intranasal route. Users of cocaine and methamphetamine smoke, snort or inject drugs. Methamphetamine is also orally ingested. Drugs such as heroin or cocaine are often administered intravenously, for example directly into a vein. The route of administration affects the following:

• Amount of psychoactive substance delivered to the brain;

- Rate at which it is delivered and eliminated;
- Intensity of the drug's effects.

There are various complications of injecting. The site of injections can cause trauma and infections and the effects include overdose, poisoning, infection, thrombosis and embolism. Key elements of how people take drugs are presented in Table 3.5.

Table 3.5 How people take addictive substances –
routes of administration

Modes of administration	Features
Oral (swallowing)	<ul><li>Most popular method of drug administration.</li><li>The slowest route – slow absorption of the drug into the blood stream.</li><li>No stigma attached, compared to smoking and injecting.</li><li>Tablet or liquid form.</li></ul>
Smoking	<ul><li>An effective route of administration.</li><li>Drug is inhaled as in the case of tobacco or heroin smoking (chasing the dragon).</li><li>Cannabis is also smoked in the form of a 'joint' which is usually mixed with tobacco.</li></ul>
Inhalation (sniffing)	<ul><li>Absorption of the drug is through the mucous membrane of the nose and mouth.</li><li>The type of drugs that are inhaled includes cocaine, tobacco snuff and volatile substances and solvents. Inhalation may also produce rapid absorption (crack cocaine).</li></ul>
Injecting	<ul><li>Drug injecting: intramuscularly or subcutaneously and/or intravenously.</li><li>Injection of drugs is less widespread than other routes of drug administration.</li><li>The most hazardous form of drug administration.</li><li>Risk of overdose because of the concentrated effect of this method.</li><li>Risk of infection from non-sterile injection methods including hepatitis B and HIV infections, abscesses, gangrene, and thromboses.</li><li>The onset of the effects of the drug is rapid when it is administered intravenously and is a major reason why drugs are often self-administered by injecting.</li><li>Drugs that are mainly injected include heroin, cocaine, amphetamines and some hypno-sedatives.</li></ul>

Summary of key points

- Pharmacological properties, individual differences and context of use influence the individual experiences of drug taking.
- Continued substance use among alcohol and drug users is driven more by physiological and psychological dependence rather than by rational decisions.
- The most common drugs that are used by recreational users are alcohol, caffeine, nicotine, cannabis, LSD and ecstasy.
- A dependent user has progressed to regular and problematic use of a psychoactive drug or has become a multiple drug user.
- Binge drinking is drinking with the intention of getting drunk.
- Chaotic use is referred to when an individual is regarded as taking a drug or drugs in a spontaneous way that tends not to follow any typical drug-using pattern.
- The routes of administration are oral, smoking, inhalation and by injection.
- Injecting drugs is less widespread than other routes of drug administration but also the most hazardous.
- The theories or models of addiction include genetic theory, neuro-pharmacological theories, psychological theory, socio-cultural theories and bio-psychosocial theory.
- The disease theory of addiction maintains that addiction is a disease due to either the impairment of behavioural and/or neurochemical processes.
- The genetic theory of addiction puts forward a genetic predisposition to alcohol or drug addiction.
- In social learning theory, in order to understand the effects of alcohol or drugs, cognitive processes must be considered in relation to other factors.
- In the bio-psychosocial theory, genetic inheritance, physiological differences, family, community, peer or social pressure are all considered.

Reflective activity 3.1

- List the theories of addiction.
- Describe briefly two theories of addiction.
- Why do people use addictive substances?
- Why do they continue with their addictive behaviours?
- Describe the patterns of substance use and misuse?
- Are these patterns applicable to non-pharmacological addictions?
- What is meant by 'binge' drinking?
- What are the routes of administration of psychoactive substances?

References

Adiran, M. (2003) 'How Can Sociological Theory Help Our Understanding of Addictions?' *Substance Use and Misuse* 38, 10, 1385–1423.

Alcohol Concern (2007) *Binge Drinking Factsheet Summary* (London: Alcohol Concern).

Bierut, L.J., Dinwiddie, S.H., Begleiter, H., Crowe, R.R., Hesselbrock, V., Nurnberger, J.I., Porjesz, B., Schuckit, M.A. and Reich T. (1998) 'Familial Transmission of Substance Dependence: Alcohol, Marijuana, Cocaine, and Habitual Smoking. A Report from the Collaborative Study on the Genetics of Alcoholism', *Archives of General Psychiatry*, 55, 11, 982–88.

Di Chiara, G. (1995) 'The Role of Dopamine in Drug Abuse Viewed from the Perspective of its Role in Motivation', *Drug and Alcohol Dependence*, 38, 2, 95–137.

Drugscope (2010) Media Guide Glossary – Chaotic use. http://www.drugscope.org.uk/resources/mediaguide/glossary, date accessed 10 January 2010.

Drummond D.C., Tiffany, S., Glautier, S. and Remington, B. (1995) 'Cue Exposure in Understanding and Treating Addictive Behaviours', in Drummond, D.C., Tiffany, S., Glautier, S and Remington, B. (eds.), *Addictive Behaviour: Cue Exposure Theory and Practice* (Chichester: John Wiley and Sons) 1–17.

Fowler, J.S., Volkow, N.D., Kassed, C.A. and Chang, L. (2007) 'Imaging the Addicted Human Brain', *Science and Practical Perspectives* 3, 2, 4–16.

Garris, P.A., Kilpatrick, M., Bunin, M.A., Michael, D., Walker, Q.D. and Wightman, R.M. (1999) 'Dissociation of Dopamine Release in the Nucleus Accumbens from Intracranial Self-stimulation', *Nature* 398, 6722, 67–69.

Ghodse, A.H. (1995) *Drugs and Addictive Behaviour* (Oxford: Blackwell Science).

Hamond, A. and Rassool, G.H. (2006) 'Spiritual and Cultural Needs: Integration in Dual Diagnosis Care', in Rassool, G.H. (ed.), *Dual Diagnosis Nursing* (Oxford: Blackwell Publishing).

Institute of Alcohol Studies (2007) *Binge drinking: Nature, Prevalence and Causes* (St Ives: Institute of Alcohol Studies).

Keane, M. (2007) 'Social Reintegration as a Response to Drug Use in Ireland: An Overview', *Drugnet Ireland*, 24, 5–6.

Kumpter, K.L., Trunnell, E.P. and Whiteside, H.O (1990) 'The Biopsychosocial Model: Applications to the Addictions Field', in Eng, R.C. (ed.), *Controversies in the Addictions Field* (Iowa: Kendall/Hunt Publishing Company) Vol. 1.

Leeds, J. and Morgenstern, M.J. (1996) 'Psychoanalytic Theories of Substance Abuse'. in Rotgers, F., Keller, D.S. and Morgenstern, J. (eds.), *Treating Substance Abuse: Theory and Technique* (New York: Guildford Press).

Merikangas, K.R., Stevens, D.E., Fenton, B., Stolar, M., O'Malley, S., Woods, S.W. and Risch, N. (1998) 'Co-morbidity and Familial Aggregation of Alcoholism and Anxiety Disorders', *Psychological Medicine*, 28, 4, 773–88.

Nader, P.W. and Czoty, M.A (2005) 'PET Imaging of Dopamine D2 Receptors in Monkey Models of Cocaine Abuse: Genetic Predisposition Versus Environmental Modulation', *American Journal of Psychiatry* 162, 1473–82.

National Institute of Alcohol Abuse and Alcoholism (NIAAA) (2004) NIAAA Council Approves Definition of Binge Drinking. *NIAAA Newsletter* 3, 3. http://pubs.niaaa.nih.gov/publications/Newsletter/winter2004/Newsletter_ Number3.pdf, date accessed 31 March 2009.

Orford, J. (1985) *Excessive Appetites: A Psychological View of Addictions* (Chichester: John Wiley and Sons).

Oyefeso, A., Ghodse, H., Keating, A., Annan, J., Phillips, T., Pollard. M. and Nash, P. (2000) Drug Treatment Needs of Black and Minority Ethnic Residents of the London Borough of Merton. Addictions Resource Agency for Commissioners (ARAC) Monograph Series on Ethnic Minority Issues (London: ARAC).

Parker, H., Aldridge, J. and Measham, F. (1998) *Illegal Leisure: the Normalization of Adolescent Recreational Drug Use* (London: Routledge).

Rassool, G.H. (1998) *Substance Use and Misuse: Nature, Context and Clinical Interventions* (Oxford: Blackwell Science).

Rassool, G.H. (2009) *Alcohol and Drug Misuse: A Handbook for Student and Health Professionals* (Oxford: Routledge).

Royal College of Psychiatrists (1987) *Drug Scenes: A Report on Drugs and Drug Dependence* (London: Royal College of Psychiatrists).

Sher, K., Walitzer, K., Wood, P. and Brent, E. (1991) 'Characteristics of Children of Alcoholics: Putative Risk Factors, Substance Use and Abuse, and Psychopathology', *Journal of Abnormal Psychology* 100, 4, 427–48.

Siegel, R. (2005) *Intoxication: The Universal Drive for Mind-Altering Substances* (Vermont: Park Street Press).

Weil, A. and Rosen, W. (2004) *From Chocolate to Morphine – Everything You Want to Know About Mind-altering Drugs* (New York: Houghton Mifflin Company).

West, R. (2006) *Theory of Addiction* (Oxford: Blackwell Publishing).

White, F.J. (2002) 'A Behavioral/Systems Approach to the Neuroscience of Drug Addiction', *The Journal of Neuroscience*, 22, 9, 3303–05.

PART 2

Pharmacological and Non-Pharmacological Addictions

Alcohol 4

Introduction

Reflective activity 4.1

Before reading this chapter, try to provide a true or false answer for each of the statements listed below. Think about some reasons as to why you chose a particular answer.

Statements	True	False
Alcohol is a central nervous system depressant.		
Alcoholism is one of the four most serious public health problems.		
It is illegal to give an alcoholic drink to a child under five years of age.		
Cannabis causes more problems than alcohol among young people in the UK.		
Men and women can drink the same amount of alcohol.		
Food in the stomach slows down the rate at which alcohol takes effect.		
Different kinds of alcoholic drinks contain different types of alcohol.		
It is dangerous to drink alcohol when taking drugs.		
Drinking water with alcohol prevents a hangover.		
Black coffee will help you to sober up after drinking too much.		
Alcohol firstly affects our sense of moral judgement, then our physical co-ordination.		
Alcohol can have a negative impact on sleep patterns and stress levels.		
A large quantity of alcohol affects respiration and heart rate.		

Statements	True	False
An average mixed drink contains nearly twice as much alcohol as a pint of beer.		
A pint of beer has the same alcohol content as a double whisky.		
Alcopops contain as much alcohol as beer.		
Pregnant women only have to worry about harming their baby if they drink alcohol heavily.		
The legal breath/alcohol limit for driving in the UK is 35 micro-grammes of alcohol per 100 millilitres of breath.		

Source: Adapted from Rassool, G.H. (2009) Alcohol and Drug Misuse: A Handbook for Students and Health Professionals (Oxford: Routledge).

When you have read this chapter, come back to this activity and consider your answers again. How many did you get right? For those you got wrong, think about the reasons for your original answer and what you know now.

Alcohol is embedded in the social and cultural fabric of Judeo-Christian societies and is actively promoted in many cultural, social and religious events. Alcohol is enjoyed by the majority of the UK and European adult population. Although, alcohol is not generally perceived as a toxic psychoactive substance with addictive potential, it has become one of the most important risks to health globally. Public health problems associated with alcohol consumption have reached alarming proportions resulting in physical, psychological, social, economic and legal consequences.

Alcohol is consumed by almost half the world's population and is a significant contributor to the global burden of disease. It is the fifth leading risk factor for premature deaths and disabilities in the world (WHO, 2009). It is estimated that 2.5 million people worldwide died of alcohol-related causes in 2004, including 320,000 young people between 15 and 29 years of age. In 2004, alcohol consumption was responsible for 3.8 per cent of all deaths in the world and 4.6 per cent of the global burden of disease as measured in dis-ability-adjusted life years.

Harmful drinking is a major avoidable risk factor for neuro-psychiatric dis-orders and other non-communicable diseases such as cardiovascular diseases, cirrhosis of the liver and various cancers. In addition, a significant proportion of the disease burden attributable to harmful drinking includes road traffic accidents and suicides (WHO, 2009). Europeans are the world's top consumers of alcohol as heavy drinking is part of the culture of Northern Europeans. In Europe, alcohol is public health enemy number three, behind only tobacco and high blood pressure, and ahead of obesity, lack of exercise or illicit drugs. UK adolescents are also the third worst binge drinkers in the EU, with more than a quarter of 15–16 year olds binge drinking three or more times in the last month (Anderson and Baumberg, 2007).

Alcohol and the law

In the United Kingdom, there are strict laws on the sale of alcohol, on whom and when people can enter a public bar, where it is sold and on buying alcohol. These restrictions apply in particular to young people. In England and Wales from late 2005, drinking establishments can apply for licences to stay open and serve alcohol for 24 hours. Police have powers to confiscate alcohol from you if you are drinking in public and can contact your parents. You can get a criminal record for offences of drunkenness. It is an offence to drive with more than the following amounts of alcohol in your body:

- 80 milligrams of alcohol in 100 millilitres of blood, or;
- 35 micrograms of alcohol in 100 millilitres of breath if a breath test is used.

Scotland's laws on alcohol are a mixture of Scottish laws and those that apply across the UK. All licensed premises operate a policy whereby young people must produce proof of their age before being served. At the same time, all licensed premises are required to display a notice stating this. People who are 18 years of age or older can buy alcohol in the same way as other adults. However, the licence holder can refuse to allow anyone under 21 on the premises if they wish (they can refuse entrance to anyone they like so long as it's not on the grounds of race, gender or disability).

Categories of alcohol misusers

There are four main categories of alcohol misusers: hazardous drinkers; harmful drinkers; moderately dependent drinkers and severely dependent drinkers. Hazardous drinkers are drinking at levels over the sensible drinking limits, either in terms of regular excessive consumption or less frequent sessions of heavy drinking. Hazardous drinkers are more likely to have the whole gamut of alcohol-related problems and may benefit from brief advice/interventions. Harmful drinkers are usually drinking at levels above those recommended for sensible drinking but show clear evidence of some alcohol-related harm.

Moderately dependent drinkers may have an insight into their problems with drinking and they may not have reached the stage of 'relief drinking' – which is drinking to relieve or avoid physical discomfort from withdrawal symptoms

(NTA, 2006). They can be described as 'chronic alcoholics' and can often be managed effectively in community settings, including medically assisted alcohol withdrawal in the community. Severely dependent drinkers may have serious and long-standing problems ('chronic alcoholism') and may have been heavy users over prolonged periods. This habit of significant alcohol consumption may be due to a desire to stop or limit the withdrawal symptoms. They have complex needs such as coexisting psychiatric problems, learning disabilities, poly-drug use or complicated assisted alcohol withdrawal; others may need rehabilitation and strategies to address the level of their dependence, or to address other issues, such as homelessness or social dislocation. However, more severely dependent drinkers may be in need of inpatient assisted alcohol withdrawal and residential rehabilitation.

Drinking behaviour, pattern and extent of use

Every week, two-thirds of adults in England drink alcohol. The average adult drinks the equivalent of 120 bottles of wine every year. Since 1970, alcohol consumption has fallen in many European countries but in England it has risen by more than 40 per cent (Donaldson, 2009). More people in 'managerial and professional' households exceeded the daily limits on their heaviest drinking day of the week (43 per cent) than those in 'routine and manual' households (31 per cent) (Office for National Statistics, 2009). Ninety-two per cent of men and 89 per cent of women reported that they had heard of measuring alcohol in units. There was less knowledge of the recommended maximum daily intake. In 2006, men were more likely to drink normal strength beer, lager and cider and less likely to drink strong beer, lager and cider and women were more likely to drink wine and less likely to drink strong beer, lager, cider and alcopops (National Statistics, 2006).

UK adults and adolescents are among the worst binge drinkers in Europe, says an Institute of Alcohol Studies report (Anderson, 2007). Several factors are contributing to a rise in binge drinking in Britain: cheaper and more accessible alcohol, changing drinking patterns, and a jump in drinking among young women. Binge drinking is a normal mode of consumption among 18–24 year old men and women, bingeing here being defined subjectively in terms of the experience of being drunk (Richardson and Budd, 2003). Over the last 10 years, binge drinking in UK girls has increased to the second highest level in Europe. Over a third of adults exceeded the daily limits for regular drinking on at least one day during the week before interview despite growing awareness of safe drinking levels, according to annual data on smoking and drinking (Office of National Statistics, 2009). Since 1998, there has been a general increase in drinking over recommended weekly limits, especially for women. Researchers also found that whilst fewer children are drinking, those that do drink are drinking much more than they did in the past (Smith and Foxcroft, 2009).

Alcohol: Health, social and economic costs

Alcohol misuse is associated with a wide range of problems, including cancer, heart disease, offending behaviour, social exclusion, domestic violence, suicide and deliberate self-harm, child abuse, child neglect and mental health problems which coexist with alcohol misuse and homelessness. In England, around 90 per cent of adults consume alcohol and the majority does not experience problems. The majority of alcohol-related deaths are due to alcoholic liver disease. Among both men and women there were more admissions in the older age groups than in the younger age groups (The Information Centre, 2009).

As well as health risks and death, alcohol misuse also has an impact on social and economic factors. Alcohol misuse imposes a greater burden on the criminal justice system than both the health service and social work services. It is estimated that the cost of alcohol-related harm to the NHS in England is £2.7 billion in 2006/07 prices (The Information Centre, 2009). It is estimated that that in 2008, there were 125,000 'alcohol-related instances of domestic violence', that an estimated 6,000 babies are born annually with fetal alcohol syndrome and that in 2006, 7,000 people were injured and 560 killed as a result of drink-driving, not including the drivers (Donaldson, 2009). The loss to the economy of premature death from alcohol misuse is around £2.4 billion each year.

Alcohol: Policy initiatives and strategies

The model of care for alcohol misusers (MoCAM) (NTA, 2006) is a framework for the treatment of adult alcohol misusers. MoCAM identifies four main categories of alcohol misusers who may benefit from some kind of intervention or treatment: hazardous drinkers; harmful drinkers; moderately dependent drinkers and severely dependent drinkers (see Chapter 2). The model of care for alcohol misusers (MoCAM) outlines the four-tiered framework of provision for commissioning evidence-based alcohol treatment in England. The key points of the four-tiered framework are presented in Table 4.1

There are a number of policy initiatives and strategies in relation to the reduction of alcohol consumption and harm amongst the population. An effective alcohol policy will be one that includes regulatory action, treatment interventions and cultural change delivered through a comprehensive strategy aimed at the whole population as well as targeting high risk groups (SHAAP, 2007). However, reducing alcohol-related harm will require a range of goals and actions that will enable a change in our drinking culture.

Table 4.1 Models of care four tier system: alcohol

Tier	Settings	Specialist settings	Intervention strategies
1	Primary health care services. Acute hospitals, e.g. A&E departments. Psychiatric services. Social services departments. Homelessness services. Antenatal clinics. General hospital wards. Police settings, e.g. custody cells. Probation services. Prison service. Education and vocational services. Occupational health services.	Specialist liver disease units. Specialist psychiatric wards. Forensic units. Residential provision for the homeless. Domestic abuse services.	Interventions include provision of: identification of hazardous, harmful and dependent drinkers. Information on sensible drinking. Simple brief interventions to reduce alcohol-related harm. Referral of those with alcohol dependence or harm for more intensive interventions.
2	Primary health care services. Acute hospitals, e.g. A&E departments. Psychiatric services. Social services departments. Homelessness services. Antenatal clinics. General hospital wards. Police settings, e.g. custody cells. Probation services. Prison service. Education and vocational services. Occupational health services.	Alcohol Services.	Alcohol-specific information, advice and support. Extended brief interventions and brief treatment to reduce alcohol-related harm. Alcohol-specific assessment and referral of those requiring more structured alcohol treatment. Partnership or 'shared care' with staff from Tier 3 and Tier 4 Provision, or joint care of individuals attending other services providing Tier 1. Interventions. Mutual aid groups, e.g. Alcoholics Anonymous Triage assessment, which may be provided as part of locally agreed arrangements.
3	Primary care settings (shared care schemes).	Community-based,	Comprehensive substance misuse assessment.

(Continued)

Table 4.1 Continued

Tier	Settings	Specialist settings	Intervention strategies
	GP-led prescribing services. The work in community settings can be delivered by statutory, voluntary or independent services providing planned care and structured alcohol treatment.	structured, planned care alcohol treatment.	Care planning. Case management. Community detoxification. Prescribing interventions to reduce risk of relapse. Psychosocial therapies and support. Interventions to address coexisting conditions. Day programmes. Liaison services, e.g. for acute medical and psychiatric health services (such as pregnancy, mental health or hepatitis services). Social care services (such as child care and housing services and other generic services).
4	Inpatient provision in the context of general psychiatric wards. Hospital services for pregnancy, liver problems, etc. with specialized alcohol liaison support.	Alcohol specialist inpatient treatment and residential rehabilitation.	Comprehensive substance misuse assessment. Care planning and review. Prescribing interventions. Alcohol detoxification. Prescribing interventions to reduce risk of relapse. Psychosocial therapies and support. Provision of information, advice and training and 'shared care' to others.

Source: Adapted from Models of Care for Alcohol Misusers (NTA, 2006).

The Alcohol Harm Reduction Strategy for England (Prime Minister's Strategy Unit, 2004) focused on the Government's aims for reducing alcohol-related harm and the costs of alcohol misuse. The strategy recognizes the need to tackle alcohol-related disorder in town and city centres, improve treatment and support for people with alcohol problems, clamp down on irresponsible promotions by the industry and provide better information to consumers about the dangers of alcohol misuse. The strategy includes a series of measures to improve the information available to individuals; to better identify and treat alcohol misuse; to prevent and tackle alcohol-related crime and disorder and to work with the industry in tackling the harms caused by alcohol. The National Alcohol Strategy is supported by the report Safe. Sensible. Social: The Next Steps in the National Alcohol Strategy (Department of Health, Home Office, Department for Education and Skills and Department for Culture, Media and Sport, 2007). This initiative sets out clear goals and actions to minimize the health harms, violence and antisocial behaviour associated with alcohol, while ensuring that people are able to enjoy alcohol safely and responsibly. It specifically focuses on the minority of drinkers who cause the most harm to themselves, their communities and their families. They are: young people under 18 who drink alcohol; 18–24 year old binge drinkers; and harmful drinkers.

In Choosing Health: Making Healthy Choices Easier (Department of Health, 2004), the report places alcohol firmly in the realm of public health practice and highlights action on reducing alcohol-related harm and encouraging sensible drinking as one of its priorities. The proposals include: a national information campaign to tackle the problems of binge drinking; training for professionals; and pilots screening and brief interventions in accident and emergency services. In addition, the report also highlighted the need for a public health approach and sets out a number of priorities for action including smoking and sexual health.

In England, as from April 2010, the first three proposed actions set up by the Government are planned to come into effect:

- Banning irresponsible promotions, such as 'all you can drink for £10' or 'women drink free' deals, that encourage people to drink quickly or irresponsibly.
- Banning 'dentist's chairs' where drink is poured directly into the mouths of customers, making it impossible for them to control the amount they are drinking.
- Ensuring free tap water is available for customers, allowing people to space out their drinks.

What is a unit of alcohol?

One unit of alcohol is 10ml (1cl) by volume, or 8g by weight, of pure alcohol. For example:

One unit of alcohol = half a pint of ordinary strength beer, lager or cider (3–4 per cent alcohol by volume [ABV]) = a small pub measure of spirits (40 per cent ABV) = a standard pub measure (50ml) of fortified wine (sherry or port) (20 per cent ABV). One and a half units of alcohol = a small glass of ordinary strength wine (125 ml) (12 per cent ABV) = a standard pub measure of spirits (35 ml) (40 per cent ABV). If you drink half a litre (500ml) – just under a pint – then you have had three units. The exact number of units in a particular drink can be calculated by multiplying the volume of the drink (number of ml) by the percentage ABV (Alcohol by Volume) and dividing by 1,000.

- For example, the number of units in a strong beer of 500ml with a 6 per cent ABV5 = 500 × 6.0 divided by 1,000 5 = 3 units.

Alcohol drinking: Recommended limits

In the United Kingdom, there are strict laws on the sale of alcohol, on who can buy alcohol and when people can enter a public bar where it is sold and on buying alcohol. These restrictions apply in particular to young people. It is an offence to drive with more than the following amounts of alcohol in your body:

- 80 milligrams of alcohol in 100 millilitres of blood, or;
- 35 micrograms of alcohol in 100 millilitres of breath if a breath test is used.

The recommended limits of alcohol drinking:

- Men should drink no more than 21 units of alcohol per week (and no more than four units in any one day).
- Women should drink no more than 14 units of alcohol per week (and no more than three units in any one day).
- Pregnant women. Advice from the Department of Health is that pregnant women and women trying to become pregnant should not drink at all.

Pharmacology of alcohol

Alcohol is based on compounds composed of carbon, hydrogen and oxygen. The three most commonly encountered alcohols are:

- Methyl alcohol (methanol).
- Isopropyl alcohol (isopropanol).
- Ethyl alcohol (ethanol).

Methanol is found in windshield wiper fluids and de-icers, antifreeze, glass cleaner, canned heat, paints, varnishes, and paint thinners and removers. Methanol (six to seven ounces) is toxic for most adults. Small amounts of isopropanol can cause permanent damage to the visual system and larger amounts are lethal. Ethanol is the alcohol found in alcoholic drinks. Some problem drinkers may consume methanol or isopropyl alcohol with potentially lethal consequences.

The enzyme alcohol dehydrogenase metabolizes the ethanol (alcohol) acetaldehyde which in turn is rapidly metabolized by another enzyme, aldehyde dehydrogenase, to acetic acid, and ultimately to carbon dioxide and water. Understanding the biochemistry of the alcohol metabolism has helped to develop pharmacological interventions such as the use of antabuse with problem drinkers. For example, the enzyme aldehyde dehydrogenase is inhibited by antabuse resulting in a toxic increase of acetaldehyde which occurs when alcohol is consumed. Acetaldehyde causes nausea and discomfort and produces an aversive reaction when alcohol is taken. Ethanol affects the central nervous system and the gastro-intestinal system including the liver, cardiovascular system, the reproductive system and the kidneys. The effects of alcohol on an individual are determined by the concentration of alcohol in the blood. This is influenced by the amount and rate of alcohol consumption, rate of absorption, genetic factors, and drinking experience.

The main neurochemical transmitters are believed to play an important role in alcohol intoxication and behaviour: gamma amino butyric acid (GABA) and its receptor, serotonin (5 HT) and dopamine. The role of neurotransmitters in the brain is to either stimulate or inhibit the flow of an impulse between neurons. Neurotransmitters like GABA act as an inhibitor whereas 5 HT and dopamine can have either the function of stimulating or inhibiting an impulse.

There is evidence implicating serotonin-5HT in the development of alcohol misuse as a result of the identification of a relationship between alcoholism and the levels of serotonin metabolites in the urine and cerebro-spinal fluid of human alcoholics (Lovinger, 1997). In addition, Lovinger suggests that abnormal serotonin levels may contribute to the development of alcohol misuse because some studies have found that the levels of chemical markers representing serotonin levels in the brain are reduced in alcoholic humans and chronically in alcohol-consuming animals.

GABA is the major inhibitory neurotransmitter in the brain in reducing the activity of the signal-receiving neuron (Cooper et al., 1991). In addition, GABA neurons are located in different areas of the central nervous system and alcohol inhibits many activities within the brain thus influencing behavioural output. Psychoactive substances such as benzodiazepine enhance GABA's actions in the brain causing sedation and intoxication that resemble the effects of alcohol. In fact, alcohol may produce some of its sedative and intoxicating effects by enhancing GABA's inhibitory function (Samson and Harris, 1992).

Dopamine regulates movement, emotion, cognition, motivation, and feelings of pleasure and alcohol seems to affect the surges of dopamine. When alcohol is taken, it increases the dopamine concentrations in the reward centres of the brain producing the normal feelings of pleasure. There is also evidence to suggest that the dopamine system is involved in a range of behavioural and neurobiological processes relevant to alcohol craving and relapse (Spanagel and Weiss, 1999; Weiss, 2005). However, it is suggested that alcohol is likely to be regulated by more than one neurobiological mechanism (Barreta et al., 2008). Alcohol not only affects the neurotransmitters individually, but also influences the interactions of these three neurotransmitters when they are working together.

Effects of alcohol

Alcohol is a psychoactive substance that depresses the central nervous system and does not have to be digested in order for absorption to occur. Alcoholic beverages with a higher concentration of alcohol such as whisky or brandy, and carbonated drinks such as champagnes are absorbed more quickly. Alcohol is absorbed in the mouth, oesophagus and the stomach but for the most part absorption of alcohol takes place in the initial part of the small intestine. Individual differences in physiology, contents of the stomach and situational factors have a significant influence on the rate of alcohol absorption.

Alcohol has a high calorific value and affects the body's ability to absorb and use nutrients effectively resulting in the problem of poor malnutrition or vitamin deficiencies in alcohol drinkers who drink hazardous levels of alcohol. There are gender differences in the way alcohol affects the bodily system. Women can become more intoxicated than men on the same amount of alcohol intake, even if they weigh the same. The fat distribution and the presence of less water in the bodies of women means that alcohol is less diluted and has greater potency within the body. Other factors such as pre-menstrual status, birth control pills and hormone replacement therapy (oestrogen) have an impact on the absorption rate of alcohol in women.

The effects of alcohol are presented in Table 4.2. Initially small amounts of alcohol produce a feeling of relaxation, euphoria and less inhibition. With increased consumption, there is cognitive, perceptual and behavioural impairment and these forms of impairment may include slurred speech, poor co-ordination, unsteady gait, uncontrolled movement of the pupils (nystagmus), poor judgment, insomnia, hangover and blackouts. Blackout is a memory impairment that occurs in anyone who drinks a large amount of alcohol in one session. Chronic alcohol use may result in significant memory problems and cognitive impairment.

Many heavy or hazardous drinkers have poor eating habits and their nutrition will not contain essential vitamins. Thiamine is essential for normal growth and development and helps to maintain proper functioning of the heart and the nervous and digestive systems. In addition, alcohol can inflame the stomach lining and impede the body's ability to absorb the key vitamins it receives. This may result in Wernicke's encephalopathy which is caused by

Table 4.2 Alcohol: effects

Street Names	• Booze, Nip, Tipple, Bevy, etc. • Found in beer, lager, alcopops, cider, wine, spirits etc.
Therapeutic Use	• As an antiseptic.
Short-Term Effects	• Effects vary according to the strength of the drink, the person's physical size and mood. • Feeling of relaxation and euphoria. • Alcohol users experience a feeling of lower inhibition. • Speech can become slurred, co-ordination is affected and emotions are heightened. • Poor judgement. • Insomnia. • Hangover.
Long-Term Effects	• Overdose can lead to loss of consciousness and alcoholic poisoning, which can be fatal. • Physical dependence can occur. • Menstrual disorders. • Fertility problems. • Fetal alcohol syndrome. • Physical problems. • Psychological problems. • Social problems.

alcohol and thiamine deficiency (Vitamin B1). However, if Wernicke's is left untreated, or is not treated in time, brain damage may result. In some cases the person may die. If treatment, with high doses of thiamine, is carried out in time most symptoms should be reversed in a few hours. If Wernicke's encephalopathy is untreated or is not treated soon enough, Korsakoff's psychosis may follow. Korsakoff's psychosis may develop gradually resulting in severe memory impairment. However, many other abilities may remain intact. Other problems associated with heavy alcohol consumption include peripheral neuropathies (lack of sensation or pain in the limbs), 'alcohol dementia', physical, immunological and psychological disorders. The features of Wernicke's encephalopathy and Korsakoff's psychosis are presented in Table 4.3.

Alcohol withdrawal syndrome

Alcohol dependence involves both physical and psychological dependence. Alcohol withdrawal syndrome is a set of symptoms observed in persons who stop drinking alcohol following continuous and heavy consumption. The milder forms of the syndrome include tremulousness, seizures, and hallucinations, typically occurring within 6–48 hours after the last drink. Recreational

Table 4.3 Wernicke's encephalopathy and Korsakoff's psychosis

Problem	Cause	Characteristics	Treatment
Wernicke's encephalopathy	Alcohol and thiamine deficiency (Vitamin B1).	• Unsteady gait (ataxia). • Involuntary, jerky eye movements. • Paralysis of muscles moving the eyes. • Drowsiness. • Confusion. • The symptoms may not always present, so diagnosis may be difficult.	High doses of thiamine.
Korsakoff's psychosis	If Wernicke's encephalopathy is untreated or is not treated soon enough.	• Damage to a large area of the cortex. • Anterograde amnesia. • Retrograde amnesia. • Confabulation (invented events which fill gaps in memory). • Apathy. • Talkative. • Repetitive behaviours.	

drinkers do not usually experience withdrawal symptoms. Hazardous or harmful drinkers who have gone through withdrawal before are more likely to have withdrawal symptoms each time they stop drinking.

Withdrawals can be physical and/or psychological (See Table 4.4). For most problem drinkers, alcohol withdrawal will not progress to the severe stage of delirium tremens (confusion and hallucination). This involves profound confusion, hallucinations, and severe autonomic nervous system overactivity, typically beginning between 48 and 96 hours after the last drink. When an individual has severe withdrawal symptoms, this can be a life-threatening condition and requires supervision under medical care.

Screening and assessment

The initial assessment or screening is usually carried out in generic settings such as in hospital or primary health care. Screening or initial assessment is a brief process that aims to determine whether an individual has a drug or alcohol problem, health related problems and risk behaviours (Rassool, 2009). A number of screening instruments have been introduced to assess alcohol problems including the FAST Alcohol Screening Test (Hodgson et al., 2002) and

Table 4.4 Alcohol withdrawal symptoms

Physical symptoms	Psychological symptoms
• Headache	• Feeling of anxiety
• Nausea	• Irritability
• Vomiting	• Emotionally volatile
• Sweating (palms and face)	• Fatigue
• Loss of appetite	• Difficulty in thinking clearly
• Insomnia	• Bad dreams
• Palpitations	• Clouding of consciousness
• Enlarged, dilated pupils	• Agitation
• Clammy skin	• Disorientation of time and place
• Tremor of hands	• Fear, suspicion and anger
• Involuntary movements of the eyelids	• Depression and suicidal behaviour
• Elevated temperature	• Paranoid delusions
• Convulsions	• A state of confusion and hallucinations (visual or tactile) – delirium tremens
• Black outs	

the CAGE questionnaire. The CAGE questionnaire is the simplest and its four questions could easily be incorporated in the routine assessment process.

- Have you ever felt that you should *cut* down your drinking?
- Have people *annoyed* you by criticizing your drinking?
- Have you ever felt bad or *guilty* about your drinking?
- Have you ever had a drink first thing in the morning to steady your nerves, or to get rid of a hangover (*eye-opener*)?

Two or more positive responses are said to identify a problem drinker. This short questionnaire concentrates on the consequences rather than on the quantity or frequency of alcohol use.

The alcohol history and assessment are a detailed account of the current presentation of an individual's alcohol drinking pattern of use. It is important to ask about the type of alcohol product, its alcohol content, and the size of glass used and their alcohol consumption on a daily or weekly basis. The assessment should then focus on the current level of dependence, risk behaviours, associated problems, source of help, and periods of abstinence and relapse. In order to ascertain the level of dependence, it is important to ask about experiences of withdrawal symptoms or any medical complications. An outline of the process of compiling an alcohol history and assessment is shown in Table 4.5.

Table 4.5 Alcohol history and assessment

• Statement of the problem	Reason for presentation (intoxication, overdose, withdrawal). Consider the individual's concerns, issues, needs or problems.
• Current alcohol use	Type, quantity, duration, frequency.
• Pattern of alcohol use	Details of alcohol taking for past week/ month.
• Current use of other substances	Prescribed, illicit or over-the-counter drugs.
• Level of dependence	Any withdrawal symptoms. Evidence of increasing tolerance.
• Associated problems	Any medical, psychiatric, social or legal problems.
• Mental state	Assess intoxication, mood, signs of psychosis, depression.
• Physical examination	Vital signs (fever, tachycardia from alcohol withdrawal or infectious complications).
• Motivation	Assess stage of change (pre-contemplation, contemplation).
• Coping strategies and strengths	Previous attempts at reduction or cessation of alcohol use. Achievements, strengths and positive aspects of the individual.
• Risk behaviours	Binge drinking. Sexual behaviour when intoxicated.
• Periods of abstinence/relapse	Duration, periods of abstinence – voluntary or enforced. Reasons for lapse or relapse.
• Sources of help	Social support systems. Statutory agencies. Local authorities. Voluntary agencies. Self-help groups.
• Reaching a diagnosis of alcohol dependence (3 of the criteria within a 12 month period (DSM-IV))	Tolerance. Withdrawal. Used in greater amounts and longer periods than intended. Inability to control use/unsuccessful attempts to cut down. Long time spent in alcohol-related activity. Reduction of social, occupational and recreational activity due to alcohol use. Continued use despite physical/psychological problems caused by alcohol use.

Source: Adapted from Rassool, G.H. and Winnington, J. (2006).

Individuals with alcohol and psychiatric problems have complex or multiple needs which are often difficult to assess comprehensively. For a detailed description see Rassool and Winnington (2006) and Rassool (2009). Alcohol can be measured directly in serum, urine and exhaled air. A number of blood tests can be undertaken to assess the presence of alcohol. Essential investigations include liver function tests (LFT), gamma-glutamyl transferase (GGT), asparate transaminase (AST) and mean corpuscles volume (MCV).

Detoxification and management of withdrawal

Detoxification is a treatment intervention where alcohol abstinence causes withdrawal symptoms. The main objectives of pharmacological interventions in alcohol withdrawal are the relief of subjective withdrawal symptoms, the prevention and management of more serious complications and preparation for more structured psychosocial and educational interventions (Rassool, 2009). The alcohol withdrawal syndrome lasts for about five days, with the greatest risk of severe withdrawal in the first 24 to 48 hours. Patients with moderate or severe withdrawal may require inpatient detoxification. Chlordiazepoxide or diazepam is usually the intervention of choice as it is safe to use and has an anti-convulsant effect which helps to safeguard against epileptic seizures. The principles of management of alcohol detoxification include a non-stimulating and non-threatening environment, monitoring of dehydration, blood pressure, dietary intake, orientating patients with time, place and people involved in treatment and sleep. Problems associated with hallucinations (tactile), delirium, altered mental states, anxiety, paranoia and depression should also be managed.

In the past few decades, preventative health education messages of sensible or controlled drinking have been part of the alcohol harm reduction strategy. Alcohol harm reduction can be broadly defined as measures that aim to reduce the incidence of problem drinking and its negative consequences. The focus of harm reduction strategies is on particular risk behaviours (such as drinking and driving, binge drinking), special populations' risk groups (such as pregnant women, young people) and particular drinking contexts (such as bars and clubs). These approaches have broadened the sphere of interest in alcohol-related harms to include social nuisance and public order problems (IHRA, 2003).

Pharmacological and non-pharmacological interventions

The intervention strategies for alcohol misuse may include pharmacological and non-pharmacological treatment. Initially, the aim of pharmacological intervention is to alleviate withdrawal symptoms and this is followed by psychosocial interventions. A structured care plan is needed to outline the needs or goals, strengths and risks identified by the assessment process and the main focus of intervention strategies. The effectiveness of the care plan is based on the engagement of the patient throughout the assessment and care planning process and the patient's active involvement in the formulation of the care plan. Both the initial care plan and a structured care plan are invaluable in the treatment journey of the patient. There is evidence to suggest that a planned and structured aftercare is effective in improving outcomes following the initial treatment of service users with severe alcohol problems (Heather et al., 2006).

The pharmacological interventions include a number of drugs that can be used to assist problem drinkers. In the last decade, naltrexone and acamprosate have been proposed for the treatment of alcohol dependence. Acamprosate's effect is dose-dependent, and although it has a few minor side-effects acamprosate reduces the craving for alcohol. In addition, there is evidence to suggest that naltrexone and acamprosate are more effective than a placebo in the treatment of alcohol disorders (Garbutt et al., 1999). Antabuse (disulfiram) is also an efficient intervention and is used for motivated problem drinkers whose goal is abstinence. The features of pharmacological and non-pharmacological intervention strategies are presented in Table 4.6

Vitamin supplements are also used during and after the treatment of alcohol problems. It is recommended that 200 mg four times a day of oral thiamine and vitamin B tablets (30 mg/day) should be prescribed as the treatment of choice for the duration of the detoxification (Royal College of Physicians, 2001). Both supplements could be continued if there is evidence of cognitive impairment (thiamine 50 mg four times a day) or poor diet (vitamin B 30 mg per day). Pharmacotherapy is also used in relapse prevention. Disulfiram taken under supervision is an effective component of relapse prevention strategies (Heather et al., 2006). Anti-craving medications such as naltrexone and acamprosate may also be used as part of psychosocial interventions, including relapse prevention.

Non-pharmacological intervention such as brief intervention can help patients reduce the risk of developing alcohol-related problems or hazardous alcohol use. The aim of the intervention is to help the patient understand that their alcohol drinking is putting them at risk and to encourage them to reduce their consumption levels (moderate drinking) rather than abstinence. There is strong evidence for the effectiveness of brief interventions in a variety of settings in reducing alcohol consumption among hazardous and harmful drinkers to low risk levels (NTA, 2006).

Brief interventions comprise a single brief advice or several short (15–30 minutes) brief counselling sessions and are designed to be conducted by non-specialist or generic health care professionals. The acronym 'FRAMES' summarizes the elements of effective brief interventions (Bien et al., 1993).

Table 4.6 Pharmacological and non-pharmacological interventions

Treatment interventions	Types	Features
Pharmacological	Naltrexone	Initial dose: 25 mg/day for 2 days. Maintenance dose: 50 mg/day. Recommendation: Monitoring of hepatic function.
	Acamprosate	Dose: patient 60 kg + : 1998 mg/day; patient less than 60 kg: 999 mg/day. Recommendation: Insist on the correct taking of medications. Hepatic monitoring.
	Disulfiram	Initial dose: 500 mg/day for 14 days. Maintenance dose: 125 to 250 mg/day. Recommendation: Monitoring of the hepatic function. Introduction only after an abstinence period from 24 to 48 hours.
	Thiamine/ Vitamin B	Thiamine 50 mg four times a day (evidence of cognitive impairment. Vitamin B 30 mg/day (poor diet).
Non-Pharmacological	Brief Interventions	'FRAMES': That is Feedback, Responsibility, Advice, Menu, Empathy and Self-efficacy. NICE (2007) recommendations: <ul><li>10–45 minutes.</li><li>Explore ambivalence about drug use and possible treatment, with the aim of increasing motivation to change behaviour.</li><li>Provide non-judgmental feedback. Supportive, non-judgmental manner.</li></ul>
	Motivational Interviewing	Advanced Counselling skills. Moderate or severe alcohol dependence users who are not willing to change their risk behaviours.
	Cognitive-Behavioural	Aims are to teach individuals how to control their responses to their environment through improving social, coping and problem-solving skills. Community reinforcement approach (CRA) – aim of engineering the service user's social environment (including the family and vocational environment).
	Social Behaviour and Network Therapy	The basic premise is to enable clients to develop positive social networks.

That is *Feedback, Responsibility, Advice, Menu, Empathy and Self-efficacy*. Brief interventions can be delivered in a supportive, non-judgmental manner rather than the more traditional confrontational styles and are associated with better outcomes. The NICE (2007) guideline on psychosocial interventions recommends that opportunistic brief interventions should be routinely provided to people who misuse alcohol with information about self-help groups based on twelve step principles such as those employed by Alcoholics Anonymous.

Other psychosocial interventions include motivational interviewing which draws heavily on basic counselling skills. Motivational interviewing is targeted for patients with moderate or severe alcohol dependence who are not willing to change their risk behaviour. Motivational interviewing increases the effectiveness of more extensive psychological treatment (Heather et al., 2006) (for more information see Chapter 30, Rassool, 2009). The use of cognitive-behavioural approaches has been found to be effective in reducing or stopping alcohol use. In the treatment for alcohol dependence, the goal of cognitive behavioural therapy is to teach the person to recognize situations in which they are most likely to drink, avoid these circumstances if possible, and cope with other problems and behaviours which may lead to their alcohol misuse. The community reinforcement approach, a form of cognitive behavioural therapy, consists of a broad range of treatment with the aim of engineering the service user's social environment (including the family and vocational environment) so that abstinence is rewarded and intoxication unrewarded (Heather et al., 2006). Social behaviour and network therapy can also be used with patients to develop positive social networks (Copello et al., 2002).

Alcoholics Anonymous, a well known self-help group, created the twelve step programme which is a set of guiding principles outlining a course of action for recovery from addiction, compulsion or other behavioural problems. The only requirement for membership is a desire to stop drinking and to achieve sobriety. Members share their experiences, strengths and hopes with each other in the hope that they may solve their common problem and help others to recover from alcohol addiction. A Cochrane Review of eight studies (Ferri et al., 2006), published between 1967 and 2005, measuring the effectiveness of AA, found no significant difference between the results of AA and twelve step facilitation approaches compared to other treatments.

Summary of key points

- Alcohol has become one of the most important risks to public health.
- Alcohol withdrawal syndrome is a set of symptoms that individuals have when they suddenly stop drinking alcohol, following continuous and heavy consumption.

- Both hazardous and harmful drinkers may benefit from advice, health information and brief interventions.
- Younger people are more likely to drink heavily above the daily consumption recommendations.
- Alcohol is absorbed in the mouth, oesophagus and the stomach. This adds to the problem of poor malnutrition or vitamin deficiencies in heavy alcohol drinkers.
- Women do not metabolize alcohol as effectively as men and they are more vulnerable to the consequences of alcohol drinking.
- Chronic alcohol use may result in significant memory problems and cognitive impairment.
- Fetal alcohol syndrome is caused by pre-natal alcohol exposure and can cause permanent damage to the baby's brain, resulting in neurological impairment of the executive functions.
- Alcohol harm reduction aims to reduce the incidence of problem drinking and its negative consequences.

Reflective activity 4.2

A 35 year old divorced and unemployed man presents with tremors (especially in the arms), headache, and nausea. He looks agitated and anxious. He usually drinks eight to 10 cans of strong lager and a half pint of spirits every day. He is also being treated for depression and has been prescribed an antidepressant, which he has not been taking regularly. He reports starting regular drinking during his student days, and has taken cannabis on various occasions. Approximately three years ago, he was hospitalized for alcohol withdrawal syndrome. He has been arrested twice for driving under the influence of alcohol. He has tried to stop drinking twice in the last few months, but resumed alcohol use when he found himself homeless.

- What would be the immediate interventions required?
- What other withdrawal symptoms or behavioural problems may be observed?
- What are the short-term goals for this patient?
- What are the long-term goals for this patient?
- Outline a care plan for this patient.

References

Anderson, P. (2007) *Binge Drinking and Europe* (St Ives: Institute of Alcohol Studies).

Anderson, P. and Baumberg, B. (2007) *Alcohol and Public Health in Europe* (St Ives: Institute of Alcohol Studies).

Barretta, S.P., Pihla, R.O., Benkefal, C., Brunelle, C., Young, S.N. and Leyton, M. (2008) 'The Role of Dopamine in Alcohol Self-administration in Humans: Individual Differences', *European Neuropsychopharmacology* 18, 6, 439–47.

Cooper, J.R., Bloom, F.E. and Roth, R.H. (1991) *The Biochemical Basis of Neuropharmacology*, 6th edn (New York: Oxford University Press).

Copello, A., Orford, J., Hodgson, R., Tober, G. and Barrett, C. (2002) 'Social Behaviour and Network Therapy: Basic Principles and Early Experiences', *Addictive Behaviours* 27, 3, 354–56.

Department of Health (2004) *Choosing Health: Making Healthy Choices Easier* (London: Department of Health).

Department of Health, Home Office, Department for Education and Skills, Department for Culture, Media and Sport (2007) *Safe. Sensible. Social. The Next Steps in the National Alcohol Strategy* (London: Department of Health/ Home Office).

Ferri, M.M.F., Amato, L. and Davoli, M. (2006) 'Alcoholics Anonymous and Other 12-step Programmes for Alcohol Dependence', Cochrane Database of Systematic Reviews 2006 (3). doi:10.1002/14651858.CD005032. pub2. http://www.mrw.interscience.wiley.com/cochrane/clsysrev/articles/ CD005032/frame.html, date accessed 15 November 2009.

Garbutt, J.C., West, S.L., Carey, T.S., Lohr, K.N. and Crews, F.T. (1999) 'Pharmacological Treatment of Alcohol Dependence: a Review of the Evidence', *JAMA* 281, 14, 1318–25.

Health and Social Care Information Centre, The (2009) *Statistics on Alcohol, England 2009* [NS] http://www.ic.nhs.uk/pubs/alcohol09, date accessed 15 January 2010.

Heather, N., Raistrick, D. and Godfrey, C. (2006) *A Review of the Effectiveness of Treatment for Alcohol Problems* (London: National Treatment Agency).

Hodgson, C.R., Alwyn, T., John, B., Thom, B. and Smith, A. (2002) 'The Fast Alcohol Screening Test', *Alcohol and Alcoholism* 37, 1, 61–66.

Information Centre (2007) *Statistics on Alcohol: England 2007* [NS] http://www. ic.nhs.uk/pubs/alcohol07, date accessed 18 January 2010.

Information Centre (2009) *Statistics on Alcohol: England 2009* [NS] http://www. ic.nhs.uk/pubs/alcohol09, date accessed 18 January 2010.

Lovinger, D.M. (1997) 'The Role of Serotonin in Alcohol's Effects on the Brain', *Alcohol Health and Research World*, 21, 2, 114–120.

National Statistics (2006) *Drinking: Adults' Behaviour and Knowledge.* Omnibus Surveys Report No 31 (London: HMSO).

National Treatment Agency (2006) *Review of the Effectiveness of Treatment for Alcohol Problems* (London: National Treatment Agency).

National Treatment Agency (2007) *Models of Care for Alcohol Misusers* (London: NTA Publications).

Office for National Statistics (2009) *Smoking and Drinking Among Adults 2007 and Drinking: Adults' Behaviour and Knowledge in 2008* (London: Crown Copyright). www.statistics.gov.uk.

Prime Minister's Strategy Unit (2004) *Alcohol Harm Reduction Strategy for England* (London: Cabinet Office).

Rassool, G.H. (2009) *Alcohol and Drug Misuse: A Handbook for Student and Health Professionals* (Oxford: Routledge).

Rassool, G.H. and Winnington, J. (2006) 'Framework for Multidimensional Assessment', in Rassool, G.H. (ed.), *Dual Diagnosis Nursing* (Oxford: Blackwell Publications).

Richardson, A. and Budd, T. (2003) *Alcohol, Crime and Disorder: a Study of Young Adults,* Home Office Research Study 263 (London: Home Office).

Royal College of Physicians (2001) *Report on Alcohol: Guidelines for Managing Wernicke's Encephalopathy in the Accident and Emergency Department* (London: The Royal College of Physicians).

Samson, H.H. and Harris, R.A. (1992) 'Neurobiology of Alcohol Abuse', *Trends in Pharmacological Science* 13, 5, 206–11.

Scottish Health Action on Alcohol Problems (SHAAP) (2007) *Alcohol: Price, Policy and Public Health Report on The Findings of The Expert Workshop on Price* (Edinburgh: SHAAP).

Sir Liam Donaldson, Chief Medical Officer (2009) *150 years of the Annual Report of the Chief Medical Officer: On the State of Public Health 2008* (London: Crown Copyright), http://www.dh.gov.uk/en/Publicationsandstatistics/Publications/AnnualReports/DH_096206, date accessed 15 December 2009.

Smith, L. and Foxcroft, D. (2009) *Drinking in the UK: An Exploration of Trends* (London: Joseph Rowntree Foundation).

Spanagel, R. and Weiss, F. (1999) 'The Dopamine Hypothesis of Reward: Past and Current Status', *Trends in Neuroscience,* 22, 11, 521–27.

Weiss, F. (2005) 'Dopaminergic Compounds: Preclinical Data', in Spanagel, R. and Mann, K. (eds.), *Drugs for Relapse Prevention of Alcoholism* (Basel: Birkhäuser) 13–23.

World Health Organization (2009) *Working Document for Developing a Draft Global Strategy to Reduce Harmful Use of Alcohol* (Geneva: World Health Organization). http://www.who.int/substance_abuse/activities/globalstrategy/en/index.html, date accessed 19 December 2009.

Opiates 5

Introduction

An opiate is a natural or synthetic psychoactive substance. The raw exudates of the opium poppy (papaver somniferum) contain a number of alkaloids including morphine and codeine. Opium appears either as dark brown chunks or in powder form, and is generally eaten or smoked. Raw opium is treated with lime and various compounds to leave partially-refined morphine and heroin is manufactured chemically from morphine. The main source of street heroin in the UK is mainly from Afghanistan, Iran and Pakistan (the Golden Crescent countries). Some of the more common opiate drugs are: codeine, heroin (diacetylmorphine), pethidine, methadone, morphine and diconal. The word opiate and opioid are used interchangeably. Opiate refers to natural drugs which produce the characteristic opiate effects whereas opioid refers to a synthetic substance derived from, or resembling, the substances in the poppy plant.

The Home Office Research Report (Hay et al., 2008) estimated the prevalence of 'problem drug use', defined as the use of opiates in England to be around 273,123. This corresponds to 8.11 per thousand of the population aged 15–64. The British Crime survey (Home Office Statistical Bulletin, 2009) reported that the use of more problematic drugs was rare within the general household population: use of heroin, methadone and opiates overall was reported by 0.1 per cent of 16 to 59 year olds.

Pharmacology of opioids

Opioid receptors are found within the central nervous system and peripheral tissues. Many of the actions of opiates are related to an alteration of the release of endogenous neurotransmitters. These opioid receptors are normally stimulated by endogenous peptides (such as endorphins, enkephalins, and dynorphins) produced in response to harmful stimulation. Opioid binding sites are classified into three receptors referred to as mu, delta and kappa receptors. However, differences in activity and efficacy appear to be related to the relative stimulation of the various opioid receptors (mu, kappa, etc.) as well as genetic differences in opioid receptor sensitivity (Trescot et al., 2008).

All three receptors produce analgesia when an opioid binds to them. However, activation of kappa receptors does not produce as much physical dependence as activation of mu receptors (Chahl, 1996). Most of the most common opioids are agonists, and create their effect by stimulating the opioid receptors. An agonist is a 'drug that binds to a receptor of a cell and triggers a response by the cell. An agonist often mimics the action of a naturally occurring substance' (Medicine.Net, 2010). It is the opposite of an antagonist which acts against and blocks an action. The development of tolerance and physical dependence with chronic administration is a characteristic feature of all opiates limiting their clinical use and creating the liability for abuse (Wing, 2009).

Heroin – drug of choice

The most popular of opiates as an illicit drug of misuse is heroin. Heroin is usually sold as a powder whose colour ranges from white, off-white and yellowish, to reddish brown, the most prevalent type now available on the UK market. Street heroin is commonly adulterated with other drugs such as paracetamol and caffeine and with dangerous substances. Heroin is usually sold in small quantities, typically a heroin bag (0.2 gram) and regular users of heroin may generally consume 1/2 gram to over 1 gram per day.

Heroin's effects are dependent on the modes of administration. The modes include: swallowing, smoking, sniffing, or injecting either subcutaneously or intravenously. Smoking is often called *'chasing the dragon'*, or *'booting'*. A small line of heroin is placed on a piece of silver foil, and heated from below. The heroin runs into a liquid, and gives off a curl of smoke, which is inhaled through a rolled tube of paper or foil. Tablets are sometimes crushed and injected. If heroin powder is injected it is generally acidified, using lemon juice, citric or ascorbic acid, heated with water, and then filtered prior to injecting. The legal status, therapeutic and non-therapeutic uses, sought-after and adverse effects are presented in Table 5.1.

In moderate doses, opiates produce a range of generally mild physical effects apart from the analgesic effect. The depressant effects reduce the activity of the nervous system including reflex functions such as coughing, respiration and heart rate. They also dilate the blood vessels thus giving a feeling of warmth. Methadone effects are similar to heroin and may be prescribed to prevent opiate withdrawal symptoms. Heroin dependence develops after repeated use over several weeks and sudden withdrawal leads to anxiety, nausea, muscle pains, sweating, diarrhoea and goose flesh. Tolerance develops quickly so that larger amounts of the same drug are needed to produce the same effect.

Table 5.1 Heroin: effects

Street Names	• Smack, junk, gear, scag, H, scat, tiger, chi, elephant, harry, dragon etc.
Colour	• Ranges from white, off-white and yellowish colour to reddish brown. • UK market: Brown heroin (Afghan).
Sold	• Heroin is usually sold in small quantities, typically £10 bags.
Modes of Administration	• Swallowed, smoked, sniffed, or injected either subcutaneously or intravenously.
Effects of Use	• Snorting heroin - onset within 3 to 5 minutes. • Smoking heroin onset almost immediate. • Intravenous injection onset results within 30 to 60 seconds. • Intramuscular or subcutaneous injection takes longer, having an effect within 3 to 5 minutes.
Legal Status	• Heroin, pethidine, morphine, dihydrocodeine and methadone are Class A controlled drugs. Codeine and dihydrocodeine are Class B but Class A if prepared for injection. Distalgesic, dextropoxyphene and buprenorphine (temgesic) are Class C.
Therapeutic Uses	• Relief of pain, treatment for diarrhoea and vomiting and as a cough suppressant. • Methadone is often prescribed to heroin addicts for maintenance or withdrawal purposes.
Non-Therapeutic Uses	• Use of illicit heroin. • Diverted pharmaceutical opiates and opioids may be formulated for injection, oral use or occasionally as suppositories.
Sought-After Effects	• Euphoria; a relaxed detachment from pain and anxiety. • A sense of calm, pleasure and profound well-being.
Adverse Effects	• Users experience nausea or vomiting on the first occasions or use after a period of abstinence. • Tolerance leading to overdose. • Withdrawal. • Risks of injecting. • Heroin dependence.

Heroin use in many cases leads to heroin addiction. However, there are also many occasional or 'controlled' heroin (and other drug) users who are capable of using the drug with informal controls/constraints on their using behaviour (Warbuton et al., 2005). A range of different strategies is used for avoiding dependence or for retaining control over their dependence. Rules are followed to enable the users to restrict the frequency and amount with which they use and to ensure that their use does not intrude into their everyday work and social routines.

Withdrawal syndrome

The withdrawal syndrome from heroin may become apparent 8 to 24 hours after the discontinuation of sustained use of the drug. The severity of the withdrawal symptoms will depend on the extent of an individual's degree of tolerance and the amount of the last consumed dose. Heroin must have been used daily for at least two to three weeks for physical withdrawals to occur. The withdrawal symptoms include: anxiety, insomnia, diarrhoea, aches, tremor, sweating, muscular spasms, sneezing and yawning. Heroin users usually complain of the so-called 'itchy blood', which often results in compulsive scratching that causes bruises and sometimes ruptures the skin leaving scabs. Heroin users who adopt 'cold turkey'; that is to quit heroin abruptly are generally more likely to experience the negative effects of withdrawal in a more pronounced manner. The common symptoms of withdrawal syndrome are presented in Table 5.2.

Table 5.2 Heroin withdrawal symptoms

Time period of withdrawal	Signs and symptoms
8–12 hours	• Yawning • Tears • Cold sweats • Runny nose
12–24 hours	• Dilated pupils • Anxiety • Irritability • Anorexia
24 hours +	• Nausea and vomiting • Abdominal cramps • Diarrhoea • Goose-bumps • Severe bone and muscle aches • Insomnia • Depression • Penile erection in males • Extra sensitivity of genitals in females • Compulsive scratching

Overdose of heroin

Death through overdose remains a significant cause of mortality amongst heroin users. Recorded rates of drug-related death due to overdose in the UK are among the highest in Europe and accounted for more than seven per cent of all deaths among those aged 15–39 years in 2004 (EMCCDA, 2007). The np-SAD Annual Report (International Centre for Drug Policy, 2009) shows that opiates/opioids (i.e. heroin/morphine; methadone; other opiates/opioid analgesics), alone or in combination with other drugs, accounted for the majority (69 per cent) of all np-SAD cases. Heroin/morphine alone or in combination with other drugs, accounted for the highest proportion (45 per cent) of fatalities, a slight decrease over the 2007 level of 46 per cent.

During a period of abstinence (for example, in treatment or in custody), tolerance diminishes quickly so that an individual can easily overdose by taking their usual dose. Overdose occurs as a result of depression of the respiratory centre in the brain, which leads to respiratory and cardiac arrest and death unless immediate medical attention is received. The symptoms of heroin overdose are presented in Table 5.3.

Injecting: Health issues

Whilst pharmaceutical heroin is not especially toxic to human organs, adulterants in street heroin may well cause more damage, especially when they are injected. The risks of injecting include vein damage and collapse, local infections,

Table 5.3 Symptoms of heroin overdose

System	Symptoms
Respiratory	• Shallow breathing • Difficulty in breathing
Circulatory	• Weak pulse • Low blood pressure
Gastro-Intestinal	• Constipation • Spasms (stomach and intestinal tracts)
Nervous	• Delirium • Drowsiness • Muscle spasticity • Disorientation • Coma
Skin	• Bluish-coloured fingernails and lips
Other	• Dry mouth • Pinpoint pupils • Discoloration of tongue

abscesses, circulatory problems, ulcers, thrombosis, infections in heart valves, and systemic infections. In addition, the use of non-sterile needles and syringes and other related equipment brings with it the risks of blood-borne viruses including hepatitis B and C, and HIV. However, most complications arise from unsterile injections and adulterated street drugs. Heroin, taken by injection, is also a risk factor in contracting hepatitis B and C, HIV and septicaemia.

An outbreak of cases of anthrax among injecting drugs users has been continuing in Scotland since December 2009 (Health Protection Agency, 2010). Anthrax is a rare and very serious bacterial infection that is acquired when spores of the anthrax bacterium get into the body. The spores can be found in soil but may also be present in contaminated supplies of street drugs such as heroin. Drug users may become infected through injecting the contaminated drugs and through the lungs by inhaling or smoking contaminated drugs. The symptoms and signs include: severe swelling or redness around a wound site, which may be painless; pain at a site where you have previously injected; an open sore or wound; pus collecting under the skin; or a more generalized and severe flu-like illness (with muscle aches, headache, tiredness and high fever) (Health Protection Agency, 2010).

Methadone

Methadone is a synthetic opioid, used therapeutically as an analgesic and in the treatment of opiate addiction. Methadone is also known as doll, red rock, juice or 'script'. Methadone is a Class A drug and it is only legal for a person to possess methadone if it has been prescribed for that individual. Methadone maintenance is commonly used as a form of treatment in the UK because it produces similar effects to heroin or morphine and could break the cycle of dependence on opiates. Methadone is considered to be the best substitute drug for opiate dependent drug users because it is easy to administer and long acting. Methadone has been proven effective for the treatment of opioid dependence and can contribute to a decreased risk of human immunodeficiency virus (HIV) transmission. It is safe and effective and is associated with no euphoric effect.

There is evidence to suggest that oral methadone substitution treatment can: help to reduce the consumption of illicit drugs; improve the health of drug users; help them to avoid the risks of overdose and infection; improve social skills and functioning; and reduce crime (Stimson and Metrebian, 2003). However, the major benefits of methadone maintenance are to relieve opiate craving, suppress the abstinence syndrome, and block the euphoric effects associated with heroin (Joseph et al., 2000).

Methadone is usually prescribed as a liquid syrup to be swallowed but it is also manufactured as tablets and ampoules for injection. There is evidence to suggest that the maintenance of individuals on a daily dose between 60mg and 120mg and higher in exceptional cases is a critical factor in improving maintenance treatment outcomes (Gossop et al., 2001). There is a tradition in the UK for doctors to prescribe injectable methadone to opiate addicts as a treatment for their addiction along with injectable heroin prescribing and this approach is known as the 'British System'.

As with other opiates, tolerance, withdrawal symptoms and dependence may develop. Although the withdrawal symptoms develop more slowly and are less acutely severe than those of morphine and heroin, they are more prolonged. Methadone withdrawal symptoms can last for several weeks or more. It is very dangerous for problem drug users to take extra methadone above the recommended dose or mix it with other depressants such as temazepam, alcohol or even heroin and this may result in overdose or death. Key elements of methadone are presented in Table 5.4.

Table 5.4 Methadone: effects

Legal Status	• Prescription of medicine only
	• Class A controlled drug
Street Name	• Meth, phy
Therapeutic Use	• Severe pain
	• Opiate dependence
Tolerance and Dependence	• Yes
Long-Term Use	• Constipation
	• Breathing difficulties
	• Regular periods affected (menstruation)
	• Risk of infection (if injected)
	• Risk of circulatory problems (if injected)
Overdose Risk	• Increases after a period of abstinence
	• Mixed with other psychoactive substances
Withdrawal Symptoms	• Nausea and vomiting
	• Increased lacrimation (tears)
	• Rhinnorrhea (runny nose)
	• High temperature
	• Tremor
	• Chills
	• Sneezing
	• Tachycardia

Assessment of opiate dependence

In order to assess the current level of heroin use, an assessment or a clinical history needs to be undertaken to examine:

- Quantity, frequency and route of administration of opiate.
- Details of opiate use for the past week/month.
- Evidence of increasing tolerance.
- Any withdrawal symptoms.
- Any medical, psychiatric, social or legal problems.
- Duration, periods of abstinence – voluntary or enforced.
- Reasons for lapse or relapse.
- Previous strategies in coping with opiate use.
- Strengths and positive aspects of the individual.
- Other risky behaviours.
- Sources of help.

A model for doing this in four 'phases' during the course of the assessment of heroin use is outlined in Preston (2009). There are a number of tools designed to assess the severity of opioid dependence. One of the tools is the Severity of Dependence Scale (SDS) (Gossop et al., 1997). This instrument is a five item questionnaire that provides a score indicating the severity of dependence on opioids. The SDS takes less than a minute to complete and has been used successfully to identify the degree of dependence by users of different drugs. A physical examination is necessary to look for signs of opiate misuse (for example, needle track marks, skin abscesses and signs of withdrawal or intoxication) and physical complications of opiate misuse. The diagnosis of opiate misuse can usually be confirmed by urinalysis or oral fluid. Morphine and codeine takes about 48 hours to be detected whereas methadone can be detected within seven to nine days. Heroin is detected in urine as the metabolite morphine.

Management and intervention strategies

Many opiate users such as heroin users manage to stop using opiates without prescribing intervention or medical assistance. Others undergo a detoxification process as part of the initial stage of the treatment plan. Detoxification is the process of allowing the body to rid itself of the opiate substance while managing the symptoms of withdrawal or 'cold turkey' (Rassool, 2009). Detoxification should be a readily available treatment option for people who are opioid dependent and have expressed an informed choice to become abstinent (NICE, 2007a). It is recommended that methadone or buprenorphine should be offered as the first-line treatment in opioid detoxification (NICE, 2007). The most rapid regime can be carried out over seven to 21 days and when there are complex needs or problems, a gradual reduction of methadone can be prescribed.

A range of psychosocial interventions are effective in the treatment of opiate dependence. Counselling and support are important both during and after withdrawal from medication. Opiate users with coexisting psychiatric disorders are recommended to undergo cognitive behavioural therapy (NICE, 2007b). Health interventions intended to about lifestyle changes, reduce exposure to blood-borne viruses and/or reduce sexual and injection risk behaviours for people who misuse opiates should be part of the treatment package. For those who require a less flexible regime, referral to self-help groups such as Narcotics Anonymous should be facilitated. Relapse prevention is a crucial aspect of the drug treatment package. Residential rehabilitation in therapeutic communities might be appropriate for those patients who are unable to achieve abstinence in other ways. A summary of the intervention strategies is presented in Table 5.5.

Table 5.5 Assessment and intervention strategies

Assessment of Opiate Dependence	• Severity of Dependence Scale (SDS) (Gossop et al., 1997).
	• Urinalysis or oral fluid swab.
Intervention Strategies	
Detoxification	• Methadone or buprenorphine.
	• Under medical and nursing supervision.
	• Rapid regime: incremental cuts in dose over 7 to 21 days.
	• Slower regimes may take several months to complete.
Psychosocial Interventions	• Counselling.
	• Support.
	• Cognitive behavioural therapy (for those with coexisting psychiatric disorders).
	• Psycho educational interventions (relating to lifestyle changes, reducing exposure to blood-borne viruses and/or reducing sexual and injection risk behaviours).
Self-Help Group	• Narcotics Anonymous.
Residential Rehabilitation	• Therapeutic communities.

Prescribing heroin for opiate dependence

Heroin has been prescribed in the UK since the 1920s for the treatment of opiate dependence. Any medical practitioner can prescribe heroin in the treatment of medical conditions, but doctors need a licence from the Home Office to prescribe it for treating addiction. However, methadone is the most common treatment for opiate dependence in the UK but not all opiate dependent people benefit from it.

The updated drug strategy (Home Office, 2002) aims to improve access to prescribed heroin. It proposes that 'all those with a clinical need for heroin prescribing will have access to it under medical provision, safeguarding against the risk of seepage into the wider community'. Large-scale trials conducted in Switzerland and the Netherlands with people with long-term heroin dependency have provided evidence that prescribing heroin can lead to health and social gains (Stimson and Metrebian, 2003). In 2005, a pilot scheme, funded by both the Home Office and the Department of Health, was initiated in three clinics where addicts inject themselves with heroin (BBC News, 2007). The injecting clinics, intended for hardened heroin addicts for whom conventional treatment has failed, have operated for about two years. Initial results show that about 40 per cent of users had 'quit their involvement with the street scene completely', had more stability in their lives and reduced criminal activities.

Table 5.6   Benefits and risks of prescribing heroin to treat opiate dependence

Benefits	Risks
• Capturing those not in treatment. • Retaining those in treatment for longer.	• Removing readiness to change. • Adverse health consequences (risk of overdose, infections, abscesses and blood-borne viruses).
• Enabling users to stop or reduce illicit heroin use. • Reducing health problems. • Reducing acquisitive crime. • Providing a stepping stone to a gradual change from heroin use to methadone, and from injecting to oral use.	• Making complementary treatment less attractive. • Potential for prescribed heroin being diverted into the illicit market. • Pharmaceutical heroin is more expensive than methadone.

Source: Adapted from Stimson and Metrebian (2009) Prescribing Heroin: What is the Evidence? (London: Joseph Rowntree Foundation).

Prescribing heroin to treat opiate dependence may benefit individuals and/ or society, but may also pose risks. The benefits and risks are presented in Table 5.6.

Reflective activity 5.1

- Discuss the therapeutic and non-therapeutic uses of heroin.
- Describe briefly the mechanism by which heroin acts.
- Describe heroin's effects via the different modes of administration
- Discuss the sought-after effects of heroin use.
- List the adverse effects of heroin.
- List the withdrawal symptoms associated with heroin use.
- Discuss the reasons why methadone is used for opiate dependent users.
- List the withdrawal symptoms associated with methadone use.
- Discuss the benefits and risks of prescribing heroin to treat opiate dependence.

Summary of key points

- The term opiate refers to any psychoactive substance of either natural or synthetic origin that has an effect similar to morphine.
- Some of the more common opiate drugs are: codeine, heroin (diacetyl-morphine), pethidine, methadone, morphine and diconal.
- Heroin is swallowed, smoked, sniffed, or injected either subcutaneously or intravenously.
- Heroin dependence develops after repeated use over several weeks and sudden withdrawal leads to anxiety, nausea, muscle pains, sweating, diarrhoea and goose flesh.
- Death through overdose remains a significant cause of mortality amongst heroin users.
- The withdrawal syndrome from heroin may become apparent eight to 24 hours after the discontinuation of sustained use of the drug.
- There is a tradition in the UK of prescribing injectable methadone or injectable heroin to opiate addicts as treatment for their addiction and this approach is known as the 'British System'.
- Methadone maintenance is commonly used as a form of treatment for opiate addiction in the UK because it produces similar effects to heroin or morphine.
- Prescribing heroin to treat opiate dependence may benefit individuals and/or society, but may also pose risks.

Reflective activity 5.2

A 24 year old single woman was admitted to an acute psychiatric unit for opiates and benzodiazepines addiction during pregnancy. Prior to admission, the patient had been injecting heroin and taking methadone and benzodiazepines orally. She was anxious to be drug free prior to the birth of her first child. She has been dependent on opiates from the age of 17 and had about six previous unsuccessful attempts at detoxification, treatment and rehabilitation. Of aetiological significance is a very disruptive early childhood with parental separation, an alcohol dependent father, behavioural problems in school, truancy and early problems with the criminal justice system, and numerous relationships with other substance misusers.

- What would be the immediate interventions required?
- What other withdrawal symptoms or behavioural problems may be observed?
- What detoxification programme may be planned for this patient?
- What are the problems associated with poly or multiple drug users?
- What are the short-term goals for this patient?
- What are the long-term goals for this patient?
- Outline a care plan for this patient.

References

BBC News (2007) *A Fix on the State*, http://news.bbc.co.uk/1/hi/magazine/7099138.stm, date accessed 25 November 2010.

Chahl, L. (1996) 'Experimental and Clinical Pharmacology: Opioids – Mechanisms of Action', *Australian Prescriber*, 19, 3, 63–65.

EMCDDA (2007) *2007 Annual Report on the State of the Drugs Problem in Europe.* EMCDDA, Lisbon. http://www.emcdda.europa.eu. National Report (2005 data) to the EMCDDA by the Reitox National Focal Point United Kingdom. New Development, Trends and In-depth Information on Selected Issues. REITOX.

Gossop, M., Best, D., Marsden, J. and Strang, J. (1997) 'Test-retest Reliability of the Severity of Dependence Scale', *Addiction*, 92, 3, 353.

Hay, G., Gannon, M., MacDougall, J., Millar, T., Eastwood, C., Williams, K. and McKeganey, N. (2008) *Estimates of the Prevalence of Opiate Use and/or Crack Cocaine Use, 2006/07*: Sweep 3 technical report (London: Home Office).

Health Protection Agency (2010) *Rise in Cases of Anthrax Infections in Heroin Injecting Drug Users.* http://www.hpa.org.uk/web/HPAweb&Page&HPAwebAutoListName/Page/1191942145757.

Home Office (2002) The Updated Drug Strategy (London: Hole Office). www.crimereduction.homeoffice.gov.uk/drugsalcohol/drugsalcohol60.htm, date accessed 12 January 2010.

Home Office Statistical Bulletin (2009) Drug Misuse Declared: Findings from the 2008/09 British Crime Survey, England and Wales (London: Crown Copyright).

IDMU (2010) Heroin Prices. http://www.idmu.co.uk/heroin-opiate-prices/, date accessed 15 January 2010.

International Centre for Drug Policy (2009) *National Programme on Substance Abuse Deaths, Drug-Related Deaths in the UK – Annual Report 2009*, http://www.sgul.ac.uk/about-st-georges/divisions/faculty-of-medicine-and-biomedical-sciences/mental-health/icdp/website-pdfs/np-SAD%2011th%20annual%20report%20Final.pdf, date accessed 10 December 2009.

Joseph, H., Stancliff, S. and Langrod, J. (2000) 'Methadone Maintenance Treatment (MMT): a Review of Historical and Clinical Issues', *Mount. Sinai Journal of Medicine* 67, 5–6, 347–64.

Medicine.Net (2010) Definition of Agonist. http://www.medterms.com/script/main/art.asp?articlekey 5 7835, date accessed 20 August 2010.

NICE (2007a) Drug Misuse: Opioid Detoxification, NICE clinical guideline 52, (London: National Institute for Clinical Excellence). From www.nice.org.uk/CG52, date accessed January 2009.

NICE (2007b) Drug Misuse: Psychosocial Interventions, NICE clinical guideline 51, London: National Institute for Clinical Excellence. From www.nice.org.uk/CG51, date accessed January 2009.

Preston, A. (2009) Phases in the Assessment of Heroin Adapted from Methadone Briefing (2009) Section 6: Assessment. http://www.drugtext.org/library/books/methadone/section6.html, date accessed 15 January 2010.

Rassool, G.H. (2009) *Alcohol and Drug Misuse: A Handbook for Student and Health Professionals* (Oxford: Routledge).

Stimson, G. and Metrebian, N. (2003) *Prescribing Heroin: What is the Evidence?* (London: Joseph Rowntree Foundation). Available at www.jrf.org.uk.

Trescot, A.M., Datta, S., Lee, M. and Hansen, H. (2008) 'Opioid Pharmacology', *Pain Physician 2008: Opioid Special Issue*, 11: S133–S153. http://www.painphysicianjournal.com/2008/april/2008;11;S133-S153.pdf.

Warburton, H., Turnbull, P.J. and Hough, M. (2005) *Occasional and Controlled Heroin Use Not a Problem?* (London: Joseph Rowntree Foundation). Available at www.jrf.org.uk.

Wing, L.M.H. (2009) 'Pharmacology of Opiates and Their Derivatives', *Australian Drug and Alcohol Review,* 6, S1, 43–49. DOI: 10.1080/09595238780000431.

6 Psychostimulants

Introduction

Reflective activity 6.1

Before reading this chapter, try to provide a true or false answer for each of the statements listed below. Think about some reasons as to why you chose a particular answer.

Statements	True	False
Stimulants were used to treat asthma and other respiratory problems, obesity and neurological disorders.		
The most common type of amphetamine is amphetamine sulphate.		
Amphetamine users quickly develop a tolerance.		
Amphetamine is a depressant psychoactive substance.		
Amphetamines keep people awake for a long period of time.		
There are no dangerous withdrawal symptoms with amphetamines.		
Heavy users of amphetamines can experience unpleasant side effects like disturbed sleep and loss of appetite.		
Crack is a smokeable form of cocaine.		
Smoking a powerful drug like cocaine may cause respiratory problems.		
With crack cocaine, the user may feel tired and depressed in the period immediately after stopping his/her use of the drug.		
Cocaine is physically addictive.		
Amyl and butyl nitrite dilates the blood vessels and makes the heart beat faster.		
Ecstasy tablets are crushed and snorted or taken in a liquid form.		
The substances cathine and cathinone in khat are closely related to amphetamine.		

Statements	True	False
Cocaethylene is produced when alcohol and cocaine are consumed together.		
Mephedrone produces stimulant effects that are comparable to those of similar drugs such as MDMA ('ecstasy').		

Source: Adapted from Rassool, G. H. (2009) Alcohol and Drug Misuse: A Handbook for Students and Health Professionals (Oxford: Routledge).

When you have read this chapter, come back to this activity and consider your answers again. How many did you get right? For those you got wrong, think about the reasons for your original answer and compare this with what you know now.

The psychoactive substances that cause an increase in activity in various parts of the nervous system are called psychostimulants. These substances produce restlessness and arousal and stimulate behaviour and are often referred to as 'uppers'. Psychostimulants are available in powder form, in a variety of tablets and capsules and as an evergreen shrub (khat). The psychostimulants covered in this chapter are: cocaine, crack cocaine, ecstasy, amphetamines and methamphetamine, amyl nitrite and khat. Not all forms of psychostimulants are illegal. Caffeine is a mild stimulant which is considered relatively safe. Other stimulants that are legal include nicotine (found in tobacco products). Historically, stimulants were used to treat asthma and other respiratory problems, obesity, neurological disorders and symptoms of depression.

There are several indications that the global problem with amphetamine-type stimulants (ATS) is worsening. Psychostimulants are being made in a growing number of countries and global seizures are increasing. It is reported that about 30 per cent of global seizures in 2007 were made in the Near and Middle East, where amphetamine use may also be significant (UNDOC, 2009). In the UK, amphetamine is the most popular psychostimulant and cocaine powder was the next most commonly used drug. Adults aged 20 to 29 were the most likely of all age groups to have taken cocaine powder and those aged 16 to 29 reported the highest levels of ecstasy use. However, adults aged 20 to 24 reported the highest level use of hallucinogens (Home Office Statistical Bulletin, 2009).

Pharmacology of psychostimulants

Psychostimulants are a group of drugs with differing structures and common actions. They exert their effects by acting on the monoamine mechanisms, the most prominent of which include the facilitation of dopamine, noradrenaline and serotonin (Riddle et al., 2005). These neurotransmitters, also referred to as catecholamines, are involved in mediating a wide range of physiological and homeostatic functions. The role of dopamine is important in the regulation of movement, cognitive processes such as attention and working memory, motivational behaviour, and mediating effects of drug abuse (Tzschentke, 2001). Noradrenaline acts on the sympathetic nervous system and is involved in mediating cardiovascular effects, arousal, concentration, attention, learning and memory (Ressler and Nemeroff, 1999). Serotonin (5-hydroxytryptamine, or 5-HT) is involved in a variety of physiological processes, including the regulation of smooth muscle function, blood pressure and both peripheral and CNS neurotransmission (Dean, 2004).

Psychostimulants may increase or enhance the activity of dopamine, noradrenaline or serotonin by either increasing release, blocking reuptake, inhibiting metabolism or acting directly on a receptor. Psychostimulants increase the release of noradrenaline, serotonin and dopamine from nerve terminals (Silvia et al., 1997; Rothman et al., 2001). Cocaine also enhances the activity of dopamine thus increasing the amount of dopamine available to act at receptors in the synapse (Silvia et al., 1997). Cocaine may also block reuptake of noradrenaline and serotonin (Rasmussen et al., 2001). MDMA is also able to enhance the release of dopamine and noradrenaline (Gold et al., 1989; Frei et al., 2001).

Amphetamines

In recent decades, amphetamine has experienced a revival in its use as a recreational drug and performance enhancer amongst young people. Amphetamine, dextroamphetamine and methamphetamine, are collectively referred to as amphetamines. The most common type is amphetamine sulphate which is illicitly manufactured and heavily diluted with adulterants (often to 15 per cent purity). Crystal amphetamine (methamphetamine hydrochloride), the street form of the drug methamphetamine, comes in clear, chunky crystals and is heated and smoked. Smokeable methamphetamine is usually called 'ice' and consists of an off-white, grey or pinkish powder which is usually smoked in a glass pipe. Amphetamines are sometimes prescribed therapeutically for a number of conditions: attention-deficit hyperactivity disorder (ADHD), traumatic brain injury, symptoms of narcolepsy and chronic fatigue syndrome. Amphetamines can also be used as a supplement to antidepressant therapy in depressive conditions. The characteristics of amphetamines are presented in Table 6.1.

Amphetamine is one of the most common psychostimulants that is used amongst young people. An occasional user may take a few weeks to consume 1/2 gram while a heavy user might consume up to six grams per day of a relatively impure substance.

Table 6.1   Characteristics of psychostimulants

Legal Status	• Amphetamines and cocaine are prescription-only medicines and controlled drugs. • Cocaine, its derivative salts and the leaves of the coca plant come under Class A of the Misuse of Drugs Act [1971]. • Amphetamine, dex- and methyl-amphetamine, phenmetrazine and methylphenidate are in Class B. • If prepared for injection the increased penalties of Class A apply.
Methods of Use	• Swallowed, sniffed or injected. (For example, amphetamine sulphate is smoked and ecstasy is taken by mouth).
Effect	• Excitement and euphoria. • Dilates the pupils of the eye. • Increased heart rate and blood pressure. • Insomnia. • Anorexia. • Mood swings. • High doses cause thought disorders and a drug-induced psychosis with hallucinations and paranoid thinking.
Dependence	• Tolerance develops quickly with amphetamines. • More pronounced psychological tolerance than physical.
Withdrawal	• Characterized by hunger, fatigue, periods of fitful sleep, increase in dreaming and depression. Depression can be prolonged and severe.
Long-term Use	• Insomnia. • Weight loss. • Exhaustion. • Severe depression. • Drug-induced psychosis.
Risk Behaviour in Pregnancy	• Congenital abnormalities. • Miscarriage. • Premature labour. • Smaller than average babies. • Babies born to mothers who continue to take stimulants during pregnancy show a withdrawal syndrome. • Withdrawal among newborn babies is characterized by shrill crying, irritability and repeated sneezing.
Overdose Risk	• Death from drug overdoses (cocaine). • Respiratory failure.

Amphetamine is swallowed, sniffed, smoked or injected. The intensity of amphetamine is based on the amount of drug taken and routes of administration. In low doses, amphetamine increases attention span and decreases impulsiveness whereas in higher doses, it decreases appetite and brings on weight loss. If amphetamine is smoked or injected, the user immediately experiences an intense 'rush' (also called a 'flash') that causes intense pleasure but only lasts a few minutes. Chronic users of amphetamines typically snort or resort to drug injection to experience the full intensity effects of the drug with the added risks of infection, vein damage, and a higher risk of overdose. The street name, legal aspects, therapeutic effects, adverse effects, withdrawal symptoms, and overdose risk are presented in Table 6.2.

Table 6.2 Amphetamine sulphate: effects

Street Name	Whizz, Sulph, Uppers, Ice ,Crystal, Glass, Amph, Billy or Sulphate.
Method of Use	Swallowed, sniffed, smoked or injected (by crushing the tablets).
Therapeutic Uses	Attention-deficit hyperactivity disorder (ADHD). Traumatic brain injury. Symptoms of narcolepsy. Chronic fatigue syndrome.
Effect	Low dose – increases attention span and decreases impulsiveness. High dose – decreases appetite and brings on weight loss. Oral form – increased wakefulness and physical activity, and decreased appetite. Smoked and injected – the user experiences an intense 'rush' (also called a 'flash').
Adverse Effects	Violent behaviour, anxiety, confusion, and insomnia. Psychotic features, including paranoia, auditory hallucinations, mood disturbances, and delusions known as amphetamine psychosis. Infection risk. Circulatory problems. Risk of cardiovascular problems.
Dependence	Psychological dependence.
Withdrawal Symptoms	Craving, nausea, irritability, depression, loss of energy, sweats, fatigue, decreased libido, decreased confidence, hyperventilation, convulsions, irregular heartbeat, insomnia, paranoia, delusions.
Overdose Risk	Overdose risk increases if amphetamine is mixed with drugs such as heroin or depressants like barbiturates or alcohol. Death from overdose is possible with large doses, but rare.

Amphetamine can cause a variety of problems, including rapid heart rate, irregular heartbeat, stroke, high blood pressure, shortness of breath, nausea, vomiting, diarrhoea and physical collapse. There may also be an increase in body temperature and convulsions, which can be lethal if not treated as an emergency. Heavy users may also display a number of psychotic features, including paranoia, auditory hallucinations, mood disturbances, and delusions known as amphetamine psychosis. The paranoid delusion may result in homicidal or suicidal thoughts. In most people, these effects disappear when they stop using the drug. The use of amphetamine is highly addictive, and, with chronic abuse, tolerance develops very quickly. Withdrawal, although not physiologically threatening, is an unpleasant experience. How severe and prolonged these withdrawal symptoms are depends on the degree of misuse.

Cocaine

In recent years, there has been considerable concern regarding the rise in cocaine use in recreational settings (for example, discos and clubs). The total number of people who used cocaine at least once in 2007, worldwide, is estimated to range between 16 and 21 million (UNDOC, 2009). In Europe, according to the European Monitoring Centre for Drugs and Drug Addiction (EMCDDA), cocaine is a growing public health issue and is the second most commonly used illicit substance among the general European population after cannabis (ECMDA, 2007). The estimated number of cocaine consumers is about 12 million Europeans with the highest prevalence levels, of over three per cent, being found in Spain, Italy, and the UK (EMCDDA, 2008; Lucena et al., 2010). In England and Wales, cocaine powder was the next most commonly used drug (after cannabis) (Home Office Statistical Bulletin, 2009).

Therapeutically, Sigmund Freud, the father of psychoanalysis, expected that cocaine would be used as a substitution therapy for morphine addiction and as a euphoriant in cases of melancholia. Cocaine had also been used as a local anesthetic in ophthalmology and dentistry.

Cocaine is a white powder derived from the leaves of the Andean coca shrub. There are three forms of cocaine: cocaine hydrochloride, freebase and crack cocaine. Freebasing consists of smoking cocaine base (or crack). Crack cocaine (rocks, ready wash, ice, base, freebase, stones) is whitish in colour and looks like irregular lumps of sugar. Crack is made by heating cocaine hydrochloride with baking soda or ammonia in water. Cocaine is often mixed with alcohol to produce cocaethylene which is highly toxic and is also toxic when mixed with cannabis or with heroin.

Cocaethylene is produced when alcohol and cocaine is combined in the body. This combination forms in the blood stream and heightens and intensifies the euphoric effect of cocaine. It also amplifies the depressive effect of alcohol. Cocaethylene affects the brain for longer and is more toxic than either drug alone. Due to the slower absorption of cocaethylene than normal alcohol, there is an increased risk of damage to the liver. Cocaethylene is associated with a greater risk of sudden death than cocaine alone (Harris et al., 2003).

The intensity and the duration of the effects of cocaine are influenced by the route of administration. 'Snorting', 'sniffing', or 'blowing' (insufflations) is the most common method of ingestion of cocaine. Chewing coca leaves mixed with an alkaline substance (such as lime or bicarbonate) has an effect within 15 to 20 minutes. With oral administration, cocaine takes approximately 30 minutes to enter the bloodstream. Snorting cocaine produces maximum physiological effects within 40 minutes and the activation period is between 5 to 10 minutes, which is similar to oral use of cocaine. Snorting cocaine can lead to rhinitis – the inflammation of the nasal membranes. In addition to runniness, addicts often suffer nosebleeds or even a loss of their sense of smell. With smoking freebase the cocaine is absorbed immediately into the bloodstream reaching the brain in about five seconds.

Cocaine users can develop a tolerance and cocaine causes both physical and psychological dependence, the severity of which depends on the route of drug administration. The psychological dependence is more of a problem than physical withdrawal symptoms. It is more severe when the drug has been injected or smoked. Withdrawal leads to strong craving and drug seeking behaviour, followed by a withdrawal syndrome. The street name, legal aspects, therapeutic effects, adverse effects, withdrawal symptoms, and overdose risk are presented in Table 6.3.

Stages in cocaine withdrawal

Cocaine withdrawal generally occurs in three phases: the 'crash', the 'withdrawal' and the 'extinction'. However, not all cocaine users may go through the three distinct phases depending on the level of cocaine consumption, the set and setting. Cocaine users who suddenly stop using cocaine may experience the crash in the first few days. Even first time users of cocaine can experience the crash, depending on dosage and length of use. The withdrawal symptoms experienced can last between nine hours and four days. The withdrawal symptoms can include:

- Agitation
- Depression
- Anxiety
- Anorexia
- Intense craving for cocaine

Table 6.3 Cocaine hydrochloride (cocaine/cocaine freebase): effects

Street Name	Coke, Snow, Crack, Freebase, Rocks, Ready Wash, Ice, Base, Stones.
Method of Use	Cocaine hydrochloride – sniffed/injected Cocaine freebase – heated and inhaled Coca leaf-chewing with an alkaline substance (such as lime or bicarbonate).
Therapeutic Uses	Cocaine had been used as a local anesthetic in ophthalmology and dentistry.
Effect	A rapid feeling of intense high. Increase alertness and energy. A feeling of well-being. Delays hunger and fatigue. Increases confidence. Stimulates sex drive. If sniffed: damage to nasal membrane; damage to septum between nostrils. If injected: circulatory problems; infection risk. If inhaled: respiratory problems; lung damage.
Adverse Effects	Extreme agitation, panic attacks and feelings of restlessness, irritability, and anxiety. Chronic use of cocaine: rhinitis (runny nose) and damage to the nasal septum. Paranoia, auditory hallucination or a full-blown cocaine psychosis.
Dependence	Yes (mainly psychological).
Withdrawal Symptoms	'Crash' or rebound dysphoria, strong craving, and drug seeking behaviour.
Overdose Risk	Hyperthermia (elevated body temperature) and convulsions occur with cocaine overdoses, and if not treated immediately, can result in death. Excessive doses whether snorted, injected, or smoked can lead to overdose which can lead to sudden death from respiratory or heart failure.

- Uncontrollable appetite
- Insomnia or prolonged, but disturbed, sleep
- Extreme fatigue and exhaustion.

During the early stage of this phase, there is a gradual return to normal sleep and mood, low levels of cocaine craving and low levels of anxiety. In the middle phase of the withdrawal, severe cravings for cocaine are experienced. This may be reinforced by cues such as cocaine paraphernalia or other environmental cues which may lead to intense craving.

The withdrawal symptoms during this phase include:

- Taste sensations
- Low energy
- Anhedonia (inability to feel pleasure)
- Anxiety
- Angry outbursts.

The final phase of cocaine withdrawal is called the extinction phase. This may last for at least six months and indefinitely for other cocaine users. Some cocaine users may experience cravings when faced with strong cues such as people, places or objects. These cravings may surface months or years after cocaine use has stopped. The person returns to a normal mood but still feels an occasional craving for cocaine. Relapse is high because of continued cravings.

Khat

Khat, an evergreen shrub (Catha Edulis), acts as a social lubricant in the Yemen, Ethiopia and Somalia. The main active substances in khat are cathine and cathinone and these are closely related to amphetamine but are of less potency. There are two main types of khat available in the UK: Mirra (Kenyan khat) and Herari (Ethiopian khat). Mirra is usually described as having the stronger effect where sometimes the stems are chewed as well, in order to enhance the potency. Herari is thought to have a milder effect and typically only the leaves would be chewed (Rees, 2007). It is transported to the UK by air and is generally preferred fresh as the leaves from the plant are most powerful when fresh. Khat loses its potency within 36–48 hours of being picked and for this reason people prefer to chew it while it is still fresh. The prevalence data on the use of khat range from 34 per cent to 67 per cent of the Somali community who identify themselves as current users of khat (ACMD, 2005). Khat users appear to have very low levels of other drug or alcohol use which may be mediated by cultural and religious beliefs. The street name, legal aspects, therapeutic effects, adverse effects, withdrawal symptoms, and overdose risk are presented in Table 6.4.

There is no evidence that khat use is a gateway to the use of other stimulant drugs, although there is however, high associated tobacco use (ACMD, 2005). Fresh leaves are chewed and dried leaves are smoked, made into a paste and chewed, or brewed in tea. The users usually chew about two ounces of leaves or stems for a number of hours, swallowing the juice. Dryness of the mouth is caused by the juice so large amounts of liquid are also drunk. Effects start about a quarter of an hour into chewing and finish up to two hours after stopping. Effects start with stimulation and talkativeness and often insomnia.

Table 6.4 Catha edulis – Khat (contains cathinone and cathine): effects

Street Name	Khat, Chat, Qat, Quaadka, Quat, Miraa, Abyssinian tea, African salad, African tea, Arabian tea, Bushman's tea, Somali tea, Boesmanstee and Kat. It is an evergreen shrub (Catha Edulis) that grows in parts of East Africa and the Middle East.
Legal Status	The khat plant is legal, but its active ingredients cathinone and cathine are Class C.
Method of Use	Chewing leaves or drinking an infusion of leaves (like tea).
Therapeutic Uses	No therapeutic use. Social and cultural significance.
Effect	Stimulation and talkativeness. This is followed by a relaxed and introspective state that can last up to 5 hours, often including insomnia.
Adverse Effects	Lethargy, irritability and general hangover. Nausea, vomiting, mouth ulcers, abdominal pain, headache, palpitations, increased aggression and hallucinations can occur. Continued use can lead to cycles of sleeplessness and irritability. Longer-term use may lead to psychiatric problems such as paranoia and possibly psychosis. Digestive problems such as constipation and stomach ulcers.
Dependence	Psychological dependence.
Withdrawal Symptoms	There is no recorded withdrawal syndrome. It would be reasonable to expect listlessness and tiredness like that experienced by other stimulant users.
Overdose Risk	There is no known record of khat resulting in overdose, although it would be likely to act with other stimulants causing palpitations and agitation. Khat is also often used with tobacco and hypno-sedatives such as benzodiazepines which brings additional associated risks.

This is then followed by periods of lethargy, irritability and general hangover. Continued use can lead to cycles of sleeplessness and irritability and can, in the longer-term, lead to psychiatric problems such as paranoia and possibly psychosis. Digestive problems such as constipation, stomach ulcers and mouth cancers have been reported frequently to affect regular users.

Ecstasy (MDMA)

Ecstasy, 3,4-Methylenedioxymethamphetamine, is a synthetic, psychoactive drug with hallucinogenic and amphetamine-like properties. Ecstasy usually comes in tablet form, powder or in capsules with different shapes and colours. The strength and contents of ecstasy tablets cannot be known accurately as all ecstasy available on the street is produced in unregulated black market laboratories and is sometimes cut with amphetamines, caffeine and other substances. The use of ecstasy by adults aged between 16 to 59 years old in 2008 was estimated at 1.8 per cent (Home Office Statistical Bulletin, 2009).

Ecstasy tablets are also crushed and snorted or taken in a liquid form through injection but swallowing is the most common way that ecstasy is used. The effects of ecstasy usually begin within 20 minutes of taking the drug, and may last up to six hours. The physiological effects that can develop include: dilated pupils, a tingling feeling, tightening of the jaw muscles, raised body temperature, increased heart rate, muscle tension, involuntary teeth clenching, nausea, blurred vision, rapid eye movement, faintness, and chills or sweating. The psychological effects can include anxiety, panic attacks, depression, sleep problems, drug craving, confused episodes and paranoid or psychotic states. Ecstasy is not physically addictive in the way that drugs like cocaine, nicotine and heroin are. Many users, however, may develop tolerance to the effects of ecstasy. Frequent ecstasy use increases tolerance very quickly. The street name, legal aspects, therapeutic effects, adverse effects, withdrawal symptoms, and overdose risk are presented in Table 6.5.

Amyl and butyl nitrite

Amyl and butyl nitrites are stimulants and are known collectively as alkyl nitrites. Amyl and butyl nitrites are clear, yellow, volatile and inflammable liquids that are sold in small brown glass bottles – or, more rarely, glass phials. It is normally snorted out of the open bottle, although some people like to get risky by inhaling a cigarette that has been dipped into the liquid (amyl nitrite is a highly volatile flammable liquid!). When the bulb is broken, it makes a snapping sound; thus they are nicknamed 'snappers' or 'poppers'. In 2008, the use of amyl nitrite by 16 to 59 year olds in England and Wales was estimated to be at 1.4 per cent (Home Office Statistical Bulletin, 2009). Therapeutically, amyl nitrite is used for heart patients and for diagnostic purposes because it dilates the blood vessels and makes the heart beat faster. The vapour is inhaled through the nose or mouth from a small bottle or tube. The immediate effects of the psychoactive substances include decreased blood pressure, followed by an increased heart rate, flushed face and neck, dizziness, and headache. At low doses, users may feel slightly stimulated; at higher amounts, they may feel less inhibited, less in control; at high doses, a user can lose consciousness.

Tolerance to the drug develops within two to three weeks of regular use, but after a few days of abstinence, this tolerance is lost. There are no reports of withdrawal symptoms or psychological dependence. The immediate effects

Table 6.5   Ecstasy/MDMA (methylenedioxymethamphetamine): effects

Street Name	Ecstasy, E, Eccy, adam, XTC, Dennis the Menace, Doves, Speckled Doves, New Yorkers, Mercedes.
Legal Status	MDMA (ecstasy) is a Class A (Schedule 1) controlled drug. This means it is an offence both to possess the drug and to supply it to others.
Method of Use	Crushed and snorted or taken in a liquid form through injection. Swallowing is the most common way that ecstasy is used.
Therapeutic Uses	Used in psychotherapy.
Effect	Stimulant with mild psychedelic effect. Possible hallucinogenic effect, particularly in high doses.
Adverse Effects	Anxiety, panic attacks and insomnia, especially in cases of long-term use, or use of large doses. Increased susceptibility to minor infections such as colds, flu and sore throats. Some female users have reported an increase in genito-urinary infections. Pre-existing conditions such as high blood pressure, glaucoma and epilepsy can be exacerbated. Evidence that ecstasy may have the potential to cause brain damage associated with mood disorders. Ecstasy increases body temperature and has a dehydrating effect. Damage to the liver.
Dependence	Psychological.
Withdrawal Symptoms	Tolerance develops with time, but not as rapidly as cocaine or amphetamine. No evidence of physical withdrawal, although after-effects of the drug can include fatigue, depression and anxiety. 'Flashbacks' following repeated use over several days have been reported.
Overdose Risk	Fatal drug reactions cause blood clots to develop in the lungs. Heat stroke or dehydration. Dilutional hyponatremia – people have drunk too much water in attempting to counteract the dehydrating effect of the drug.

of nitrites are dizziness, relaxation of muscles, increased heart rate, low blood pressure, feeling flushed, blurred vision, headaches, vomiting, burning feeling (mouth and nose) and death (due to existing heart problems or low blood pressure). The long-term effects include reduced resistance to infections and the suppression of the immune system.

Mephedrone

Mephedrone, also known as 4-methylmethcathinone (4-MMC), is a stimulant drug and research chemical of the phenethylamine, amphetamine, and cathinone chemical classes. Mephedrone or 'meow meow' has emerged on the so-called 'legal highs' market and reportedly produces stimulant effects that are comparable to those of similar drugs such as MDMA ('ecstasy'). The drug is sold in high street 'head shops' (which sell bongs and rolling paraphernalia) and on the Internet as a plant food or 'research chemical'. Effects include euphoria, alertness, talkativeness and feelings of empathy. However, users can have the same adverse effects of stimulants including convulsions, breathing problems, nose bleeds, depression, psychosis and, in some cases, even death.

In April 2010, all cathinone derivatives, including mephedrone, methylone and methadrone, were designated Class B drugs under the Misuse of Drugs Act 1971. Class B drugs, which include cannabis and amphetamine sulphate, carry a maximum sentence of five years for possession or 14 years for supply.

Assessment and management of psychostimulants

Assessment and management of a patient presenting with acute psychostimulant toxicity can be a demanding and potentially dangerous activity. It is important during the assessment phase to keep the initial assessment brief, to provide clear orientations, to offer clients treatment options, to involve significant others and convey empathy (CSAT-SAMSHA, 2001). The assessment should include a thorough physical examination and mental state examination. This is supported by urinalysis to confirm the use of a stimulant.

The stimulant users may become extremely agitated and violent, displaying erratic and unpredictable behaviour. The patients may also experience panic attacks, delirium, irritability, confusion, tactile, auditory and visual hallucinations. Physical restraints may be necessary to ensure both safety for the staff and the patient, and to control the situation so that physical assessment and interventions can be undertaken. Clear protocols should be established in dealing with potentially aggressive or abusive patients and staff should be trained in this competence. Set firm boundaries with respect to aggressive or counter-productive behaviour.

Pharmacological treatment

Research evidence on the efficacy of pharmacological treatment for amphetamine users is limited. It has been reported that a number of potential treatments have been studied and pharmacological treatment with fluoxetine, amlodipine, imipramine and desipramine appear to have very limited benefits for amphetamine dependence (Scottish Advisory Committee on Drug Misuse, 2002). It is further suggested that fluoxetine may decrease craving in the short-term and imipramine may increase the duration of adherence to treatment.

Dexamphetamine sulphate has been prescribed in England and Wales for long-term amphetamine injectors. In England and Wales between 900 and 1,000 amphetamine users are prescribed dexamphetamine and 60 per cent of specialists in drug dependence consider that dexamphetamine has a role in treating amphetamine dependence (Merrill et al., 2004). A two centre randomized controlled trial of dexamphetamine substitution as a treatment of amphetamine dependence (Merrill et al., 2004) supports the Department of Health's current clinical guidelines that dexamphetamine substitution should remain a specialist treatment/intervention carried out by experienced practitioners. Dexamphetamine substitution therapy should be part of a complete treatment package incorporating psychosocial interventions and providing clinical monitoring procedures (urine analysis, blood pressure checks and mental state examination).

In relation to cocaine treatment, the UK Department of Health Guidelines (Department of Health, 2007) clearly states in their guidelines that substitute stimulant prescribing does not have demonstrated effectiveness and, accordingly, should not ordinarily be provided. A meta-analysis of desipramine shows a benefit (compared to the placebo) for promoting abstinence among cocaine users, but no effect on their retention in treatment (Levin et al., 1991). Desipramine (Norpramin, Pertofane) is a tricyclic antidepressant. There is also currently no evidence to support the clinical use of carbamazepine (Tegretol, Tegretol XR, Equetro, Carbatrol) in the treatment of cocaine dependence. Antidepressants have also been used in the treatment of cocaine dependence. Antidepressants, such as fluoxetine, can be effective in the management of major depressive episodes associated with stimulant use. There is no evidence that antidepressants have any effect on the withdrawal symptoms from stimulants (Department of Health, 2007). Overall, there is no strong evidence to support any single treatment for cocaine or amphetamine users. However, there is also no evidence to prove that such treatments are ineffective (Scottish Advisory Committee on Drug Misuse, 2002).

Non-pharmacological treatments

Psychosocial interventions have most commonly been used to treat psychostimulant users, in part because of the absence of a strong evidence base demonstrating the effectiveness of pharmacotherapies. Kamieniecki et al., (1998) reported the use of inpatient programmes, therapeutic communities, twelve step programmes, peer interventions, behavioural strategies, cognitive-behavioural interventions and acupuncture with psychostimulant users. Counselling forms the basis of most community-based treatments for psychostimulant users. Cognitive behavioural therapy (CBT) is currently used with psychostimulant users as part of the treatment package, especially in treatment intended to prevent relapse.

Studies have found that an abstinence-based psychosocial treatment approach, linking counselling and social support, has the greatest impact on cocaine misuse (NICE, 2007b). There is also evidence to suggest that contingency management approaches have been found to be more successful at promoting abstinence (NICE, 2007b). Complementary therapy such as acupuncture has been used in the treatment of psychostimulants. However, there is little clear evidence of the effectiveness of acupuncture for the treatment of psychostimulant dependence as a stand-alone intervention. A recent randomized controlled trial of the use of acupuncture in the treatment of cocaine addiction does not support the use of acupuncture as a stand-alone treatment, or when only minimum psychosocial treatments are provided (Margolin et al., 2002).

Harm reduction

The clinical management of stimulant misuse is not nearly as effective as that for opiate dependence, where treatments such as methadone and buprenorphine routinely enable substantial reductions in drug usage in the majority of individuals (Seivewright et al., 2005). A harm reduction approach for stimulant users needs to focus on safer sex and safer drug use. Stimulant users are more frequent injectors than opiate users and, in addition, have lowered sex inhibition and thus can be involved in unsafe sex. Drug information should include education about health risks, advice on safer sexual practices and the provision of clean injecting equipment (See Chapter 16 on Harm Reduction).

Emergency interventions with psychostimulant users

Psychostimulant users present to Accident and Emergency Departments with the following symptoms:

- Toxicity – seizures, collapsed lung, cardiac arrhythmias, or respiratory failure, with cardiovascular complications.
- Neurological – collapse, convulsions, cerebrovascular accident.

- Psychological – agitation, paranoia, confusion, hallucinations, aggression.
- Problems associated with injecting behaviour (blood-borne virus transmission, complications from injecting).
- Premature labour.

Toxic or fatal stimulant overdose are seldom seen in chronic, high-dose, intravenous stimulant users, probably because tolerance develops rapidly. However, most stimulant overdose fatalities occur in users who accidentally ingest large amounts as in the case of body packers. The symptoms of a psycho stimulant overdose are presented in Table 6.6.

Stimulant users who present with life-threatening medical conditions and toxic drug levels should be treated with life-saving techniques that respond to the severity of problems. Psychostimulant users who show acute neurological symptoms such as epileptic seizures or rapidly elevating vital signs require immediate intervention. There are no specific antidotes or antagonists to stimulant overdose available. The fundamental principles, in the management of the unconscious patient, are to maintain the airway, breathing and circulation. Urine or blood screening are performed to confirm diagnosis. If the patient is conscious, induced vomiting or gastric lavage with charcoal may reduce drug absorption if the drug was ingested less than four hours previously. CT scans and lumbar puncture should therefore be performed on the confused, unconscious or otherwise neurologically impaired psychostimulant user. If the patient shows signs of hyperthermia, it is important to correct elevated body temperature by cooling the patient with body ice packs, electric fan techniques, or cooling blankets to avoid uncontrolled

Table 6.6 Symptoms of psychostimulants overdose

Symptoms	
• Pressure, tightness or pain in chest.	• Racing pulse.
• Difficulty breathing.	• Grossly enlarged pupils.
• Headache, ringing in the ears.	• Muscle cramps.
• Dizziness.	• Inability to urinate.
• Vomiting.	• Nausea and vomiting.
• Cramps.	• Shaking, or seizures.
• Foaming at the mouth.	• Hallucinations.
• Profuse sweating, or failure to sweat.	• Panic.
• Irritability.	• Loss of consciousness.
• Confusion.	
• Hostility.	

hyperthermia. Treat seizures like status epilepticus with intravenous diazepam or other benzodiazepine.

The management of emergency situations resulting from the use of cocaine and crack involve the use of diazepam (psychiatric/psychological effects), aspirin and nitrates (cardiovascular effects) and oxygen (respiratory effects). In dealing with psychostimulant psychosis, an antipsychotic medication may be prescribed in the short-term.

Summary of key points

- The psychoactive substances that cause an increase in activity in various parts of the nervous system are called psychostimulants.
- Psychostimulants are available in powder form, in a variety of tablets and capsules and as an evergreen shrub.
- Amphetamine is swallowed, sniffed, smoked or injected (by crushing the tablets).
- If amphetamine is smoked or injected, the user immediately experiences an intense 'rush' (also called a 'flash').
- There are three forms of cocaine: cocaine hydrochloride, freebase and crack cocaine.
- Cocaine users can develop a tolerance and cocaine causes both physical and psychological dependence.
- Injecting cocaine has the added risks of infection, vein damage, and a higher risk of overdose.
- Smoking cocaine base is a more potent way of administration than snorting and produces a 'rush' similar to the experience of injecting cocaine.
- Many cocaine and crack users also take other drugs, including heroin. Alcohol is often mixed with cocaine to produce cocaethylene which is highly toxic.
- Cocaine withdrawal generally occurs in three phases: the 'crash', the 'withdrawal' and the 'extinction'.
- Khat generally produces talkativeness, mild euphoria and hallucinations.
- With khat, nausea, vomiting, mouth ulcers abdominal pain, headache, palpitations, increased aggression and hallucinations can occur.
- Ecstasy – the user experiences euphoric feelings, and feelings of empathy, relaxation and meaningfulness.
- The adverse effects of ecstasy include tiredness, confusion, anxiety and depression.
- Some people may develop tolerance to the effects of ecstasy and using larger amounts will increase the severity of undesirable effects, rather than increase the pleasurable effects.

- Mephedrone or 'meow meow' has emerged on the so-called 'legal highs' market and reportedly produces stimulant effects that are comparable to those of similar drugs such as MDMA ('ecstasy').

Reflective activity 6.2

JW is a 21 year old single employed man who lives with his parents. He was referred for assessment by his local substance misuse services. He uses amphetamine sulphate two to three times per day, and every day uses roughly three grams. He had been snorting amphetamine for the past few months but used to inject. His current drug use includes cannabis (about 1/8 ounce per day) and half a bottle of spirits. In the last two months, his alcohol consumption has increased. He has lost weight, has a poor appetite and has poor sleep patterns. He had brief episodes of paranoid psychosis and labile moods with periods of irritability, fatigue, and depressed mood associated with suicidal thoughts.

- What would be the immediate interventions required?
- What other withdrawal symptoms or behavioural problems may be observed?
- What are the short-term goals for this patient?
- What are the long-term goals for this patient?
- What treatment interventions and/or strategies may be planned for this patient?
- Outline a care plan for this patient.

References

Advisory Council on the Misuse of Drugs (ACMD) (2005) *Khat (Qat): Assessment of Risk to the Individual and Communities in the UK* (London: Home Office).

CSAT-SAMSHA (2001) Keys Based on TIP 33 *Treatment for Stimulant Use Disorders*, CSAT's Knowledge Application Program 2001, US Department of Health and Human Services, Substance Abuse and Mental Health Services Administration Center for Substance Abuse Treatment, www.samhsa.gov.

Dean, A. (2004) 'Pharmacology of Psychostimulants', Chapter 3 in Baker, A., Lee, N.K. and Jenner, L. (eds.), *Models of Intervention and Care for Psychostimulant Users*, 2nd Edition, National Drug Strategy Monograph Series No. 51 (Canberra: Australian Government Department of Health and Ageing).

Department of Health (England) and the devolved administrations (2007) *Drug Misuse and Dependence: UK Guidelines on Clinical Management* (London: Department of Health (England)), the Scottish Government, Welsh Assembly Government and Northern Ireland Executive.

EMCDDA Statistical Bulletin (2007) European Monitoring Centre for Drugs and Drug Addiction (EMCDDA). *Cocaine and Crack Cocaine: a Growing Public Health Issue* (Lisbon: EMCDDA).

European Monitoring Centre for Drugs and Drug Addiction (EMCDDA) (2008) *Annual Report on the State of the Drugs Problem in Europe.* Available at http://www.emcdda.europa.eu/publications/annual-report/2008, date accessed 10 December 2009.

Frei, E., Gamma, A., Pascual-Marqui, R., Lehmann, D., Hell, D. and Vollenweider, F.X. (2001) 'Localization of MDMA-induced Brain Activity in Healthy Volunteers using Low Resolution Brain Electromagnetic Tomography (LORETA)', *Human Brain Mapping,* 14, 3, 152–65.

Gold, L.H., Hubner, C.B. and Koob, G.F. (1989) 'A Role for the Mesolimbic Dopamine System in the Psychostimulant Actions of MDMA', *Psychopharmacology,* 99, 1, 40–47.

Harris, D.S., Everhart, E.T., Mendelson, J. and Jones, R.T. (2003) 'The Pharmacology of Cocaethylene in Humans Following Cocaine and Ethanol Administration', *Drug Alcohol and Dependence,* 72, 2, 169–82.

Home Office Statistical Bulletin (2009) *Drug Misuse Declared: Findings from the 2008/09 British Crime Survey. England and Wales* (London: Home Office), http://www.homeoffice.gov.uk/rds/pdfs09/hosb1209.pdf.

IDMU (2010a) *Amphetamine Prices.* www.idmu.co.uk/amphetamine-prices-2008.htm, date accessed 12 January 2010.

IDMU (2010b) *Ecstasy Prices.* www.idmu.co.uk/ecstasy-prices/, date accessed 12 January 2010.

Kamieniecki, G., Vincent, N., Allsop, S. and Lintzeris, N. (1998) *Models of Intervention and Care for Psychostimulant Users.* Monograph Series No. 32. NCETA (Canberra: Commonwealth Department of Health and Family Services).

Levin, F.R. and Lehman, A.F. (1991) 'Meta-analysis of Despiramine as an Adjunct in the Treatment of Cocaine Addiction', *Journal of Clinical Psychopharmacology* 11, 6, 371–78.

Lucena, J., Blanco, M., Jurado, C., Rico, A., Salguero, M., Vazquez, R., Thiene, G. and Basso, C. (2010) 'Cocaine-related Sudden Death: a Prospective Investigation in South-west Spain', *European Heart Journal* 31, 3, 318–29; doi:10.1093/eurheartj/ehp557.

Margolin, A., Kleber, H.D., Avants, S.K., Konefal, J., Gawin, F., Stark, E., Sorensen, J., Midkiff, E., Wells, E., Jackson, R., Bullock, M., Culliton, P.D., Boles, S. and Vaughan, R. (2002) 'Acupuncture for the Treatment of Cocaine Addiction: a Randomised Controlled Trial', *JAMA* 287, 1, 55–63.

Merrill, J., McBride, A., Pates, R., Peters, L., Tetlow, A., Roberts, C., Arnold, K., Crean, J., Lomax, S., and Deakin, B. (2004) *Dexamphetamine Substitution as a Treatment of Amphetamine Dependence: A Two- Centre Randomised Controlled Trial,* UK Department of Health Drug Misuse Research Initiative, http:// dmri.lshtm.ac.uk/docs/mcbride_es.pdf, date accessed 15 December 2009.

NICE (2007a) *Drug Misuse: Psychosocial Interventions.* NICE clinical guideline 51 (London: National Institute for Health and Clinical Excellence).

NICE (2007b) *Community-Based Interventions to Reduce Substance Misuse Among Vulnerable and Disadvantaged Children and Young People* (London: National Institute for Health and Clinical Excellence).

Rasmussen, S.G., Carroll, F.I., Maresch, M.J., Jensen, A.D., Tate, C.G. and Gether, U. (2001) 'Biophysical Characterization of the Cocaine Binding Pocket in the Serotonin Transporter Using a Fluorescent Cocaine Analogue as a Molecular Reporter', *Journal of Biological Chemistry,* 276, 7, 4717–23.

Rees, P. (2007) Briefing Paper 2: Khat, March 2007. http://www.phleicester.org. uk/Documents/trs/Khat%20briefing%20Paperl.pdf, date accessed 8 February 2010.

Ressler, K.J. and Nemeroff, C.B. (1999) 'Role of Norepinephrine in the Pathophysiology and Treatment of Mood Disorders', *Biological Psychiatry,* 46, 9, 1219–33.

Riddle, E.L., Fleckenstein, A.E. and Hanson, G.R. (2005) 'Role of Monoamine Transporters in Mediating Psychostimulants Effects', *The AAPS Journal,* 7, 4, E847–851. doi:10.1208/aapsj070481. PMID 16594636.

Rothman, R.B., Baumann, M.H., Dersch, C.M., Romero, D.V., Rice, K.C., Carroll, F.I. and Partilla, J.S. (2001). 'Amphetamine-type Central Nervous System Stimulants Release Norepinephrine More Potently Than They Release Dopamine and Serotonin', *Synapse,* 39, 1, 32–41.

Scottish Advisory Committee on Drug Misuse (2002) *Psychostimulant Working Group Report.* http://www.scotland.gov.uk/Publications/2002/08/15141/9093, date accessed 15 January 2010.

Seivewright, N., McMahon, C. and Egleston, P. (2005) 'Stimulant Use Still Going Strong – Revisiting Misuse of Amphetamines and Related Drugs', *Advances in Psychiatric Treatment,* 11, 4, 262–69.

Silvia, C.P., Jaber, M., King, G.R., Ellinwood, E.H. and Caron, M.G. (1997) 'Cocaine and Amphetamine Elicit Differential Effects in Rats with a Unilateral Injection of Dopamine Transporter Antisense Oligodeoxy Nucleotides', *Neuroscience,* 76, 3, 737–47.

Tzschentke, T.M. (2001) 'Pharmacology and Behavioral Pharmacology of the Mesocortical Dopamine System', *Progress in Neurobiology,* 63, 3, 241–320.

UNDOC (2009) *World Drug Report 2009.* United Nations Office of Drugs and Crime, Vienna. www.unodc.org.

7 Cannabis

Introduction

Reflective activity 7.1

Before reading this chapter, try to provide a true or false answer for each of the statements listed below. Think about some reasons as to why you chose a particular answer.

Statements	True	False
THC is the psychoactive ingredient in cannabis.		
The effects of cannabis last for a maximum of 14 hours.		
A common form of cannabis is Hash Oil.		
The name of the active chemical in cannabis is Delta-9 ethanol dehydrogenase.		
Cannabis has little effect on the ability to drive a car.		
Cannabis is less damaging to the ability to drive a car than alcohol.		
Cannabis impairs co-ordination and judgement resulting in an inability to drive.		
Cannabis causes little risk of lung cancer.		
Cannabis affects the brain by affecting memory and learning.		
Cannabis is physically addictive.		
Cannabis is a central nervous system stimulant.		
Cannabis is a gateway drug.		
Large doses of potent cannabis can cause 'toxic psychosis' when swallowed.		
Research suggests that there is no link between cannabis use and pregnancy.		

Statements	True	False
Memory problems associated with cannabis use are due to THC's actions on the hippocampus.		
Men are more likely than women to become regular users of cannabis.		

When you have read this chapter, come back to this activity and consider your answers again. How many did you get right? For those you got wrong, think about the reasons for your original answer and compare this with what you know now.

Cannabis is derived from a bushy plant, Cannabis Sativa, and is the most commonly used psychoactive substance in the world. The street names for the substance can vary around the country as some names are based on where it comes from, for example, Afghan, homegrown, Moroccan etc. Cannabis is the largest illicit drug market by far, including roughly 143–190 million annual consumers with cannabis production taking place in at least 172 countries and territories (UNDOC, 2007). The production of cannabis resin (also known as hashish) is concentrated in North Africa (Morocco) and in the South-West Asia/Middle East region, particularly in Afghanistan and Pakistan. Cannabis is used as a relaxant or mild intoxicant and is marketed in different forms:

- Hash or Hashish (resin which is scraped from the plant and then compressed into blocks).
- Herbal cannabis, also known as marihuana.
- Cannabis oil, prepared from the resin (whose potency is high).

Cannabis is the most commonly consumed illicit drug in all European countries. The EMCDDA (2009) reports that around 74 million Europeans (15–64 years) have tried cannabis in their lifetime, around 22.5 million of them having used it in the last year. However, cannabis popularity is declining, particularly among the young, but the numbers of regular and intensive cannabis users in Europe are less encouraging. Up to 2.5 per cent of all young Europeans could be using cannabis on a daily basis, representing a large population at risk and in potential need of assistance (EMCDDA, 2009).

The global number of people who used cannabis at least once in 2007 is estimated to be between 143 and 190 million persons (UNDOC, 2009). Cannabis is the type of drug most likely to be used by adults; 7.9 per cent of 16–59 year olds used cannabis in the last year in 2008/09. This psychoactive drug also remains the substance most likely to be used by young people; 18.7 per cent of respondents aged 16–24 had used cannabis in the last year in 2008/09 (The Information Centre, 2009). Cannabis is usually retailed in ounces (28 grams) or fractions of ounces, 1/4 ounce (7 grams), 1/2 ounce (14 grams). The retail price varies depending on whether it is sold in herbal (grass) or resin form.

Pharmacology of cannabis

Cannabinoid receptors are termed CB1 and CB2 receptors and have been found in animal and human brains and peripheral nerves (Devane, 1988; Munro, 1993). An endogenous substance named anandamide was isolated from the pig brain but had different chemical structures from plant cannabinoids (Devane et al., 1992). THC (Tetrahydrocannabinol), known as delta-9-tetrahydrocannabinol (Δ^9-THC), is the main psychoactive ingredient found in the cannabis plant. THC has been shown to increase the release of dopamine from the nucleus accumbens and prefrontal cortex (Tanda et al., 1997). Aston (2001), in a review of the pharmacology of cannabis, suggested that this effect, which is common to many drugs of misuse (including heroin, cocaine, amphetamine and nicotine), may be the basis of its reinforcing properties and its recreational use. It is reversed by naloxone, suggesting an opioid link. There is also evidence to suggest that cannabinoids derived from herbal cannabis interact with endogenous cannabinoid systems in the body causing impairments of psychomotor performance (Aston, 2001).

Features of cannabis

Cannabis contains more than 400 chemicals and the two powerful active ingredients are: THC (Δ – tetrahydrocannabinol), and CBD (cannabidiol) and both substances are classed as cannabinoids. THC is concentrated in the resin at the top of the plant. 'Skunk' (which has a particularly strong smell), 'sinsemilla' (a bud grown in the absence of male plants and which has no seeds), and 'netherweed' contain on average two to three times the amount of the active compound, THC. Cannabis is usually taken by mixing and smoking the substance with tobacco. Usually these substances are mixed. Sometimes they are smoked as a cigarette (joint), in a pipe, brewed in a drink or mixed with food. Cannabis smokers usually regulate the dose by the mode of ingesting the drug. The street name, legal aspects, therapeutic effects, adverse effects, withdrawal symptoms, and overdose risk are presented in Table 7.1.

Table 7.1 Cannabis: effects

Street Name	Bhang, Black, Blast, Blow, Blunts, Bob Hope, Bush, Dope, Draw, Ganja, Grass, Hash, Hashish, Hemp, Herb, Marijuana, Pot, Puff, Northern Lights, Resin, Sensi, Sinsemilla, Shit, Skunk, Smoke, Soap, Spliff, Wacky Backy, Weed, Zero.
Legal Status	Cannabis is controlled under the Misuse of Drugs Act [1971] (Class C). Cannabinol, cannabinol derivatives, and cannabis resin are also regulated under Class B under the statute. It is illegal to cultivate, produce, supply or possess the drug, unless a Home Office licence has been issued for research use or other special purposes. It is an offence to allow any premises to be used for cultivating, producing, supplying, storage or smoking of cannabis.
Method of Use	Usually, cannabis is mixed with tobacco and smoked. Cannabis is smoked in a pipe, brewed in a drink or mixed with food.
Therapeutic Uses	Cannabis is indicated for the treatment of anorexia associated with weight loss in patients with AIDS, and to treat mild to moderate nausea and vomiting associated with cancer chemotherapy.
Effect	Influenced to a large extent by the expectations, motivation and mood of the user. Intense feeling of relaxation, talkativeness, bouts of hilarity, relaxation and greater sensitivity to sound and colour. Concentration and mental and manual dexterity are impaired.
Adverse Effects	Apathetic, sluggish, and neglecting their appearance (chronic users). Bronchitis and other respiratory problems. Perceptual distortion, panic attack. Cannabis may also induce psychosis. Psychiatric problems may precipitate a temporary exacerbation of symptoms.
Dependence	No physical dependence. Psychological need for the drug.
Withdrawal Symptoms	A cannabis withdrawal syndrome has been characterized, but its clinical significance remains uncertain. The withdrawal symptoms include increased anger and aggression, anxiety, depressed mood, irritability, restlessness, sleep difficulty and strange dreams, decreased appetite, and weight loss.
Overdose Risk	No overdose risk.

The effects of cannabis usually start just a few minutes after smoking and last from about one hour to several hours depending on how much is consumed. There is no hangover of the type associated with alcohol use. Whilst under the influence of cannabis, concentration and mental and manual dexterity are impaired, making tasks such as driving or any procedure requiring accuracy or precision both difficult and dangerous. People chronically intoxicated on cannabis appear apathetic and sluggish. There may be particular risks for people with respiratory or heart disorders. The long-term effects include other respiratory conditions such as emphysema, and heart disease, and while not inevitable, are definite possibilities for anyone who regularly smokes tobacco. It can also make asthma worse and is a risk factor for anyone with cardiovascular problems.

Perceptual distortion may also occur, especially with heavy use. If the drug is used while an individual is anxious or depressed, these feelings may be accentuated leading to a feeling of panic. It has been reported that a growing number of medical health practitioners are convinced that cannabis use increases susceptibility to mental illness, accounting for 14 per cent of UK psychosis cases (Moore et al., 2007). Heavy use, particularly with strong varieties (skunk), can lead to psychosis. Heavy users of cannabis with personality disturbance or psychiatric problems may precipitate a temporary exacerbation of symptoms. Generally people who smoke cannabis are more likely to use other drugs, and people who smoke tobacco and drink are also more likely to try cannabis. However, there is no evidence that the use of one drug actually causes people to use another (escalation theory).

The concept of amotivational syndrome in relation to the long-term effects of cannabis remains a controversial entity in the literature. Amotivational syndrome includes a collection of features said to be associated with substance use, including apathy, loss of effectiveness, diminished capacity to carry out complex or long-term plans, low tolerance for frustration, impaired concentration, and difficulty in following routines. The consensus of opinion regarding the relationship of cannabis use and amotivational syndrome is that the syndrome may simply reflect chronic cannabis intoxication, the user's personality, attitudes, or developmental stage.

Withdrawal syndrome of cannabis?

There is now a growing consensus of the existence of a cannabis dependence syndrome which is consistent with other classic psychoactive drugs of addiction. There are now stronger risks of developing a tolerance and experiencing withdrawal symptoms with cannabis cessation due to the potency of the drug. A cannabis withdrawal syndrome has been characterized, but its clinical significance remains uncertain (Vandrey et al., 2008). The findings of the study (Vandrey et al., 2008) suggest that withdrawal symptoms associated with cannabis were of about the same severity as those associated with tobacco withdrawal. Tobacco withdrawal, but not cannabis withdrawal, is included in the current DSM-IV. These results are consistent with other evidence suggesting cannabis withdrawal is clinically important and warrants detailed description in the DSM-Vand ICD-11 (Vandrey et al., 2008). Symptoms typically begin within the first 24 hours after cessation of the drug, peak within the first week, and last about one to two weeks. The withdrawal symptoms of cannabis can be somewhat characterized as the opposite of the intoxicating effects of the drug. Other additional symptoms of cannabis withdrawal can include headache, nausea, anxiety, paranoia, irritability or aggression.

Assessment of cannabis use

Assessment may comprise compiling a drug history of the current clinical presentation of an individual's cannabis pattern of use. Obtain a good history to indicate that cannabis use is impairing the patient's ability to function either physiologically or psychologically. The assessment should focus on the current pattern of cannabis use, the quantities and associated problems. In order to ascertain the level of dependency, it is important to ask about experiences of withdrawal symptoms or any psychological complications. An outline of the assessment should include the following:

• Consider the statement of the need/problem.
• Type, quantity and frequency of cannabis use.
• Details of drug taking for past week/month.
• Prescribed, illicit or over-the-counter drugs.
• Evidence of increasing tolerance and withdrawal symptoms.
• Risk behaviour (sexual behaviour when intoxicated).
• Duration, periods of abstinence – voluntary or enforced.
• Reasons for lapse or relapse.
• Previous strategies in coping with the use of the drug.

A mental state or psychiatric assessment should be undertaken when psychiatric symptoms are evident. With cannabis-induced psychotic disorders, there are two types of psychotic disorder: one features delusions, the other hallucination. A careful history is required to establish whether the patient has a pre-existing psychotic disorder or whether symptoms arose after cannabis consumption. Those individuals presenting with anxiety or panic reactions with experience of perceptual distortions and intensified sensations are typically inexperienced users who react to novel experiences (Johns, 2001). Studies reported that individuals with cannabis use disorder have a high rate of other substance misuse disorders (Miller et al., 1990) as well as other types of axis disorders such as depression, anxiety state and psychosomatic symptoms (Troisi et al., 1998).

There are a number of self-administered instruments in the assessment of cannabis use. Cannabis dependent individuals presenting for treatment typically report cannabis craving. The Marijuana Craving Questionnaire (MCQ) (Heishman et al., 2003) can be used to measure cue-elicited craving in cannabis dependent individuals presenting for treatment. For the diagnosis of cannabis dependence, the DSM-IV criteria should be used. The Severity of Dependence Scale (SDS) (Gossop, 1997) has also been adapted to assess the psychological aspects of cannabis dependence. There is also the World Health Organization's screening instrument, the Alcohol, Smoking and Substance Involvement Screening Test (ASSIST) (Henry-Edwards et al., 2003) to identify persons with hazardous or harmful use of a range of psychoactive substances including cannabis.

Management and intervention strategies

There is a widespread consensus that cannabis dependence does not require treatment because the withdrawal syndrome of cannabis is so mild that most users can quit or cease to use without requiring medical assistance. However, there are a number of cannabis users who seek help and treatment for their addiction. The treatment strategies include: brief interventions, health education, harm reduction, assistance with withdrawal symptoms, relapse prevention and psychological interventions. Psychological therapies using motivational interviewing, cognitive-behavioural and relapse prevention techniques seem to be effective in reducing use with about one-fifth of participants in the studies achieving abstinence (Maddock and Babbs, 2006). Pharmacological therapies for cannabis misuse have been little studied.

Psychological interventions

Brief interventions are those practices that aim to provide information about the individual's cannabis use, information about personal risks associated with current drug use patterns, and general information about cannabis related risks and harms. In addition, it would nudge them and motivate an individual to do something about it. The key component of effective brief interventions is the provision of clear advice regarding the harms associated with continued use of cannabis. The users should also be provided with self-help resources to enable them to cut down or stop their cannabis use. The final component of effective brief interventions is to encourage patients' confidence that they are able to make changes in their substance use behaviour. Brief interventions with cannabis users have been found to reduce the frequency and/or quantity of cannabis used. These positive changes in patterns of use are reported to have resulted in improved health and social functioning (Lang, 2000).

Rollnick and Miller (1995) described motivational interviewing as more focused and goal-directed than non-directive counselling. In motivational interviewing, the counsellor takes a directive approach to the examination and resolution of ambivalence, which is its central purpose. Motivational interviewing is employed when the patients show no or little commitment to change their behaviour. It is a technique that does not require an in-depth counselling knowledge but involves a non-judgmental approach, open-ended questioning and reflective listening. Various tools and strategies have been developed to help apply these principles and these include pencil and paper exercises, structured questions and focused reflections (Mason, 2006). The four principles of motivational interviewing are: express empathy, develop discrepancy, roll with resistance and support self-efficacy. McCambridge and Strang (2004) reported reductions in the use of cannabis, cigarettes and alcohol among young people in the UK after just one session of motivational interviewing.

Relapse Prevention is a cognitive behavioural technique centred on the teaching of coping skills. There is good evidence of the effectiveness of specific relapse prevention in the treatment of drug and alcohol problems and psychosocial functioning (NTA, 2006a; 2006b). The techniques used to teach coping skills include identification of specific situations where coping inadequacies occur, and the use of instruction, modeling, role-plays and behavioural rehearsal. Exposure to stressful situations is gradually increased as adaptive mastery occurs. An important part of any plan should include assertiveness work and social inclusion.

Many of the studies into the efficacy of psychological interventions have demonstrated that they are effective in helping users to stop or reduce their use of cannabis (Budney et al., 2000; Stephens et al., 2000; Copeland et al., 2001; Marijuana Treatment Project Research Group, 2004). However, the vast majority of participants continue to use at the end of treatment. There are limited studies conducted in the UK.

Assistance with withdrawal symptoms

There are no pharmacological therapies for cannabis misuse and there has been limited research in this area. There are some suggestions that fluoxetine and buspirone are associated with reduced cannabis use, and nefazadone may help alleviate withdrawal symptoms (McRae et al., 2003). Most users of cannabis do not require assistance with medication during the detoxification or withdrawal from cannabis. Some cannabis users may need help with pharmacotherapy to alleviate severe agitation, restlessness, irritability insomnia or nightmare. These patients may be prescribed Benzodiazepines-Diazepam 4–10 mg tds for a short duration. This should be complemented with psychosocial and educational interventions.

Status of cannabis

In the UK, cannabis has been classified and reclassified a number of times and currently its status is a Class B drug. The rationale behind such a move was to protect the public and to prevent the consequences of cannabis use on young people's mental health because of research linking heavy use of the drug with schizophrenia and other mental health problems. This shift in reclassification of cannabis went against the Advisory Council on the Misuse of Drugs' (ACMD) recommendations.

The health effects of cannabis have often been the focus of debate on the legal status of cannabis. It has been argued that the scientific investigation and deliberation on the health effects would resolve decisions on whether to legalize or not (Farrell and Ritson, 2001). There is a wide consensus on the adverse physical and psychological effects of cannabis. However, when compared to the morbidity and mortality caused by other psychoactive legal substances such as alcohol and tobacco, cannabis is nowhere near the same level and status.

Currently, psychoactive substances are regulated according to classification systems that claim to relate to the harms (physical, psychological and social) and risks of each drug. However, a study by Nutt et al. (2007) showed that socially accepted drugs such as alcohol and tobacco were judged more harmful than cannabis, and substantially more dangerous than the Class A drugs LSD, 4-methylthioamphetamine and ecstasy. Nutt et al. (2007) proposed that drugs should be classified by the amount of harm that they do, rather than the sharp A, B and C divisions in the UK Misuse of Drugs Act.

Advocates of legalization argue that cannabis is not only less harmful than legal substances like alcohol and tobacco, but has been proven to be effective in certain medical conditions. There is evidence to suggest that cannabis will bring about relief for sufferers and some aspects of disability for multiple sclerosis (Zajicek et al., 2005) and other medical conditions such as glaucoma. Thus, the legal status of cannabis should be determined on health grounds. Opponents of legislation claimed that the legalization of cannabis would far outweigh its benefits and will act as a precursor to increased addiction. In the advancement of the argument against the legalization or decriminalization, Farell and Ritson (2001) suggested that one of the key determinants of legal status is likely to be social and moral attitudes to a range of psychoactive substances.

There is also the argument about individual choice and freedom of choice in a democratic society. The state should be less paternalistic about legislating against something which harms only the actual consumer. In contrast, legislation to control the psychoactive substance is necessary to prevent or reduce harm caused by cannabis. There is evidence that cannabis itself can induce significant levels of dependence (Hall and Solowij, 1998) and affects not only the individual consumer but significant others. In the longer term, as Farrel and Ritson (2001) suggest the issue of cannabis in relation to a range of medical disorders will be seen as a medicinal matter, as is the case with homoeopathy and other complementary medicines.

Summary of key points

- Cannabis has two powerful active ingredients – THC and CBD (cannabidiol) and both substances are classed as cannabinoids.
- Cannabis is the most commonly used psychoactive substance in the world.
- In England and Wales, cannabis remains the most widely used drug.
- Herbal cannabis, also known as marijuana or grass is a weaker preparation of dried plant material.
- It is an offence to allow any premises to be used for cultivating, producing, supplying, storage or the smoking of cannabis.
- The concept of Amotivational Syndrome in relation to the long-term effects of cannabis, remains a controversial entity in the literature. It may simply reflect chronic cannabis intoxication.
- Brief interventions comprise of a single brief advice or several short (15–30 minutes) counselling sessions.
- Motivational interviewing takes the form of 'directive, client-centred counselling for eliciting behaviour change by helping clients to explore and resolve ambivalence'.
- Patients may need support to identify risks associated with their substance misuse and a relapse prevention plan is based on the identified risk factors.

Reflective activity 7.2

A 28 year old married painter and decorator comes to see you seeking help with his use of cannabis. He reports using cannabis on a daily basis for the last 10 years. He smokes about 5 gm of cannabis a week and about 40 cigarettes. During the weekend, he drinks about five to eight pints of strong beer. He says that due to his heavy smoking, he is unable to play rugby as he suffers from breathlessness. He has tried to give up both cannabis and tobacco on several occasions but always has a relapse. His partner does not like him being stoned all the time as he has refused to go out due to his mild social anxiety. On stopping cannabis use, he says that he suffers from headaches, irritability, mood swings and insomnia.

- What would be the immediate interventions required?
- What other withdrawal symptoms or behavioural problems may be observed?
- What are the short-term goals for this patient?
- What are the long-term goals for this patient?
- How would you advise him to stop using cannabis and tobacco?

References

Aston, H.C. (2001) 'Pharmacology and Effects of Cannabis: a Brief Review', *The British Journal of Psychiatry*, 178, 2, 101–06.

Budney, A., Higgins, S., Radanovich, K. and Novy, P. (2000) 'Adding Voucher-based Incentives to Coping Skills and Motivational Enhancement Improves Outcomes During Treatment for Marijuana Dependence', *Journal of Consulting and Clinical Psychology* 68, 6, 1051–61.

Copeland, J., Swift, W., Roffman, R. and Stephens, R. (2001) 'A Randomised Controlled Trial of Brief Interventions for Cannabis Use Disorder', *Journal of Substance Abuse Treatment* 21, 2, 55–64.

Devane, W.A., Dysarz, F.A., Johnson, M.R., Melvin, L.S. and Howlett, A.C. (1988) 'Determination and Characterisation of a Cannabinoid Receptor in Rat Brain', *Molecular Pharmacology*, 34, 5, 605.

Devane, W.A., Hanus, L., Breuer, A., Pertwee, R.G., Stevenson, L.A., Griffin, G., Gibson, D., Mandelbaum, A., Etinger, A. and Mechoulam, R. (1992) 'Isolation and Structure of a Brain Constituent That Binds to the Cannabinoid Receptor', *Science* 258, 5090, 1946–49. DOI: 10.1126/science.1470919.

EMCDDA (2009) Annual Report 2009: The State of the Drugs Problem in Europe (Lisbon: European Monitoring Centre for Drugs and Drug Addiction), http://www.emcdda.europa.eu.

Farrell, M. and Ritson, B. (2001) 'Cannabis and Health', *The British Journal of Psychiatry*, 178, 2, 98.

Gossop, M., Best, D., Marsden, J. and Strang, J. (1997) 'Test-Retest Reliability of the Severity of Dependence Scale', *Addiction*, 92, 3, 353.

Hall, W. and Solowij, N. (1998) 'Adverse Effects of Cannabis', *Lancet*, 352, 9140, 1611–16.

Heishman, S.J., Evans, R.J., Singleton, E.G., Levin, K.H., Copersino, M.L. and Gorelick, D.A. (2003) 'Reliability and Validity of a Short Form of the Marijuana Craving Questionnaire', *Drug and Alcohol Dependence*, 102, 1–3, 35–40.

Henry-Edwards, S., Humeniuk ,R., Ali, R., Monteiro, M. and Poznyak, V. (2003) Brief Intervention for Substance Use: A Manual for Use in Primary Care. (Draft Version 1.1 for Field Testing), (Geneva: World Health Organization).

IDMU (2010) Cannabis Prices 2008. (Wigan, The Independent Drug Monitoring Unit). http://www.idmu.co.uk/

Johns, A. (2001) 'Psychiatric Effects of Cannabis', *British Journal of Psychiatry* 178, 2, 116–22.

Lang, E. (2000) 'Report of an Integrated Brief Intervention with Self-defined Problem Cannabis Users', *Journal of Substance Abuse Treatment*, 19, 2, 111–16.

Maddock, C. and Babbs, M. (2006) 'Interventions for Cannabis Misuse', *Advances in Psychiatric Treatment* 12, 6, 432–39.

Marijuana Treatment Project Research Group (2004) 'Brief Treatments for Cannabis Dependence: Findings from a Randomized Multisite Trial', *Journal of Consulting and Clinical Psychology*, 72, 3, 455–66.

Mason, P. (2006) 'Motivational Interviewing', in Rassool, G.H. (ed.), *Dual Diagnosis Nursing* (Oxford: Blackwell Publications).

McCambridge, J. and Stràng, J. (2004) 'The Efficacy of Single-session Motivational Interviewing in Reducing Drug Consumption and Perceptions of Drug-related Risk and Harm Among Young People: Results from a Multi-site Cluster Randomized Trial', *Addiction*, 99, 1, 39–52.

McRae, A.L., Budney, A.J. and Brady, K.T. (2003) 'Treatment of Marijuana Dependence: a Review of the Literature', *Journal of Substance Abuse Treatment*, 24, 4, 369–76.

Miller, N.S., Klahr, A.L., Gold, M.S., Sweeney, K., Cocores, J.A. and Sweeney, D.R. (1990) 'Cannabis Diagnosis of Patients Receiving Treatment for Cocaine Dependence', *Journal of Substance Abuse* 2, 1, 107–11.

Moore, T., Zammit, S., Lingford-Hughes, A., Barnes, T., Jones, P., Burke, M. and Lewis, G. (2007) 'Cannabis Use and Risk of Psychotic or Affective Mental Health Outcomes: a Systematic Review', *The Lancet*, 370, 9584, 319–28.

Munro, S., Thomas, K.L. and Abu-Shaar, M. (1993) 'Molecular Characterization of Peripheral Receptor for Cannabinoids', *Nature*, 365, 6441, 61–65.

NTA (2006a) *Treating Drug Misuse Problems: Evidence of Effectiveness* (London: National Treatment Agency).

NTA (2006b) *Review of the Effectiveness of Treatment for Alcohol Problems* (London: National Treatment Agency).

Nutt, D., King, L.A., Saulsbury, W. and Blakemore, C. (2007) 'Development of a Rational Scale to Assess the Harm of Drugs of Potential Misuse', *Lancet*, 24, 369 (9566), 1047–53.

Rollnick, S. and Miller, W.R. (1995). 'What is Motivational Interviewing?' *Behavioural and Cognitive Psychotherapy* 23, 4, 325–34.

Stephens, R.S., Roffman, R.A. and Curtin, L. (2000) 'Comparison of Extended Versus Brief Treatments for Marijuana Use', *Journal of Consulting and Clinizcal Psychology*, 68, 5, 898–908.

Tanda, G., Pontieri, F.E. and Di Chiara, G. (1997) 'Cannabinoid and Heroin Activation of Mesolimbic Dopamine Transmission by a Common μ_1 Opioid Receptor Mechanism', *Science*, 276, 5321, 2048–50. DOI: 10.1126/science. 276.5321.2048.

The NHS Information Centre (2009) Statistics on Drug Misuse: England 2009, The Information Centre for Health and Social Care, Lifestyles Statistics. www.ic.nhs.uk.

Troisi, A., Pasini, A., Saracco, M. and Spalletta, G. (1998) 'Psychiatric Symptoms in Male Cannabis Users Not Using Other Illicit Drugs', *Addiction* 93, 4, 487–92.

UNDOC (2007) *World Drug Report 2007*. http://www.unodc.org/india/world_drug_report_2007.html, date accessed 15 November 2009.

Vandrey, R.G., Budney, A.J., Hughes, J.R. and Liguori, A. (2008) 'A Within-Subject Comparison of Withdrawal Symptoms During Abstinence from Cannabis, Tobacco, and Both Substances', *Drug and Alcohol Dependence*, 92, 1–3, 48–54.

Zajicek, J.P., Sanders, H.P., Wright, D.E., Vickery, P.J., Ingram, W.M., Reilly, S.M., Nunn, A.J., Teare, L.J., Fox, P.J. and Thompson, A.J. (2005) 'Cannabinoids in Multiple Sclerosis (CAMS) Study, Safety and Efficacy Data for up to 12 Months Follow-up', *Journal of Neurology, Neurosurgery and Psychiatry* 76, 12, 1664–69.

Hallucinogens and Other Psychoactive Substances

8

Introduction

Reflective activity 8.1

Before reading this chapter, try to provide a true or false answer for each of the statements listed below. Think about some reasons as to why you chose your particular answers.

Statements	True	False
Hallucinogens refer to a group of drugs causing hallucinogenic experiences.		
The following drugs are hallucinogens: LSD, PCP, GHB and ecstasy.		
Most hallucinogenic drugs cause hallucinations.		
The effects of LSD start about 30 minutes after taking it.		
Acid, microdots, dots, tabs or trips are slang names for LSD.		
LSD is associated with physical dependence.		
Ecstasy refers to which of the following drugs? MDMA.		
Ecstasy tablets contain amphetamine.		
The effects of ecstasy start about 10 minutes after taking it.		
The following are considered 'Club Drugs': ecstasy, rohypnol and ketamine.		
The effects of ecstasy may cause psychological dependence.		
GHB Gammahydroxybutyrate is a Class C drug.		
The effects of GHB start in anything from 10 to 60 minutes.		
In terms of physical and social harm GHB is more dangerous than alcohol.		
Regular use of GHB can cause psychological dependence.		
Special K is known as PCP.		
The effects of injecting ketamine start in anything from 10 to 15 minutes.		
Psilocybin is known as magic mushroom.		

Statements	True	False
The effects of injecting psilocybin start immediately.		
Benzodiazepines and barbiturates are prescription-only medicines and are Class C and B controlled drugs respectively.		
Hypno-sedatives are a drug of misuse not only among the illicit drug population but among the population in general.		
Some organic based (volatile) substances produce effects similar to alcohol or anaesthetics when their vapours are inhaled.		

When you have read this chapter, come back to this activity and consider your answers again. How many did you get right? For those you got wrong, think about the reasons for your original answer and compare this with what you know now.

This chapter examines the hallucinogens, hypno-sedatives and over-the-counter drugs. The term hallucinogens refers to a diverse group of drugs, whether natural or synthetic, such as LSD (Lysergic Acid Diethylamide), psilocybin (liberty cap mushrooms), amanita muscaria (fly agaric mushrooms), morning glory seeds and mescaline (peyote cactus), PCP (phencyclidine) and ketamine. Hallucinogens are psychoactive substances that induce an alteration in perception, thought, emotion and consciousness.

Most hallucinogenic drugs, with the exception of dimethyltryptamine and atropine, do not consistently cause hallucinations. Hallucinations are defined as false sensations that have no basis in reality (Parish et al., 2009). These substances are more likely to cause a modification of normal perception with changes in mood or in thought than actual hallucinations. The individual is usually quite aware of the illusive and personal nature of their perceptions. In England and Wales, the proportion of 16 to 59 year olds who use tranquillizers was estimated at 0.7 per cent, use of hallucinogens (LSD and magic mushrooms) was estimated at 0.6 per cent, as was the use of ketamine (Home Office Statistical Bulletin, 2009).

Pharmacology of hallucinogens

It is well recognized that hallucinogens are psychoactive substances that cause hallucinations, which are profound distortions in a person's perception of reality. It is stated that hallucinogens produce their effects by initially disrupting the interaction of nerve cells and the neurotransmitter serotonin (Fantegrossi et al., 2008). Serotonin is involved in the control of behavioural, perceptual, and regulatory systems, including mood, hunger, body temperature, sexual behaviour, muscle control, and sensory perception.

Evidence from laboratory studies suggests that LSD, like hallucinogenic plants, acts on certain groups of serotonin receptors designated the 5-HT2 receptors, and that its effects are most prominent in two brain regions: one is the cerebral cortex, an area involved in mood, cognition, and perception; the other is the locus ceruleus, which receives sensory signals from all areas of the body and has been described as the brain's 'novelty detector' for important external stimuli (NIDA, 2001). One of the hallucinogens, PCP acts mainly through a type of glutamate receptor in the brain that is important for the perception of pain, responses to the environment, and learning and memory. In the brain, PCP also alters the actions of dopamine, a neurotransmitter responsible for the euphoria and 'rush' associated with many misused drugs (NIDA, 2001).

LSD (Lysergic Acid Diethylamide)

Lysergic Acid Diethylamide, known as LSD, an odourless, colourless, and tasteless powder, is derived from a fungus that grows on rye and other grains. The substance comes in many forms: liquid, tablets or capsules, squares of gelatine or blotting paper. The blotting paper is divided into small decorated squares, with each square representing one dose (50–150 micrograms). The methods of use include: swallowing, sniffing, injecting and smoking. The effects of LSD tend to start about half an hour after taking it and last up to 12 hours or sometimes even longer, depending on the dosage. The street name, legal aspects, therapeutic effects, adverse effects, withdrawal symptoms, and overdose risk are presented in Table 8.1.

Table 8.1 LSD: effects

Street Name	Acid, Microdots, Dots, Tabs, Trips.
Legal Status	Class A controlled drug
Method of Use	Swallowed, sniffed, injected or smoked.
Therapeutic Uses	Depression, treatment of obsessive-compulsive disorders, alcohol dependence and opiate addiction. Psychotherapy.
Effect	Dependent on the user's prior experience, mood, expectations and setting. Profound alteration in mood, sensation and consciousness, intensified sensory experiences, perceptual distortions, confusion of time, space, body image and boundaries (blending of sight and sound).
Adverse Effects	Panic, confusion, impulsive behaviour and unpleasant illusions (bad trip), flashbacks and may precipitate psychotic reactions.

(Continued)

Table 8.1 Continued

	In a 'bad trip', the user may experience strong feelings of anxiety, paranoia, panic or fear. Physiological effects: elevated heart rate, increased blood pressure, and dilated pupils, higher body temperature, sweating, loss of appetite, sleeplessness, dry mouth, and tremors. Hallucinations (Eg tactile insects are crawling on the skin). Delusions.
Dependence	No physical dependence.
Withdrawal Symptoms	No withdrawal symptoms.
Overdose Risk	No overdose risk. But physiological and psychological risks.

Frequent, repeated doses of LSD are unusual and therefore tolerance is not commonly seen. Any tolerance developed quickly goes away once regular use is stopped. There is no physical dependence or withdrawal symptoms associated with recreational use of LSD. LSD is not considered an addictive drug since it does not produce compulsive drug-seeking behaviour.

GHB (gammahydroxybutyrate)

GBH, a central nervous depressant, is a colourless liquid, with a slightly salty taste. As it is colourless and odorless, GHB has been used in many cases of drug-related sexual assault and is also used by body-builders and athletes. GHB is difficult to detect because traces of the drug quickly leave the body. GHB is marketed on the Internet as a sleep aid, weight loss product and as an aid for insomnia. The drug is usually sold in small 30ml plastic containers (costing approx. £15) and consumed in capfuls. GHB is sometimes sold as 'liquid ecstasy', but is not related to ecstasy. The drug can take anything from 10 minutes to an hour to take effect and the effects can last from 1.5 to 3 hours or even longer. A Science and Technology Committee Report found the use of GHB to be less dangerous than tobacco and alcohol in terms of social harms, physical harm and addiction (The Stationery Office, 2006). The street name, legal aspects, therapeutic effects, adverse effects, withdrawal symptoms, and overdose risk are presented in Table 8.2.

Users of GHB enjoy an alcohol-like intoxication with potent positive sexual effects. When combined with alcohol, GHB can lead to respiratory depression and death. With higher doses, the adverse effects as the dosage increases can lead to disorientation, nausea, confusion, a numbing of the muscles or muscle spasms and vomiting. At high doses, convulsions, coma and respiratory collapse

Table 8.2 GHB: effects

Street Name	Liquid ecstasy, GBL, BDO, GBH, Blue Nitro, Midnight Blue, Renew Trient, Reviarent, SomatoPro, Serenity, Enliven.
Legal Status	Class C controlled drug
Method of Use	Oral.
Therapeutic Uses	Historically: General anesthetic, hypnotic, treatment of depression and insomnia. Treatment for acute alcohol withdrawal and medium to long-term detoxification (Italy).
Effect	Recreational dose: euphoria, increased enjoyment of movement and music, increased libido, increased sociability, intoxication.
Adverse Effects	Nausea and vomiting, desire to sleep, giddiness, slurred speech, dizziness, respiratory depression, drowsiness, agitation, visual disturbances, depressed breathing, amnesia, convulsions, unconsciousness, death.
Dependence	Physical dependence.
Withdrawal Symptoms	Convulsions, paranoia and hallucinations. Insomnia, restlessness, anxiety, tremors, sweating, loss of appetite, tachycardia, chest pain, high blood pressure, muscle and bone aches, sensitivity to external stimuli, inability to sleep.
Overdose Risk	Yes. Within 15 minutes, users may have a loss of consciousness or an actual coma.

can occur, often requiring emergency care. Driving or operating machinery while under the influence of GHB increases the risk of physical injury or accident to the user and to others. Regular use of GHB can cause physical dependence. The withdrawal symptoms will subside after 2–21 days depending on the doses and frequency of use. Withdrawal from GHB may cause symptoms similar to acute withdrawal from alcohol or barbiturates (delirium tremens) and can cause convulsions, paranoia and hallucinations.

Ketamine

Ketamine is a drug used in human and veterinary medicine primarily for the induction and maintenance of general anesthesia but acts as a depressant and a hallucinogenic. Ketamine is used as a recreational drug due to its capability to produce a sense of detachment from one's physical body. It is sold in either powdered or liquid form and can be inhaled, injected or mixed in drinks.

The effects are evident in about 10–15 minutes and last about one hour. The drug is often mixed with other psychoactive substances such as cocaine and ecstasy to enhance their potency. It is also possible to smoke ketamine mixed with cannabis and tobacco. With intravenous use, the onset of the effects of ketamine is immediate. Ketamine users report euphoria, anxiety or mood lability and sensations ranging from a pleasant feeling of floating to being separated from their bodies. Some ketamine users' experiences involve a terrifying feeling of almost complete sensory detachment known as the 'K-hole'. The street name, legal aspects, therapeutic effects, adverse effects, withdrawal symptoms, and overdose risk are presented in Table 8.3.

A few deaths have occurred through overdose, heart or respiratory failure and large doses can lead to loss of consciousness. With large or repeat doses hallucinations occur, for example, a loss of sense of time, feeling disconnected from the body and near-death experiences. In a study of 10 ketamine users, there is some evidence to suggest that long-term use may result in damage to the liver or urinary bladder, or even acute renal failure (Chu et al., 2007). However, more robust research needs to be undertaken with larger samples to confirm the above findings.

There is growing concern that users are taking higher doses of the drug and more people are injecting the substance (Drugscope, 2009). Some drug services are also reporting an increase in the number of young people using ketamine.

Table 8.3   Ketamine: effects

Street Name	Special K, Green, Super K, Vitamin K.
Legal Status	Class C controlled drug.
Method of Use	Inhaled, injected or mixed in drinks or combined with tobacco or marijuana and smoked.
Therapeutic Uses	Human anesthesia and veterinary medicine.
Effect	Euphoria, anxiety, mood lability. Sensations ranging from a pleasant feeling of floating to being separated from their bodies. Sensory detachment (likened to a near-death experience), similar to a 'bad trip' on LSD, are called the 'K-hole'.
Adverse Effects	Withdrawn state (disassociation), ataxia, dysarthria, muscular hypertonicity, myoclonic jerks. Severe hypertension and mild respiratory depression. Anxiety, dysphoria, depression, disorientation, insomnia, flashbacks, hallucinations, and psychotic episodes. A withdrawal syndrome with psychotic features has been described following discontinuation of long-term ketamine use
Dependence	No dependence.
Withdrawal Symptoms	No withdrawal symptoms.
Overdose Risk	Yes. Heart or respiratory failure.

Psilocybin

Psilocybin ('magic mushrooms') is from the same chemical family so its effects are similar. LSD is usually sold as dried mushrooms or in substances made from mushrooms. In its pure form, psilocybin is also a white powder. There is a variety of wild fungi native to the UK and the most common one is the Liberty Cap. Other sources of hallucinogens include amanita muscaria (fly agaric mushrooms) and mescaline which is derived from the peyote cactus. Psilocybin can be eaten fresh, cooked or brewed into a 'tea'. It usually takes about 30–50 mushrooms to produce a hallucinogenic experience similar to that experienced with LSD.

The physical effects of psilocybin are usually experienced within 20 minutes of ingestion and can last for six hours. The street name, legal aspects, therapeutic effects, adverse effects, withdrawal symptoms, and overdose risk are presented in Table 8.4.

The sought-after effects are similar to LSD, but the hallucinogenic trip is often milder and shorter. Small quantities cause relaxation and slight changes in mood but larger quantities can cause perceptual changes, distortion of body

Table 8.4 Psilocybin: effects

Street Name	Magic Mushroom
Legal Status	Psilocybin or psilocybin containing mushrooms are now a Class A drug under the Drugs Act 2005 including 'fungus (of any kind) which contains psilocin or an ester of psilocin'. This does not include fly agaric which is still legal.
Method of Use	Ingested orally. Brewed as a tea or added to other foods to mask their bitter flavour. Coat the mushrooms with chocolate (to disguise the flavour).
Therapeutic Uses	No therapeutic use.
Effect	Similar to LSD, but the hallucinogenic trip is often milder and shorter. Relaxation and slight changes in mood.
Adverse Effects	Stomach pain, nausea and vomiting, shivering, a numbing of the mouth, muscle weakness, diarrhoea, dizziness, drowsiness, and panic reactions. Perceptual changes, distortion of body image and hallucinations.
Dependence	Tolerance builds up with mushrooms in so far as the user needs to space out 'trips' to get the desired effects.
Withdrawal Symptoms	No withdrawal symptoms.
Overdose Risk	Some poisonous mushrooms can cause death or permanent liver damage within hours of ingestion.

image and hallucinations. Some people eat poisonous mushrooms thinking they are mushrooms containing psilocybin. This can be very dangerous as some poisonous mushrooms can cause death or permanent liver damage within hours of ingestion. Fly agaric mushrooms often cause nausea and stomach pain. Tolerance builds up with mushrooms in so far as the user needs to space out 'trips' to get the desired effects.

PCP (Phencyclidine)

PCP, a pure white crystalline powder, is most often called 'angel dust'. It was first developed as an anaesthetic in the 1950s but was discontinued for therapeutic use because of its hallucinatory effects. It has a distinctive bitter chemical taste. It is often sold on the illicit drug market in a variety of tablet, capsule, and coloured powder forms that are normally snorted, smoked, or orally ingested. Depending upon how much and by what route PCP is taken, its effects can last approximately 4–6 hours. The street name, legal aspects,

Table 8.5 PCP: effects

Street Name	Angel dust.
Legal Status	Class A controlled drug.
Method of Use	Snorted, smoked, or orally ingested.
Therapeutic Uses	Intravenous anesthetic.
Effect	Alterations in thought, mood, sensory perception and changes in body awareness. Feelings of detachment from reality, including distortions of space, time, and body image. Another episode may produce hallucinations, panic, and fear.
Adverse Effects	Nausea, blurred vision, dizziness, decreased awareness, numbness, slurred speech, loss of co-ordination, rapid and involuntary eye movements, exaggerated gait, shallow and rapid breathing, increased blood pressure, elevated heart rate, increased temperature, memory loss, difficulties with speech and thinking, depression, and weight loss. Convulsions, coma, hyperthermia, and death. A temporary schizophrenic-type psychosis may last for days or weeks. Auditory hallucinations, image distortion, severe mood disorders, and amnesia may also occur.
Dependence	Tolerance. PCP is addictive – its repeated misuse can lead to craving and compulsive PCP-seeking behaviour.
Withdrawal Symptoms	Violence, muscle rigidity, convulsions, coma, psychosis.
Overdose Risk	Yes. Violent or suicidal.

therapeutic effects, adverse effects, withdrawal symptoms, and overdose risk are presented in Table 8.5.

PCP is sometimes sprinkled on cannabis, mint, parsley or oregano and smoked. PCP has been sold as mescaline, THC, or other psychoactive drugs. Interactions with other central nervous system depressants, such as alcohol and benzodiazepines, can lead to coma. High doses of PCP can also cause seizures, coma, and death (though death more often results from accidental injury or suicide during PCP intoxication). PCP causes the development of tolerance and strong psychological dependence. Recent research suggests that repeated or prolonged use of PCP can cause a withdrawal syndrome when drug use of PCP is stopped.

Assessment and management of hallucinogens

Health care professionals regularly encounter patients seeking treatment for problems relating to the use of hallucinogens and others are brought to the Accident and Emergency Department as a result of hallucinogenic experiences and adverse effects. Different hallucinogen abuse has an effect on a variety of organ systems. Some hallucinogenic drugs such as PCP (Phencyclidine) have been known to cause muscle rigidity, seizures, and coma. Anticholinergics have been associated with delirium, tachycardia, hypertension, and seizures. LSD (e.g., lysergic acid diethylamide) rarely causes significant physical complications. Hallucinogens do not have a typical withdrawal pattern but are deemed to be psychologically addictive rather than physically addictive. However, when considering hypno-sedatives, the withdrawal from the psychoactive substances can lead to grand mal seizures.

Assessment of hallucinogenic use may be undertaken by observation of the patients' clinical signs, use of checklists and the use of a rating scale (Riba et al., 2001). The management of these patients includes support, reassurance and the reduction of panic attacks. It is important for health care professionals to be non-judgemental in order to enhance the therapeutic relationship. In relation to PCP intoxication, the phase tends to last from eight to 24 hours including the management of agitated behaviour, seizures, and hyperthermia. Vital signs including temperature are closely monitored during this acute phase. If the delirium is severe and compromises patient or staff safety, haloperidol (Haldol) in doses of 1 to 4 mg IM every 2 to 4 hours has proved useful in reducing the anxiety and lessening the psychotic symptoms. Phenothiazines are contraindicated for the first week after PCP ingestion (because PCP is somewhat anticholinergic and because PCP is often contaminated with belladonna alkaloids) (Long, 2009). As a result of gastrointestinal complication with PCP, activated charcoal (1 g/kg) may be administered and repeated every four hours for several doses in most symptomatic patients. Some patients intoxicated with PCP have been known to demonstrate violent behaviour and, on occasions, physical restraints and sedation may be a necessity. Benzodiazepines are usually effective in managing, agitated behaviour, aggressive behaviour, anxiety and the treatment of epileptic fits. As there are no recognized withdrawal symptoms from the use of LSD, psychosocial interventions are the focus of treatment strategies. Counselling and cognitive behavioural interventions are usually indicated in the psychological treatment of those who have been using LSD. Benzodiazepines are usually prescribed for withdrawal symptom management of LSD and anti-depressants such as SSRIs for depression or associated mood disorders.

Hypno-sedatives

The hypno-sedatives include both hypnotics and minor tranquillizers. The barbiturates are: tuinal, membutal, sodium amytal, phenobarbitone etc. and minor tranquillizers (benzodiazepines): valium (diazepam) librium, ativan, mogadon, temazepam etc. Others include heminevrin, chloral hydrate etc. According to the 2008 INCB report (2007 data only), the highest per capita consumption of prescribed barbiturates has been reported by countries in Europe. For the sedative/hypnotic type (including mainly barbiturates) the countries with the highest rates of use included France, Belgium, Ireland, Finland, the UK, Italy and Luxembourg. The street name, legal aspects, thera-peutic effects, adverse effects, withdrawal symptoms, and overdose risk are presented in Table 8.6.

Hypno-sedatives are a drug of misuse not only among the illicit drug population but among the population in general. Barbiturates are usually swallowed as tablets but can be injected for both medical and non-medical pur-poses. Valium, temazepam and mogadon are the most commonly prescribed minor tranquillizers (for daytime anxiety relief) and hypnotics (to promote sleep). Temazepam is a popular drug of choice to inject along with heroin. The original use of barbiturates as a sedative/hypnotic is no longer recommended because of adverse reactions and the risk of dependence. Barbiturates such as phenobarbital are used in the treatment of epilepsy and other types of convul-sions. Phenobarbital may be used in the treatment of withdrawal symptoms in neonates of mothers suffering from poly-drug use during pregnancy. It is the substance of choice for the treatment of neonatal abstinence syndrome in cases of combined dependence or benzodiazepine dependence (EMCDDA, 2009a).

Benzodiazepine combined with the use of alcohol increases the risk of a fatal overdose because both act as central nervous system depressants. This potential risk can occur when opiates are taken with benzodiazepines as part of a pattern of poly-drug use. A significant number of problem drug users

Table 8.6 Hypno-sedatives: effects

Street Name	Downers, Barbs, Tranx, Amytal, Downers, Nembutal, Phenobarbital, Reds, Red birds, Red devils, Seconal, Tuninal, Yellowjackets. Benzodiazepines: Rohypnol, Roofies, Flunitrazepam, Ruffies, Roches, R-2, Valium.
Legal Status	Benzodiazepines (Class C) – prescription-only medicines. Barbiturates (Class B) – prescription-only medicines.
Method of Use	Oral or injected.
Therapeutic Uses	Anaesthesia and in the treatment of epilepsy and, rarely nowadays, insomnia. Minor tranquillizers are often prescribed for the relief of anxiety and stress.
Effect	Similar to alcohol intoxication. Euphoria and disinhibition.
Adverse Effects	Slurred speech, stumbling, confusion, reduction of inhibition, lowering of anxiety and tension, and impairment of concentration, judgement and performance. The common reactions from minor tranquillizers include fatigue, drowsiness, and ataxia. In addition, other effects may include constipation, incontinence, urinary retention, dysarthria, blurred vision, hypotension, nausea, dry mouth, skin rash, and tremor.
Dependence	Physical and psychological dependence.
Withdrawal Symptoms	Barbiturates and minor tranquillizers are highly addictive and withdrawal symptoms include anxiety, headaches, cramps in the abdomen, pains in the limbs and even epileptic fits. Withdrawal of barbiturates is life-threatening and should always be medically supervised.
Overdose Risk	In the case of overdose, respiratory failure and death may result if these drugs are mixed with alcohol or with each other. Injecting these drugs is particularly hazardous with an increased risk of overdose, gangrene and abscesses.

swallow, snort or inject high doses of benzodiazepines to enhance the euphoriant effects of opiates or to minimize unpleasant effects of psychostimulants. The concomitant use of benzodiazepines and opiates is a major risk factor in drug-related deaths (EMCDDA, 2009b).

Assessment and management of hypno-sedatives

The assessment of the patient is undertaken, if possible, to ascertain the type and dosage of hypno-sedatives used. If the patient has taken an overdose of a hypno-sedative, care and management are implemented in the same way as with any drug intoxication. The management of a patient with a hypno-sedative overdose includes:

- Maintain an adequate airway and ventilation.
- Stabilize and maintain the blood flow and blood pressure.
- Consider inducing emesis, performing lavage, and administering activated charcoal to a patient who has orally ingested the drug, depending on the time of ingestion and level of consciousness.
- Monitor vital signs.

Benzodiazepines are the most commonly misused psychoactive substances but they produce less respiratory depression than barbiturates. However, benzodiazepine overdose is most dangerous in combination with other hypno-sedatives. The pharmacological treatment of benzodiazepine intoxication is with the use of antagonist, flumazenil. Withdrawal symptoms in long-term benzodiazepine users and seizures in patients who have taken an overdose of tricyclic antidepressants and benzodiazepines can occur with flumazenil; these symptoms are avoidable by utilizing slow flumazenil dose titration (Weinbroum et al., 1997). Flumazenil should be administered in an initial IV dose of 0.2 mg given over 30 seconds, followed by a second 0.2 mg IV dose if there is no response after 45 seconds. This procedure can be repeated at one minute intervals up to a cumulative dose of 5 mg. In patients who are physically dependent on benzodiazepines, slowly administer repeated doses of flumazenil (Sola et al., 2010).

For those who have overdosed on barbiturates, intravenous sodium bicarbonate is administered to alkalinize the urine and increase the rate of barbiturate excretion. In severe cases, dialysis may be essential. Vital signs and urine pH (maintained at 7.5) should be monitored. Close observation is required for those who have attempted suicide with hypno-sedative or barbiturate overdose. Referral to a psychiatrist is required to assess the patient's mental and psychological state.

Dealing with hypno-sedative withdrawal syndromes

Both hypno-sedatives and benzodiazepines exhibit cross-dependence and the key principle is to withdraw the psychoactive agent slowly to avoid epileptic seizure. It is important to determine the patient's drug tolerance level. The use of a long-acting barbiturate such as phenobarbital is chosen in preference to other sedatives because it has a longer half-life. An initial dose of 30–60 mg of phenobarbital is administered and the detoxified drug is repeated at hourly or two hour intervals as needed for 2–7 days after the patient has received similar 24-hour doses for 2 consecutive days. The 24-hour stabilizing dose is given in divided doses every 3–6 hours. This index dose is then tapered reducing subsequent daily doses by 30–60 mg/day (Stern et al., 2004). Vital signs and withdrawal symptoms should be monitored.

For those patients who cannot cope with mild withdrawal effects, an alternative is to replace short-acting benzodiazepines (e.g., Alprazolam) with an equivalent dosing of a longer-acting drug (e.g., Clonazepam) (Stern et al., 2004). The following is a commonly used benzodiazepine equivalence schedule. Diazepam 10 mg is approximately equivalent to the following drugs and doses (Kaplan et al., 2009):

- Alprazolam – 1 mg
- Chlordiazepoxide – 25 mg
- Clonazepam – 0.5–1 mg
- Lorazepam – 2 mg
- Oxazepam – 30 mg
- Temazepam – 20 mg

It is important to medicate rapidly for long-term users of sedative-hypnotics with severe withdrawal symptoms. The withdrawal should be undertaken under close medical observation especially if the patient has been using high doses of hypno-sedatives, has a history of withdrawal seizures or delirium tremens, or has a concurrent medical illness (Kaplan et al., 2009).

Volatile substances

Lighter fuel refills, glues, aerosols and typewriter correction fluids/thinners, dry cleaning fluids, de-greasing compounds etc. are products which are subjected to misuse. The use of volatile substances is thought to be usually confined to short periods during early adolescence and may be superseded by the use of other psychoactive substances (such as alcohol and cannabis) as age and disposable income increase access to alternatives (EMCDDA, 2009c). A report (St George's University of London, 2007) reveals that in 2007 there were 58 deaths in the UK associated with volatile substances. In 2007, butane from all sources accounted for 46 of the 58 deaths and of these butane cigarette lighter refills formed the largest group. Three deaths in 2007 were attributed to asphyxia (a condition of deficient supply of oxygen to the body) associated with the inhalation of nitrous oxide (more commonly known as 'laughing gas') (St George's University of London, 2007).

The mode of use depends upon the volatile compound and also the nature of the product that contains it. Gases may be inhaled directly from cigarette lighter refills. In order to remove the non-volatile components of the substance, aerosols may be sprayed through fabric (e.g. a towel or socks). Solvents, such as toluene, may be poured onto a handkerchief or into a bag and the vapour inhaled. Glue is usually poured into a plastic bag which is palpated as the vapour is inhaled. Helium, often from disposable cylinders purchased from shops selling party balloons can also be fed into a plastic bag covering the head (EMCDDA, 2009c). The street name, legal aspects, therapeutic effects, adverse effects, withdrawal symptoms, and overdose risk are presented in Table 8.7.

Table 8.7 Volatile substances: effects

Street Name	Solvents, Inhalants, Glue, Gas, Thinners, Hair Sprays, Tolly, Huff, Dusting, Chroming.
Legal Status	The Intoxicating Substances Supply Act (England and Wales) (1985) makes it an offence to supply a young person under 18 years with a substance which the supplier knows or has reason to believe will be used 'to achieve intoxication'. In Scotland, the common law provides for a similar offence of 'recklessly' selling solvents to children knowing that they are going to inhale them. An amendment to the Consumer Protection Act (The Cigarette Lighter Refill (Safety) Regulations 1999) made it an offence to 'supply any cigarette lighter refill canister containing butane or a substance with butane as a constituent part to any person under the age of eighteen years'.
Method of Use	The mode of use depends upon the volatile compound and also the nature of the product that contains it. Inhaled.
Therapeutic Uses	Some volatile substances are used in human and veterinary medicine as anaesthetics.
Effect	Effects are experienced within a matter of minutes. Users typically experience a sensation akin to taking alcohol. Giggly and disorientated, possibly being uncoordinated and feeling dizzy. Nausea is not uncommon.
Adverse Effects	Depressed respiration rate, depressed heart rate, loss of co-ordination, disorientation, loss of consciousness, drowsy, hangover, heart failure, damage to brain, kidneys and liver, exhaustion, amnesia, loss of concentration, weight loss, depression, accidental death.
Dependence	Tolerance and psychological dependence.
Withdrawal Symptoms	Occasional mild physical withdrawal symptoms, such as headaches, have been noted. However, psychological rather than physical dependence is more common.
Overdose Risk	Deaths result from accidents, choking on vomit or suffocation. Deaths are often sudden, and often a mechanism of death involving cardiac arrest appears to be the cause.

The effects of some substances such as butane last only a few minutes, requiring frequent repeated doses, whereas toluene is much longer acting (more like alcohol) requiring less frequent doses. Sniffers of volatile substances heighten the desired effect by increasing the concentration of the vapour and excluding air. For example, by sniffing from a bag or by placing a plastic bag over the head while inhalation takes place. The inhaled solvent vapours are absorbed quickly through the lungs and rapidly reach the brain. Part of the effect is the reduction in oxygen intake. Respiratory rate and heart rate are depressed and repeated or deep inhalation can result in an 'overdose', causing disorientation, loss of control, and unconsciousness. The effects appear quickly and disappear, usually less than 45 minutes after sniffing being stopped. There may be a hangover effect with headache and poor concentration for about a day.

Sniffing solvents may cause intoxication similar to the effects of alcohol. So a sniffer may become drowsy, confused, aggressive, may have accidents while they are intoxicated and suffer serious health consequences. Chronic misuse of aerosols and cleaning fluids can cause renal and hepatic damage, loss of control of movement, weight loss, depression and tremor. These symptoms usually clear when sniffing ceases. Tolerance can develop but physical dependence does not constitute a significant problem. Psychological dependence occurs in susceptible youngsters with concomitant family or personality problems. These individuals are also more prone to become 'lone sniffers' instead of the usual pattern of sniffing in groups.

The mortality related to solvent sniffing has become a significant cause of death of young males. Most deaths are believed to occur from 'sudden sniffing death syndrome' (SSDS), an irregular and rapid heart rhythm brought on by the use of volatile substances and anoxia or hypercapnia (i.e. a high concentration of carbon dioxide in the blood), and a sudden stimulus that produces an epinephrine (adrenaline) release (EMCDDA, 2009c). Deaths also may result from asphyxiation, particularly if a plastic bag is used to inhale the compound (e.g. when inhaling glue). Deaths from trauma may occur, particularly with the longer acting compounds, e.g. toluene.

Over-the-counter drugs (OTC)

In recent years there has been an increasing trend in the use of over-the-counter (OTC) drugs for their non-medical therapeutic effects. The use of non-prescription drugs for self-medication is now available widely in pharmacies, in retail outlets and on the Internet. These are depressants such as codeine linctus, Colles Browne's mixture, Gee's Linctus, kaolin and morphine. The stimulants include Fenox, Mercocaine, lozenges, Sinutads, Sudafed and Do-Do. Travel sickness remedies such as Kwells containing hallucinogenic compounds are also available over-the-counter. In the context of over-the-counter (OTC) drugs, misuse is defined as using an OTC product for a legitimate medical reason but in higher doses or for a longer period than recommended, for example, taking more of a painkiller than recommended to treat headache (Hughes et al., 1999).

In a study by Wazaify et al., (2005) on the awareness of the misuse potential of some OTC drugs, the majority of participants were highly aware of the misuse of OTC drugs, with the majority naming painkillers as the products most liable for abuse. OTC medicines such as painkillers, sleeping aids, cough mixtures and laxatives being the main categories reported. This supports the findings from a community pharmacy survey which identified opioid-containing products (kaolin and morphine), antihistamines and laxatives as being prone to misuse (Hughes et al., 1999). It has been suggested that by monitoring the usage of certain OTC products, in addition to data recording and education, safe and effective use of such medicines can be promoted (Wazaify et al., 2005).

Ecstasy (MDMA)

3,4-Methylenedioxymethamphetamine, better known as ecstasy, is a synthetic, psychoactive drug with hallucinogenic and amphetamine-like properties. It is often categorized as a hallucinogen, as in some respects it resembles LSD. MDMA is manufactured from the components of methylamphetamine and safrole (a nutmeg derivative). It usually comes in tablet form, powder or in capsules in different shapes and colours. Swallowing is the most common way that ecstasy is taken. Ecstasy tablets are also crushed and snorted or taken in a liquid form through injection.

The main use of ecstasy has been as a 'dance' or 'rave culture' drug. The effects of ecstasy take about half an hour to kick in and tend to last between three and six hours, followed by a gradual comedown. The strength and contents of ecstasy tablets cannot be known accurately as all ecstasy available on the street is produced in unregulated black market laboratories. Ecstasy is sometimes cut with amphetamines, caffeine and other substances. Pills sold as 'ecstasy' often contain no MDMA and are instead made from an amphetamine ('speed') base. Less than one per cent remains in the body after 48 hours and this amount will not be detectable in blood or urine samples. However, ecstasy users may test positive for amphetamines in a standard drug test.

The street name, legal aspects, therapeutic effects, adverse effects, withdrawal symptoms and overdose risk are presented in Table 8.8.

Ecstasy was first manufactured in Germany in 1914 as an appetite suppressant, although it was never actually marketed for this purpose. It has been used in a limited way as an adjunct to various types of psychotherapy in order to facilitate the therapeutic process. In addition, the drug has also been used

Table 8.8   Ecstasy/MDMA (methylenedioxymethamphetamine): effects

Street Name	Ecstasy, E, Eccy, adam, XTC, Dennis the Menace, Doves, Speckled doves, New Yorkers, Mercedes.
Legal Status	MDMA (ecstasy) is a Class A (Schedule 1) controlled drug. This means it is an offence both to possess the drug and to supply it to others.
Method of Use	Crushed and snorted or taken in a liquid form through injection. Swallowing is the most common way that ecstasy is taken.
Therapeutic Uses	Use in psychotherapy.
Effect	Stimulant with mild psychedelic effect. Possible hallucinogenic effect, particularly in high doses.
Adverse Effects	Anxiety, panic attacks and insomnia, especially in cases of long-term use, or use in large doses. Increased susceptibility to minor infections such as colds, flu and sore throats. Some female users have reported an increase in genito-urinary infections. Pre-existing conditions such as high blood pressure, glaucoma and epilepsy can be exacerbated. There is evidence that ecstasy may have the potential to cause brain damage associated with mood disorders. Ecstasy increases body temperature and has a dehydrating effect. Damage to the liver.
Dependence	Psychological
Withdrawal Symptoms	Tolerance develops with time, but not as rapidly as with cocaine or amphetamines. No evidence of physical withdrawal, although after-effects of the drug can include fatigue, depression and anxiety. 'Flashbacks' following repeated use over several days have been reported.
Overdose Risk	Fatal drug reactions can cause blood clots to develop in the lungs. Heat stroke or dehydration. Dilutional hyponatremia where people have drunk too much water in an attempt to counteract the dehydrating effects of the drug.

to some extent with terminally ill patients in order to help them come to terms with their situation and to communicate or ventilate their feelings more easily.

The effects start after about 20–60 minutes after use and can last several hours. Users describe ecstasy as making them empathic, producing a temporary state of openness with an enhanced perception of colours and sound. The user experiences euphoric feelings, and feelings of empathy, relaxation and meaningfulness. Tactile sensations are enhanced for some users, making physical contact with others more pleasurable. The user experiences euphoria which plateaus for two to three hours before wearing off. Ecstasy can also cause mild hallucinogenic effects.

There are usually three phases associated with ecstasy use. There is the 'coming up' effect when the user experiences a sudden amphetamine-like rush. This rush is accompanied by mild nausea. It is immediately followed by the plateau of intoxication where the user may feel good, happy and relaxed. The final phase is the 'coming down' where the user may feel physically exhausted, depressed or irritable. The effects of ecstasy usually begin within 20 minutes of taking the drug, and may last up to six hours. The physiological effects that can develop include: dilated pupils, a tingling feeling, tightening of the jaw muscles, raised body temperature, increased heart rate, muscle tension, involuntary teeth clenching, nausea, blurred vision, rapid eye movement, faintness, and chills or sweating. The psychological effects can include anxiety, panic attacks, depression, sleep problems, drug craving, confused episodes and paranoid or psychotic states.

The adverse effects of ecstasy include tiredness, confusion, anxiety and depression. With higher doses the user can feel anxious and confused, and co-ordination can be impaired, making driving or a similar activity very dangerous. If taken regularly over the period of a few days the user can experience panic attacks, temporary paranoia or insomnia. The use of this particular drug may be more hazardous for individuals that have heart conditions, hypertension, blood clotting disorders, a history of seizures or any type of psychiatric disorder. Ecstasy should not be used in combination with amphetamines, mono amine oxidase inhibitor drugs, alcohol or diuretics. Recent research findings also link MDMA use to long-term damage to those parts of the brain critical to thought and memory. It is believed that the drug causes damage to the neurons that use the chemical serotonin to communicate with other neurons.

Some people may develop tolerance to the effects of ecstasy and using larger amounts will increase the severity of undesirable effects, rather than increase the pleasurable effects. There is evidence that people can become psychologically dependent on ecstasy and it can be very difficult for them to stop or decrease their use. At present, there is no conclusive evidence that people can become physically dependent on ecstasy.

Overdose and death

Overdose from ecstasy can occur. It is usually characterized by very high body temperature and blood pressure, hallucinations and an elevated heartbeat. This is especially dangerous for those who have an existing heart condition or breathing problems, and for people with depression or some other psychological disorder. Sudden death through overheating, dehydration, heavy alcohol consumption or drinking too much water has led to collapse, convulsions or renal failure. However, drinking too much water in an attempt to stay 'safe' is more dangerous. Some, often inexperienced, users have died after drinking as much water (dilutional hyponatremia) as they physically could. The excess water causes the brain to swell inside the skull, which puts pressure on the brain stem and leads to coma and death. Because of these ill-effects, it is advised that users should wear light, loose clothing, drink plenty of non-alcoholic fluids and stop dancing when they feel exhausted, which could help reduce the possible complications of the drug. There is always a danger of the drug being contaminated by other substances such as amphetamine mixtures, LSD and ketamine. About ten ecstasy-related deaths have been reported in the UK each year for the past several years. Although the number of deaths is relatively low compared to drugs such as heroin or alcohol, there is still cause for concern.

Summary of key points

- Hallucinogens are psychoactive substances that induce an alteration in perception, thought, emotion and consciousness.
- LSD comes in many forms: liquid, tablets or capsules, squares of gelatine or blotting paper. LSD can be swallowed, sniffed, injected or smoked.
- There is no physical dependence or withdrawal symptoms associated with recreational use of LSD.
- The effects of the drug may cause panic, confusion, impulsive behaviour and unpleasant illusions (bad trip), flashbacks and may precipitate psychotic reactions.
- Users of GHB enjoy an alcohol-like intoxication with potent positive sexual effects.
- At high doses of GHB, convulsions, coma and respiratory collapse can occur.
- Withdrawal from GHB may cause symptoms similar to acute withdrawal from alcohol or barbiturates (delirium tremens) and can cause convulsions, paranoia and hallucinations.
- Ketamine is used as recreational drug due to its capability to produce a sense of detachment from one's physical body.
- With very high doses, coma and severe hypertension may occur; deaths are unusual.

- Psilocybin usually takes about 30–50 mushrooms to produce a hallucinogenic experience similar to that experienced with LSD.
- Higher doses cause perceptual changes, distortion of body image and hallucinations.
- Some people eat poisonous mushrooms thinking they are mushrooms containing psilocybin.
- High doses of PCP can cause convulsions, coma, hyperthermia, and death.
- Recent research suggests that repeated or prolonged use of PCP can cause withdrawal syndrome when drug use is stopped.
- Hypno-sedatives are drugs of misuse not only among the illicit drug population but among the population in general.
- Benzodiazepines and barbiturates are prescription-only medicines and are Class C and B controlled drugs respectively.
- Barbiturates are depressant drugs and their effects are similar to alcohol intoxication.
- Some organic based substances produce effects similar to alcohol or anesthetics when their vapours are inhaled.
- After inhalation of volatile substances, effects are experienced within a matter of minutes.
- Over-the-counter drugs are taken in large doses and often combined with other drugs to obtain the desired effects.
- The amphetamine derivatives in decongestants may be used as a stimulant, and cough linctuses and diarrhoea drugs treatment may be used for their opiate content.

Reflective activity 8.2

An adolescent was brought to the Accident and Emergency Department with disturbing visual hallucinations, anxiety, panic reaction, agitation and paranoid delusions. His friends are not forthcoming with information other than to say they were in a dance club.

- What would be the immediate interventions required?
- The vital signs indicate the patient has tachycardia, hypertension, and hyperthermia. Other signs may include sweating, ataxia, and vomiting. What does this suggest?
- What treatment interventions and/or strategies may be planned for this patient?
- What health education messages would you give to him and his friends?

References

Chu, P.S.K., Kwok, S.C., Lam, K.M., Chu, T.Y., Chan, S.W.H., Ma, W.K., Chui, K.L., Yiu, M.K., Chan, Y.C., Tse, M.L. and Lau, F.L. (2007) 'Street Ketamine – Associated Bladder Dysfunction: a Report of Ten Cases', *Hong Kong Medical Journal* 13, 4, 311–13.

Drugscope (2009) DrugScope Highlights Concerns Over Trends in Ketamine Use (London: Drugscope). www.drugscope.org.uk.

EMCDDA (2009a) Barbiturates. http://www.emcdda.europa.eu/publications/drug-profiles/barbiturates, date accessed 10 December 2009.

EMCDDA (2009b) 2009 Annual Report on the state of the drugs problem in Europe (Lisbon, EMCDDA), http://www.emcdda.europa.eu/publications/searchresults?action=list&type=PUBLICATIONS&SERIES_PUB=w36, date accessed 15 January 2010.

EMCDDA (2009c) Volatile Substances. http://www.emcdda.europa.eu/publications/drug-profiles/volatile, date accessed 10 December 2009.

Fantegrossi, W.E., Murnane, K.S. and Reissig, C.J. (2008) 'The Behavioral Pharmacology of Hallucinogens', *Biochemical Pharmacology* 75, 1, 17–33.

Home Office Statistical Bulletin (2009) Drug Misuse Declared: Findings from the 2008/09 British Crime Survey. England and Wales, (London: Home Office), http://www.homeoffice.gov.uk/rds/pdfs09/hosb1209.pdf.

Hughes, G.F., McElnay, J.C., Hughes, C.M. and McKenna, P. (1999) 'Abuse/Misuse of Non-prescription Drugs', *Pharmacy World and Science*, 21, 6, 251–55.

International Narcotics Control Board (2008) *Psychotropic Substances: Statistics for 2007 – Assessments of Annual Medical and Scientific Requirements for Substances in Schedules II, III and IV of the Convention on Psychotropic Substances of 1971* (New York: United Nations).

Kaplan, H.I., Sadock, B.J. and Ruiz, P. (2009) *Kaplan and Sadock's Comprehensive Textbook of Psychiatry*, 9th edn (Philadelphia: Lippincott Williams and Wilkins).

Le Secretariat Permanent a'la Politique de Prevention. 'La problématique des smart drugs en Belgique', V.S.P.P. Ministère de l'Intérieur, B 1040 Brussels. http://bdoc.ofdt.fr/pmb/opac_css/index.php?lvl=notice_display&id=31637.

Long, P.W. (2009) Phencyclidine Dependence. www.mentalhealth.com, date accessed 14 September 2010.

National Institute on Drug Abuse (2001) Research Report – Hallucinogens and Dissociative Drugs. NIH Publication Number 01-4209. www.drugabuse.gov.

Parish, B.S., Richards, M.E. and Cameron, S. (2009) *Hallucinogens* http://emedicine.medscape.com/article/293752-overview, date accessed 18 August 2010.

Riba, J., Rodríguez-Fornells, A., Strassman, R.J. and Barbanoj, M.J. (2001) 'Psychometric Assessment of the Hallucinogen Rating Scale', *Drug and Alcohol Dependence*, 63, 3, 215–23.

St George's, University of London (2007) *VSA Report 22: Trends in Deaths Associates with Abuse of Volatile Substances 1971–2007*, Division of Community Health Sciences, London.

Sola, C.L., Chopra, A. and Rastogi, A. (2010) *Sedative, Hypnotic, Anxiolytic Use Disorders*. http://emedicine.medscape.com/article/290585-overview, date accessed 14 September 2010.

Stern, T.A., Fricchione, G., Cassem, N.H., Jellinek, M.S. and Rosenbaum, J.F. (2004) 'Drug Addicted Patients', in *Massachusetts General Hospital Handbook of General Hospital Psychiatry*, 5th edn (St. Louis: Mosby Press).

The Stationery Office (2006) *Science and Technology Committee Report Drug Classification Making a Hash of it?* Fifth Report of Session 2005–06, 176 (London: The Stationery Office).

Wazaify, M., Shields, E., Hughes, C.M. and McElnay, J.C. (2005) 'Societal Perspectives on Over-the-counter (OTC) Medicines', *Family Practice* 22, 2, 170–76.

Weinbroum, A.A., Flaishon, R., Sorkine, P., Szold, O. and Rudick, V. (1997) 'A Risk-benefit Assessment of Flumazenil in the Management of Benzodiazepine Overdose', *Drug Safety*, 17, 3, 181–96.

Synthetic Drugs: Smart or 'Eco Drugs' and 'Spice'

Reflective activity 9.1

Before reading the chapter, state whether you think the statements are true or false. Consider the reasons for your answers.

Statements	True	False
Smart drugs are defined as substances used or abused, presenting stimulating, sedating or hallucinogenic effects.		
Spice refers to a blend of plant or herbal ingredients, including Indian Warrior and Lion's Tail.		
Eco drugs, such as hallucinogenic mushrooms, kava kava and yohimbe are synthetic substances that can produce a psychotropic or physical effect.		
No legal action has been taken in the UK to ban or otherwise control Spice products.		
The use of herbal mixtures is perceived as having some risk of psychological dependence.		
A number of Spice products, sometimes sold as a mix of air-freshening herbs or incense, can be bought on the Internet, in head shops and smart shops.		
Smart drugs are reported to enhance sexual behaviour, physical endurance, muscle power, and emotional intelligence.		
Eco drugs such as kava kava and yohimbe are vegetable substances that can produce a psychotropic or physical effect.		

When you have read this chapter, come back to this activity and consider your answers again. How many did you get right? For those you got wrong, think about the reasons for your original answer and compare this with what you know now.

Smart or eco drugs

Smart drugs, smart products or eco drugs are new substances that are composed of multiple ingredients. Smart drugs are referred to as substances taken with the purpose of enhancing cognitive functions and may have stimulating or hallucinogenic effects (Rassool, 2009). An alternative definition of smart drugs are that they are substances used or abused, presenting stimulating, sedating or hallucinogenic effects, comparable to those observed with known drugs but promoted as safe, healthy and harmless substitutes for illicit drugs (Limbergen and Vrijsen, 1997). These substances are also called 'cognitive enhancers' or 'nootropics'. ('Nootropic' comes from the Greek – 'noos' = mind and 'tropos' = changed, toward, turn). Therapeutically, cognitive enhancing drugs are used to treat neuropsychiatric disorders, Alzheimer's disease, schizophrenia and attention deficit hyperactivity disorder, so as to improve the quality of life and well-being for patients and their significant others.

However, there are a growing number of people who use these substances in the hope of improving their mental or cognitive functioning or to enhance sexual behaviour, physical endurance, muscle power, and emotional intelligence. Smart drugs are being marketed on many internet web sites, and in books, magazines and newspaper articles detailing the supposed effects of these substances. They are being promoted as mind enhancers, mind boosters, brain boosters, intelligence boosters and as safe, healthy and harmless substitutes for illicit drugs.

These substances are classified as:

- Smart drugs – improving cognitive functions.
- Smart drinks and nutrients.
- Smart products – herbal mixtures and food additives which mimic the effects of illicit drugs such as ecstasy.
- Eco drugs – herbs, plants and mixtures of both. Some hallucinogenic or euphoric effects are linked with their use.
- Energizing drinks – high caffeine content with guarana and taurine.

Their effects can vary considerably. Some smart products are highly stimulating, and others induce a mild form of excitement and/or euphoria. Eco drugs, such as hallucinogenic mushrooms, kava kava and yohimbe are vegetable substances that can produce a psychotropic or physical effect. It is not always clear which laws and regulations apply to these substances. In addition, there is limited evidence about the effects of these substances and the risks involved and the long-term safety in using these substances.

Legal highs

Europe is faced with an increasingly complex and volatile synthetic drug market as suppliers are now highly innovative in their growing sophistication in marketing legal alternatives to illicit drugs (so-called 'legal highs') (EMCDDA, 2009). The appearance of synthetic cannabinoids marks the latest stage in the development of 'designer drugs', according to the EMCDDA report on the state of the drugs problem in Europe (EMCDDA, 2009). The Internet is now marketing these 'legal alternatives' to controlled drugs. In 2009, the EMCDDA surveyed 115 online shops in 17 European countries. The majority of the online retailers identified were based in the UK (37 per cent), Germany (15 per cent), the Netherlands (14 per cent) and Romania (7 per cent). Among the new products on sale in 2009 are 'party pills' containing legal alternatives to the newly-controlled substance BZP (EMCDDA, 2009). There is growing concern in the European Union regarding the online marketing of 'Spice'.

Spice

Spice refers to a blend of plant or herbal ingredients, including Indian Warrior and Lion's Tail. In addition, there are many other herbal preparations for which the claim is made that they have a similar make-up to 'Spice' – e.g. Yucatan Fire, Smoke, Sence, ChillX, Highdi's Almdröhner, Earth Impact, Gorillaz, Skunk, Genie, Galaxy Gold, Space Truckin, Solar Flare, Moon Rocks, Blue Lotus, Aroma, Scope, etc. A number of Spice products, sometimes sold as a mix of air-freshening herbs or incense, can be bought on the Internet, in head shops and smart shops. A 2008 EMCDDA study into 'legal highs' sold via the web, found that Spice was frequently offered as a smoking blend (i.e. 37 per cent of online shops investigated) (Hillebrand et al., 2010). Different blends and flavours are marketed under a variety of names including: Spice silver, Spice gold, Spice diamond, Spice tropical synergy and Spice Yucatan fire. Spice comes packaged in small sealed pouches holding 3 gm (less than an eighth of an ounce).

One of the main attractions in the use of Spice products is that it can have similar effects to those produced by cannabis. This may be due to the fact that a new psychoactive substance, JWH-018 (Naphthalen-1-yl-(1-pentylindol-3-yl) methanon), a synthetic cannabinoid receptor agonist, has been identified in at least three Spice products – gold, silver and diamond (Drugnet Europe, 2009b). In June 2009, HU-210 was identified for the first time in three 'Spice' products in the United Kingdom.

The government's Advisory Council on the Misuse of Drugs (ACMD, 2009) warns that Spice Gold, which is advertised as a herbal high and an 'aromatic potpourri', in reality contains synthetic chemicals that mimic the effects of some of the more powerful active ingredients in cannabis. The ACMD also recommends that, with named exemptions, the synthetic cannabinoids are placed in Schedule 1 of the Misuse of Drugs Regulations on the grounds they have no recognized medicinal use. The ACMD also recommends that nabilone, as a component of an existing medicinal product (cesamet) should be placed in Schedule 2 of the Misuse of Drugs Regulations (2001).

Responding to potential health concerns, the UK has taken legal action in order to ban or otherwise control Spice products. A number of psychoactive substances have been classified under the Misuse of Drugs Act 1971 (Amendment) Order 2009 which came into force on 23rd December 2009. Synthetic cannabinoid receptor agonists has been added to Part 2 of Schedule 2 to the Misuse of Drugs Act 1971 ('the Act') which specifies drugs which are subject to control as Class B drugs under the Act. In addition, the Order adds Gamma-butyrolactone (GBL), 1,4–butanediol (1,4–BD), 15 anabolic steroids, two non-steroidal agents, Oripavine, 1–benzylpiperazine (BZP) and a group of substituted piperazines to Part 3 of Schedule 2 to the Act which specifies drugs which are subject to control as Class C drugs under the Act (OPSI, 2009).

Physical and social harms

Due to the novelty of some of the compounds of the psychoactive substances, there is limited literature about the harms caused to the user. However, the EMCDDA recently published a briefing paper that sets out the key issues and identifies potential harms (EMCDDA, 2009). Currently, there is no robust evidence about the public health implications of the consumption of these mixtures.

However, concerns have been raised that some of these herbal mixtures may contain constituents that may be harmful to health. The findings of a self-administered study showed that some of the effects include reddened conjunctivae, significant increase of pulse rates, dry mouth, moderate behavioural impairment and an alteration of mood and perception. The effects continued for about six hours under slow attenuation (Auwärter et al., 2009). The whole next day, some minor after-effects were still noticeable. In addition, there are reports of the effects of herbal mixtures on the cardiovascular and nervous system which cause paranoia and panic attacks, short-term loss of consciousness and psychomotor agitation (ACMD, 2009). Due to the high potency of synthetic cannabinoids, it is possible for a user to have an overdose.

The use of herbal mixtures must also be perceived as having some risk of psychological dependence. Other harms include the triggering of psychological problems or may involve additional problems for users with pre-existing psychiatric conditions. It is assumed that as it is difficult to estimate the current societal harms, it is plausible to expect that the societal harms have the same potential as cannabis.

Summary of key points

- Smart drugs, smart products or eco drugs are new substances that are composed of multiple ingredients.
- Smart drugs are substances used or abused, presenting stimulating, sedating or hallucinogenic effects.
- Smart drugs are being marketed as mind enhancers, mind boosters, brain boosters, intelligence boosters and as safe, healthy and harmless substitutes for illicit drugs.
- Eco drugs, such as hallucinogenic mushrooms, kava kava and yohimbe are vegetable substances that can produce a psychotropic or physical effect.
- The appearance of synthetic cannabinoids marks the latest stage in the development of 'designer drugs'.
- Spice refers to a blend of plant or herbal ingredients, including Indian Warrior and Lion's Tail.
- A number of Spice products, sometimes sold as a mix of air-freshening herbs or incense, can be bought on the Internet, in head shops and smart shops.
- The Advisory Council on the Misuse of Drugs warns that Spice Gold, which is advertised as a herbal high and an 'aromatic potpourri', in reality contains synthetic chemicals that mimic the effects of some of the more powerful active ingredients in cannabis.
- The UK has taken legal action to ban or otherwise control Spice products.
- There is limited literature about the harms caused by herbal mixtures to the user.
- Concerns have been raised that some of these herbal mixtures may contain constituents that may be harmful (physical, social and psychological) to health.

Reflective activity 9.2

You are required to give a short presentation to a group of adolescents on the dangers of synthetic drugs. What would you include in your presentation?

References

ACMD (2009) Consideration of the Major Cannabinoids Agonists (London: Home Office).

Auwarter, V., Dresen, S., Weinmann, W., Muller, M., Putz, M. and Ferreiros, N. (2009) 'Spice and Other Herbal Blends: Harmless Incense or Cannabinoid Designer Drugs?' *Journal of Mass Spectrometry* 44, 5, 832–37.

DRUGNET Europe (2009) Concerns Expressed Over Spice. January–March 2009 (Lisbon: EMCDDA). http://www.emcdda.europa.eu/publications/drugnet/online/2009/65/article6, date accessed 15 March 2010.

EMCDDA (2009) Annual Report 2009: the State of the Drugs Problem in Europe (Lisbon: EMCDDA).

Hillebrand, J., Olszewski, D. and Sedefov, R. (2010) 'Legal Highs on the Internet', *Substance Use Misuse* 45, 3, 330–40.

OPSI (2009) 2009 No. Dangerous Drugs. The Misuse of Drugs Act 1971 (Amendment) Order 2009. http://www.opsi.gov.uk/si/si2009/draft/ukdsi_9780111486610_en_1, date accessed 15 January 2009.

Van Limbergen, K. and Vrijsen M. (1997) 'La Problématique des Smart Drugs en Belgique', V.S.P.P. Ministère de l'Intérieur, B 1040 Brussels.

Tobacco and Nicotine 10

Introduction

Reflective activity 10.1

Before reading this chapter, try to provide a true or false answer for each of the statements listed below. Think about some reasons as to why you chose a particular answer.

Statements	True	False
Tobacco smoking is not an addictive substance.		
Smoking can hamper the sexual function of both men and women.		
Smoking causes stomach ulcers.		
Smoking helps to reduce a person's stress level.		
Chewing tobacco does not have health risks because it is smoke-free.		
Switching to light or low tar cigarettes will save me.		
Smoking a cigar is better for you than smoking a cigarette.		
Some people gain weight when they quit smoking.		
Chewing tobacco does not have the same adverse effects as smoking tobacco.		
Even when a smoker inhales, two-thirds of the smoke from the cigarette goes into the environment.		
Children who breathe second-hand smoke are more likely to develop asthma.		
When one person smokes in a room, everyone smokes because they are inhaling second-hand smoke.		
Second-hand smoke is more dangerous for children than adults because children breathe faster and their lungs are not as developed.		

When you have read this chapter, come back to this activity and consider your answers again. How many did you get right? For those you got wrong, think about the reasons for your original answer and compare this with what you know now.

Tobacco smoking is highly addictive and is one of the most widely used psychoactive substances. The contents of cigarettes contain the most toxic and carcinogenic substances. Nicotine is found in chewing tobacco and the smoke from cigarettes, cigars and pipes which contain thousands of chemicals, including nicotine. It is the single greatest cause of preventable illness and premature death. Tobacco smoking is the second major cause of death in the world and is responsible for one third of cancer, one seventh of cardiovascular disease and most chronic lung disease in adults (WHO, 2002). It is reported that smoking is on the rise in the developing world but falling in developed nations and smoking-related diseases kill one in ten adults globally.

In the European Union, it is estimated that tobacco consumption kills 650,000 people a year while a further 80,000 are killed by passive smoking (Europa-Eu, 2007). Women under 65 in the UK have the worst death rate from lung cancer of all EU countries and the second worst death rate from heart disease after women in Ireland. The United Kingdom (UK) has high rates of death due to smoking compared to most other countries in the European Union (EU). It is estimated that around 13 million adults in the UK smoke cigarettes; that is 22 in every 100 people aged 16 and over. More men than women smoke. But the gap has closed in the last 60 years. In 2006, 23 in every 100 men and 21 in every 100 women smoked (ONS, 2006). In Great Britain, the highest rates of smoking are in the 20–24 age group, with 31 per cent of people of this age recorded as smokers (Cancer Research UK, 2009). The latest figures for 2007 show that around 9.5 million adults in Britain smoke cigarettes and a further one million people smoke pipes/cigars (ONS, 2008; ASH, 2007). One in five deaths in the UK are due to smoking and more than 120,000 people in the UK die each year from smoking-related causes (Department of Health, 1998).

The health and risk factors associated with active cigarette smoking include cancer, cardiovascular disease, respiratory diseases, and the impairment of sexual health and maternal health. In addition to its direct health effects, tobacco leads to malnutrition, increased health care costs and premature death – the 'Features of Tobacco Smoking' are presented in Table 10.1.

Pharmacology of tobacco smoking

The physical dependence of nicotine addiction is well documented. The rationale for the self-medication hypothesis is that it modulates the negative effects of withdrawal symptoms or acts as positive reinforcement in specific situations. Nicotine acts on nicotinic cholinergic receptors in the brain to release dopamine and other neurotransmitters that sustain addiction (Benowitz, 2008). It is thought that the increased levels of dopamaine in the reward system of the central nervous system are responsible for the addiction caused by nicotine

Table **10.1** Tobacco smoking: effects

Street Name	Fags, Smoke, Ciggy, Cancer Stick, Cig, and many others.
Legal Status	It is illegal to sell tobacco products to anyone under the age of 18.
Method of Use	Smoking, Sniffing, Chewing.
Therapeutic Uses	It has no medicinal or therapeutic uses.
Effect	Enhancing mood and performance. Produces rewarding effects in the relief of stress. Increases performance and concentration on minor tasks. Reduces aggression and irritability.
Adverse Effects	Headache, dizziness, insomnia, abnormal dreams, nervousness, gastrointestinal (GI) distress, dry mouth, nausea, vomiting, dyspepsia, diarrhoea and musculoskeletal symptoms. Increase in blood pressure. Acceleration of heart rate. Smokers are more likely to suffer from heart disease, blood clots, cancer, strokes, bronchitis, circulation problems, ulcers and sexual health problems.
Dependence	A physical dependence develops quite quickly along with psychological dependency and quitting can be extremely difficult.
Withdrawal Symptoms	Physical: Dryness of the mouth, nausea, sore throat, drowsiness, cough problems, headache, tiredness, postnasal drip, bleeding in the gums, stomach pain, constipation, hunger pangs, increased appetite, increased weight gain, insomnia, tightness/stiffness in the chest. Psychological: craving, restlessness, feeling of loneliness, inability to concentrate, anger, irritability, anxiety, depression.
Overdose Risk	A small dose of pure nicotine injected directly into the bloodstream would kill a person within one hour.

consumption. Tobacco smoke contains the monoamine oxidase inhibitors (MAOI) harman, norharman, anabasine, anatabine, and nornicotine. These compounds significantly decrease MAO activity in smokers (Fowler et al., 1998; Herraiz et al., 2005). Nicotine also has an affinity for melanin (skin pigmentation) and it has been suggested to underlie the increased nicotine dependence and lower smoking cessation rates in darker pigmented individuals.

Nicotine and addictive behaviour

Addiction to nicotine sustains cigarette smoking and is responsible for the remarkable intractability of smoking behaviour (Department of Health et al., 1998). A report on nicotine addiction found that nicotine complied with the established criteria for defining an addictive substance (Royal College of Physicians, 2000). The Report stated that nicotine is a highly addictive substance, to a degree similar or in some respects exceeding addiction to heroin or cocaine. It is suggested that most smokers do not smoke out of choice but because they are addicted to nicotine.

The World Health Organization International Classification of Diseases (ICD)-10 (World Health Organization, 1992) and the Diagnostic and Statistical Manual of Mental Disorders (DSM-IV), (American Psychiatric Association, 1995) provide a suitable framework for determining the addictive or dependent nature of nicotine and smoking. The features of nicotine addictions (DSM-IV or ICD-10 definitions) include:

- A strong desire to take the drug.
- A higher priority given to drug use.
- Continued use despite harmful consequences.
- Tolerance.
- Withdrawal.

On present evidence, it is reasonable to conclude that nicotine delivered through tobacco smoke should be regarded as an addictive drug, and tobacco use as the means of nicotine self-administration (Royal College of Physicians, 2000). The medical and psychological effects of tobacco smoking are presented in Table 10.2.

Table 10.2 Medical and psychological effects of tobacco smoking

	Effects
Cardiovascular diseases	Coronary heart disease: acute myocardial infarction, chronic ischemic heart disease. Angina attacks. Risk factor for stroke in association with high blood pressure. Arteriosclerosis. Smoking tends to increase blood cholesterol levels.
Respiratory diseases	Eighty three per cent (83%) of deaths are from chronic obstructive lung disease, including bronchitis. A close relationship exists between cigarette smoking and chronic cough and mucus hyper secretion. The majority of cigarette smokers suffer from chronic bronchitis, pulmonary emphysema and bronchial asthma.
Cancer	Smoking causes 84% of deaths from lung cancer. Risks of cancers of the mouth, pharynx, larynx, bladder, pancreas, kidney, stomach, and is associated with cancer of the cervix.

(Continued)

Table 10.2 Continued

	Effects
Sexual Health	Impairs fertility in both women and men. Smokers take longer to conceive than non-smokers. Earlier menopause than non-smokers. Women smokers who take oral contraceptives have approximately ten times the risk of a heart attack, stroke or other cardiovascular disease compared to non-smokers.
Maternal Smoking and Pregnancy	Fetal and perinatal mortality, low birth weight. Pregnancy complications including miscarriage, stillbirth, ectopic pregnancy and cot death. Affect the child's long-term growth, behavioural characteristics and educational achievement.
Smoking and Diabetes Type 2	Smoking is linked to a significantly increased risk of developing type 2 diabetes.[1] Previous research has linked smoking to insulin resistance – a condition which often leads to diabetes.
Psychological	Anxiety disorders. Depression. Aggression.

Source: [1]Willi, C., Bodenmann, P., Ghali, W.A., Faris, P.D. and Cornuz, J. (2007) 'Active Smoking and the Risk of Type 2 Diabetes. A Systematic Review and Meta-analysis', *Journal of the American Medical Association*, 298, 22, 2654–64.

Public health strategy

The WHO Framework Convention on Tobacco Control (WHO FCTC) (WHO, 2003), the first global public health treaty, was developed in response to the globalization of the tobacco epidemic. The treaty asserts the importance of supply and demand reduction and addresses tobacco industry marketing campaigns and cigarette smuggling that is often co-ordinated by the tobacco industry in many countries. In the report *Smoking Kills – A White Paper on Tobacco (The Stationery Office, 1999)*, the Government's Strategy in England is to focus on the reduction of smoking behaviours so as to improve health in Britain. The main strategy, as part of public health improvement, aims to reduce smoking among children and young people; to help adults – especially the most disadvantaged – to give up smoking and to offer particular help to pregnant women who smoke. A comprehensive service, provided by the National Health Service, has been implemented to help smokers to give up with added treatment including nicotine replacement therapy (NRT).

In England, 1 July 2007 became a landmark day for public health policy. A new law was introduced to make virtually all enclosed public places and workplaces in England smoke free. The findings of an evaluation of the health benefits of a smoke free England found compliance with smoke free legislation has been consistently high and the general public and businesses support the smoke free law and have quickly adapted to its requirements (Department of Health 2008). Air quality in pubs has improved dramatically from 'unhealthy' average levels to smoke free levels that are comparable to outdoor air. Local National Health Service (NHS) Stop Smoking Services have experienced over 20 per cent increased demand as smokers have benefited from the more supportive environment to quit smoking.

Harmful effects of tobacco smoke

Tobacco smoke contains three main constituents: tar, carbon dioxide and nicotine. Tar comprises 4,000 different organic chemicals, including carcinogens, and is the toxic chemical found in cigarettes. The rating of the type of cigarette is determined by the concentration of tar. For example, high tar cigarettes contain at least 22 milligrams (mg) of tar; medium tar cigarettes from 15 mg to 21 mg; and low tar cigarettes 7 mg or less of tar. However, the actual tar exposure, and hence health risk, from smoking low tar brands may be almost the same as for conventional cigarettes (Jarvis and Bates, 1999). Tar is present in all cigarettes and tends to increase as the cigarette is burnt down. This means that the end of cigarette may contain as much as twice the amount of tar as the first puffs. On exhalation, the brown sticky substance paralyses the cilia in the lungs, and contributes to lung diseases such as emphysema, chronic bronchitis and lung cancer.

Nicotine, a main toxic component of cigarette smoking, is highly addictive. The average cigarette yields at least 8 mg to 20 mg of nicotine (depending on the brand), while a cigar may contain up to 40 mg of nicotine. Nicotine, although poisonous, is absorbed very slowly when it is inhaled. Nicotine is broken down in the liver to produce cotinine and nicotine oxide. In order to test whether or not someone has been smoking in the past day or two, the screening of the individual's urine would confirm the presence of cotinine. Nicotine can increase the heart rate and blood pressure and the stickiness of the blood platelets.

Carbon monoxide is a colourless, odourless gas which is one of the harmful gases included in tobacco smoke. Carbon monoxide enters the blood stream and its toxicity stems from its binding to haemoglobin to form carboxyhaemoglobin. Smokers tend to have a reduced amount of haemoglobin available and an increased number of red blood cells. In smokers, where the oxygen-carrying capacity of the blood is reduced, disease of the peripheral circulation can have adverse health effects.

For smokers of cigars or pipes, the same amounts of carcinogens and toxic chemicals found in cigarette smoke are also found in pipe and cigar tobacco. Pipe and cigar smokers reduce their health risks because they often smoke less than cigarette smokers and they usually do not inhale. However, pipe and cigar smokers have nearly the same risk as cigarette smokers for developing cancers of the mouth, throat, voice box, oesophagus and bladder. Pipe smokers also have a high risk of lip cancer. Chewing tobacco and snuff are called smokeless tobacco. The health risks include damage to the delicate lining of the mouth and throat, heart disease, stroke and cancer. For those who smoke cigarettes and use smokeless tobacco, the risks are highest for developing cancer of the mouth and throat.

Health benefits of quitting smoking

One of the key factors for people who wish to quit smoking is their health concerns. About two in three smokers want to stop smoking. There is evidence to suggest that smoking cessation has major and immediate health benefits for men and women of all ages (US Department of Health and Human Services, 1990). The benefits apply to persons with and without smoking-related disease. Improvement in overall health gains will be gained through smoking cessation.

- Nicotine withdrawal symptoms disappear after one month.
- Reduces the risk of coronary heart disease, COPD (chronic obstructive pulmonary disease) and peripheral vascular disease.
- Reduces the risk of stroke.
- A reduction of risk between 30 and 50 per cent for lung cancer has been reported after 10 years abstinence. Bladder cancer and cervical cancer risks are also substantially lower after a few years of abstinence.
- Reduces the risk of impotence, fertility problems, optic neuropathy, cataract, macular degeneration, psoriasis, gum disease, tooth loss, osteoporosis and Raynaud's phenomenon (discolorations of the fingers and/or the toes).
- Women who stop smoking before becoming pregnant have infants of the same birth weight as those born to women who have never smoked.
- The risk of death of former smokers compared to that for continuing smokers begins to decline shortly after giving up until after some 15 years of abstinence.

Assessment

The process of compiling a smoking history involves asking basic questions including the amount and type of cigarette smoked on a regular basis, the number of months or years as a smoker and previous attempts to quit. Key components of compiling a smoking history include:

- Number of years as a smoker?
- How soon is the first cigarette smoked after waking?

- Does the person crave a cigarette when in a no smoking area or situation?
- Examine any previous attempts to quit.
- Assess suitability for various types of intervention.
- Discuss concerns, for example, withdrawal discomfort.
- Measure expired carbon monoxide levels (ECO).

It is important to assess the suitability for interventions. For example, the combination of nicotine replacement therapy (NRT) and behavioural support. The treatment interventions need to be discussed with the patient and to ensure the patient has realistic expectations of the efficacy of the treatment. Part of the assessment is to take the ECO level (measuring carbon monoxide) as carbon monoxide levels are an indicator of the amount of tobacco smoke inhaled by an individual smoker (Foulds, 1996). Using an ECO monitor where clients can see one of the positive effects of not smoking can add a major incentive towards quitting (Mills, 1998).

Patients with nicotine dependence suffer from withdrawal symptoms with the sudden stopping or reduction of smoking or other tobacco use. The physio logical and psychological effects of nicotine withdrawal are presented in Table 10.3. The extent of withdrawal symptoms of nicotine is dependent on the duration of smoking and number of cigarettes smoked and may begin within a few hours after the last cigarette, quickly driving people back to tobacco use. The withdrawal symptoms peak within the first few days of smoking cessation and may subside within a few weeks or may persist for months. Depressed

Table 10.3 The physiological and psychological effects of nicotine withdrawal

Physiological	Psychological
• Dryness of the mouth	• Craving
• Nausea	• Restlessness
• Sore throat	• Feeling of loneliness
• Drowsiness	• Inability to concentrate
• Cough problems	• Anger
• Headache	• Irritability
• Tiredness	• Anxiety
• Postnasal drip	• Depression
• Bleeding in the gums	
• Stomach pain	
• Constipation	
• Hunger pangs	
• Increased appetite	
• Increased weight gain	
• Insomnia	
• Tightness/stiffness in the chest	

smokers appear to experience more withdrawal symptoms on quitting, are less likely to be successful at quitting, and are more likely to relapse.

Treatment interventions

NICE (2006) has recommended that everyone who smokes should be advised to quit and that where a service user presents with a smoking-related disease, cessation advice may be linked to their medical condition. It is important for a health care professional to advise all patients who want to quit of the option to be offered a referral to an NHS Stop Smoking Service. The NHS Stop Smoking Service (SSS) typically combines behavioural support, delivered in a group or individual setting, with pharmacotherapy (nicotine replacement therapy or bupropion). The Cochrane reviews found no difference in efficacy between individual and group treatments, so preference must be given to group approaches where practicable as they are considerably more cost-effective, though some smokers prefer the individual approach (Lancaster and Stead, 1999a; 1999b; Stead and Lancaster, 1999). Psychological and pharmacological interventions play an integral role in smoking cessation treatment. Self-help materials are also provided to complement the psychological interventions.

Brief interventions

The psychological techniques of brief interventions involves opportunistic advice, discussion, negotiation or encouragement interventions and typically take between five and 10 minutes and may include opportunistic advice to stop or an assessment of the patient's commitment to quit. This should be supplemented by pharmacotherapy and/or behavioural support, the provision of self-help material and referral to the NHS Stop Smoking Services.

Self-help

Self-help leaflets and information are also valuable as part of self-interventions in the strategy to quit smoking. There is some evidence to suggest that self-help information has a small but significant effect in comparison with no intervention (Stead and Lancaster, 1999a; 1999b). An interesting development based on computing technology is to personalize advice to individual smokers (Strecher et al., 1994). There are also many online guides (available through the Internet) which give useful tips about smoking cessation.

Pharmacological interventions

The main forms of pharmacological treatment covered are nicotine replacement therapy (NRT) and the antidepressant bupropion. The aims of NRT are to reduce withdrawal symptoms by replacing the nicotine from tobacco smoking. There is evidence that all forms of NRT made it more likely that a person's attempt to quit smoking would succeed (Stead et al., 2008). The chances of stopping smoking were increased by 50 to 70 per cent.

Bupropion, an alternative to nicotine-based treatment, is an effective intervention and should be offered as a treatment option for patients requesting help with smoking cessation. However, bupropion is unsuitable for pregnant women, people with a history of seizures or eating disorders) for which nicotine replacement may be considered. Bupropion is not recommended for smokers under the age of 18 years, as its safety and efficacy have not been evaluated for this group. Varenicline (Champix, Pfizer) has also been recommended as an option for smokers who have expressed a desire to quit smoking (NICE, 2007).

NRT is available as:

- Transdermal patch (varying doses, 16 hours and 24 hours duration);
- Gum (2 mg and 4 mg);
- Sublingual tablet (2 mg);
- Nasal spray (0.5 mg per dose, usually administered two doses at a time);
- Inhalator/inhaler;
- Lozenge (1, 2 and 4 mg).

Social support

Social support is believed to be an important component of any treatment interventions. Social support from friends, family, co-workers, and significant others has long been acknowledged as a key factor in helping individuals cope with stressful situations (Dormann and Zapf, 1999). A meta-analysis by Viswesvaran and Schmidt (1992) concluded that cessation programs incorporating social support, social norms, and self-esteem enhancement were more effective than treatment programmes without these elements.

Relapse prevention

Many people lapse and relapse after quitting smoking. Relapse is the major problem, eroding the success rates of 50–60 per cent at one month to 20–30 per cent one year later (Hajek, 1989). Relapse interventions are used to help people avoid relapse and these are usually focused on teaching the skills to cope with temptations to smoke. This approach and others have not been shown to be helpful, either for people who quit on their own, or with the help of a cessation treatment, or who quit because they were pregnant or in hospital (Royal College of Physicians, 2000). The findings of a review of the Cochrane analysis on the use of behavioural interventions (Hajek et al., 2009) showed that at the moment there is insufficient evidence to support the use of any specific behavioural intervention for helping smokers who have successfully quit for a short time to avoid relapse. The review concluded that extended treatment with varenicline may prevent relapse and that extended treatment with bupropion is unlikely to have a clinically important effect.

Summary of key points

- The contents of a cigarette contain the most toxic and carcinogenic substances.
- There is evidence to suggest that tobacco smoking is addictive.
- The Government's strategy is to see a reduction in smoking among children and young people and to offer particular help to pregnant women who smoke.
- The health and risk factors associated with active cigarette smoking include cancer, cardiovascular disease, respiratory diseases, type 2 diabetes, sexual health and maternal health.
- The extent of withdrawal symptoms of nicotine is dependent on the duration of smoking and number of cigarettes smoked.
- Nicotine Withdrawal Symptoms occur with the sudden stopping or reduction of smoking or other tobacco use.
- The NHS Stop Smoking Service provides counselling and support to smokers wanting to quit, complementing the use of stop smoking aids such as nicotine replacement therapy (NRT) and bupropion (Zyban).
- Both pharmacological and psychological interventions are part of the treatment interventions to aid smoking cessation.
- The aims of NRT are to reduce withdrawal symptoms associated with stopping smoking by replacing the nicotine from tobacco smoking.

Reflective activity 10.2

A 60 year old woman with stable angina and a history of depression smokes 20 cigarettes daily. She would like to stop smoking but is concerned about weight gain. She has tried to quit several times on her own without success.

- What would be the brief interventions required initially?
- What other withdrawal symptoms or behavioural problems may be observed?
- What would you discuss with her about the benefits of smoking cessation?
- Identify the psychological interventions that may be used with the patient?
- Identify the pharmacological interventions that may be used with the patient?

References

Action on Smoking and Health UK (ASH) Factsheet No. 1: *Smoking Statistics: Who Smokes and How Much*. March 2007. Available at http://www.ash.org. uk/information/facts-and-stats/essential-information, date accessed 20 January 2010.

American Psychiatric Association (1995) *Diagnostic and Statistical Manual of Mental Disorders*, 4th edn (Washington: APA).

Cancer Research UK (2009) *Lung Cancer and Smoking Statistics*. Available at http://info.cancerresearchuk.org/cancerstats/types/lung/smoking/, date accessed 20 January 2010.

Department of Health, Department of Health and Social Services, Northern Ireland, The Scottish Office Department of Health, Welsh Office (1998) *Report of the Scientific Committee on Tobacco and Health* (London: The Stationery Office).

Department of Health (2008) *Smoke Free England – One Year On* (London: Department of Health). This document is available to download at www. dh.gov.uk/tobacco.

Dormann, C. and Zapf, D. (1999) 'Social Support, Social Stressors at Work, and Depressive Symptoms: Testing for Main and Moderating Effects with Structural Equations in a Three-Wave Longitudinal Study', *Journal of Applied Psychology*, 84, 6, 874–84.

Europa-Eu (2007) http://europa.eu, date accessed 12 December 2009.

Foulds, J. (1996) 'Strategies for Smoking Cessation', *British Medical Bulletin* 52, 1, 157–73.

Fowler, J.S., Volkow, N.D., Wang, G.J., Dewey, S.L., MacGregor, R., Schlyer, D., Gatley, SJ, Schutz, B., Schafer, M.K., Eiden, L.E. and Weihe, E. (1998) 'Neuropharmacological Actions of Cigarette Smoke: Brain Monoamine Oxidase B (MAO B) Inhibition', *J Addict Dis* 17, 1 23–34. Doi:10.1300/J069v17n01_03.

Hajek, P. (1989) 'Withdrawal-oriented Therapy for Smokers', *British Journal of Addiction*, 84, 6, 591–98.

Hajek, P., Stead, L.F., West, R., Jarvis, M. and Lancaster, T. (2009) 'Relapse Prevention Interventions for Smoking Cessation', *Cochrane Database of Systematic Reviews* 2009, Issue 1. Art. No.: CD003999. DOI: 10.1002/14651858.CD003999. pub3.

Herraiz, T. and Chaparro, C (2005) 'Human Monoamine Oxidase is Inhibited by Tobacco Smoke: Beta-carboline Alkaloids Act as Potent and Reversible Inhibitors', *Biochem. Biophys. Res. Commun.* 326, 2, 378–86. Doi: 10.1016/ j.bbrc.2004.11.033.

Jarvis, M. and Bates, C. (1999) Why Low Tar Cigarettes Don't Work and How the Tobacco Industry Has Fooled the Smoking Public. 1999 Edition.

http://www.ash.org.uk/media-room/press-releases/tobacco-industry-deceit-on-low-tar-cigarettes-revealed, date accessed 12 December 2009.

Lancaster, T. and Stead, L.F. (1999a) Individual Behavioural Counselling for Smoking Cessation (Cochrane Review). In: The Cochrane Library, Issue 2 (Oxford: Update Software).

Lancaster, T. and Stead, L.F. (1999b) Self-help Interventions for Smoking Cessation (Cochrane Review). In: The Cochrane Library, Issue 2 (Oxford: Update Software).

Mills, C. (1998) 'Nicotine Addiction: Health Care Interventions', in Rassool, G.H. (ed.), *Substance Use and Misuse: Nature, Context and Clinical Interventions* (Oxford: Blackwell Publications).

NICE (2006) *Brief Interventions and Referral for Smoking Cessation in Primary Care and Other Settings*, Public Health Guidance No 1 (London: National Institute for Clinical Excellence).

NICE (2007) Varenicline: Guidance for Smoking Cessation, TA123 (London: National Institute for Clinical Excellence).

ONS (Office for National Statistics) (2006) *General Household Survey 2006. Smoking and Drinking Among Adults*. Available at http://www.statistics.gov.uk, date accessed 20 January 2010.

ONS (Office for National Statistics) (2008) *General Household Survey: Smoking and Drinking Among Adults 2007*. http://www.statistics.gov.uk/StatBase/Product.asp?vlnk=5756, date accessed 10 January 2010.

Royal College of Physicians (RCP) (2000) *Nicotine Addiction in Britain. A Report of the Tobacco Advisory Group of the Royal College of Physicians* (London: RCP).

Stead, L.F. and Lancaster, T. (1999) Group Behaviour Therapy Programmes for Smoking Cessation (Cochrane Review). In: The Cochrane Library, Issue 2 (Oxford: Update Software).

Stead, L.F., Perera, R., Bullen, C., Mant, D. and Lancaster, T. (2008) Nicotine Replacement Therapy for Smoking Cessation. Cochrane Database of Systematic Reviews 2008, Issue 1. Art. No.: CD000146. DOI: 10.1002/14651858. CD000146.pub3.

Strecher, V., Kreuter, M., Den Boer, D., Kobrin, S., Hospers, H.J. and Skinner, C.S. (1994) 'The Effects of Computer-tailored Smoking Cessation Messages in Family Practice Settings', *Journal of Family Practice*, 39, 3, 262–70.

The Stationery Office (1999) *Smoking Kills – A White Paper on Tobacco*. Cm.4177, The Stationery Office, London.

US Department of Health and Human Services (1990) *The Health Benefits of Smoking Cessation*. US Department of Health and Human Services. Public Health Service, Center for Disease Control. Center for Chronic Disease Prevention and Health Promotion. Office on Smoking and Health. DHHS Publication No. (CDC) 90-8416.

Viswesvaran, C. and Schmidt, F.L. (1992) 'A Meta-Analytic Comparison of the Effectiveness of Smoking Cessation Methods', *Journal of Applied Psychology*, 77, 4, 554–61.

World Health Organization (1992) *International Statistical Classification of Diseases and Related Health Problems, 10th revision* (Geneva: WHO).

World Health Organization (2002) *Global Smoking Statistics for 2002* (Geneva: WHO).

World Health Organization (2003) *WHO Framework Convention on Tobacco Control* (Geneva: WHO).

Eating Disorders 11

Introduction

Reflective activity 11.1

Before reading this chapter, try to provide a true or false answer for each of the statements listed below. Think about some reasons as to why you chose a particular answer.

Statements	True	False
There is no similarity between physical addiction to various chemicals and eating disorders.		
Eating disorders are a range of complex syndromes with physical, psychological, behavioural and social features.		
There are no physical complications in eating disorders.		
It is estimated that about one million people in the UK live with an eating disorder regardless of their age, sex or cultural background.		
Eating disorders have been regarded as a developmental or biological disorder.		
Personality traits also appear to be significant in the development of eating disorders.		
Anorexia usually develops over time and most commonly starts in the mid-thirties.		
In anorexia, there is no obsession with eating, food and weight control.		
Anorexics are always in a state of denial.		
Anorexics have no coexisting psychiatric and physical illnesses.		
One feature of bulimia nervosa is the nature of bingeing which provides an explanation for the absence of severe weight loss.		

Statements	True	False
People with Body Dysmorphic Disorder (BDD) are preoccupied or obsessed with real or imagined flaws, usually the skin, hair and nose.		
Compulsive over-eating is one of the eating disorders where the individual eats according to emotional cues.		
People with eating disorders smoke cigarettes to suppress their appetite.		
Eating disorders and substance misuse have a number of characteristics in common.		
Psychiatric disorders such as post traumatic stress disorder, obsessive-compulsive disorder, mood disorders and personality disorders are found among those with eating disorders.		

When you have read this chapter, come back to this activity and consider your answers again. How many did you get right? For those you got wrong, think about the reasons for your original answer and compare this with what you know now.

There is a strong argument that eating disorders are a form of addictive behaviour. Clinically, the addictive behaviours that define eating disorders and alcohol and drug misuse are very similar. Several researchers imply that there is a similarity between physical addiction to various chemicals and eating disorders (Engs, 1996; Lerner, 2006; Marlatt and Witkiewitz, 2008). The major eating disorders are anorexia nervosa and bulimia nervosa. Four classes of eating disorders, which cluster in families have been found: anorexia nervosa with obsessive-compulsive symptoms, anorexia nervosa without obsessive-compulsive symptoms, anorexia and bulimia nervosa, and bulimia nervosa with self-induced vomiting (Keel et al., 2004). There are other eating disorders which are similar to anorexia or bulimia but with slightly different characteristics. Other eating disorders include Binge Eating Disorder, Body Dysmorphic Disorder (BDD), Compulsive over-eating, Compulsive Exercising, Eating Disorder Not Otherwise Specified (ED-NOS), Night Eating Syndrome, Pica Prader-Willi Syndrome, and Sleep Eating Disorder (SED-NOS).

Eating disorders are a range of complex syndromes with physical, psychological, behavioural and social features. Eating disorder is characterized when an individual 'experiences severe disturbances in eating behaviour, such as extreme reduction of food intake or extreme over-eating, or feelings of extreme distress or concern about body weight or shape' (NIMH, 2009). Eating disorders are psychological illnesses with acute physical complications. The negative impact of the disorders have devastating consequences for the sufferers and their significant others as recovery is extremely difficult. The psychological effects on the sufferer include having low self-esteem, feelings of shame and/or secrecy and sufferers are in constant denial. The long-term disabilities include negative effects on employment, fertility, relationships and parenting (NICE, 2004).

It is estimated that about one million people in the UK live with an eating disorder regardless of their age, sex or cultural background. Young women are most likely to develop an eating disorder, particularly those aged 15 to 25 but older women and men of all ages also get eating disorders (NIMH, 2009). Eating disorders frequently coexist with other psychiatric disorders such as depression or anxiety disorders and addictive behaviours, for example, alcohol and drug misuse. The mortality rates among people with eating disorders are high due to the effects of chronic physical complications of eating disorders and suicide. Anorexia nervosa has the highest mortality rate of any psychiatric disorder of adolescence (NICE, 2004).

Common features of eating disorders and addiction

Individuals with addictive behaviours and eating disorders display similar features. Different types of addiction resemble one another (though there are also differences), and individuals often switch from one to another. It is stated that these common characteristics satisfy all the clinical and biological criteria for conventional addictive behaviours such as smoking, alcoholism and cocaine misuse (Davis and Claridge, 1998; Davis et al., 1999). These characteristics find direct parallels in the core eating disorder behaviours such as dieting, over-exercising and binge eating, all of which tend to become increasingly excessive over time (Davis, 2001). The common features of addictive behaviours and eating disorders include:

- Compulsive nature of the behaviour.
- Common psychobiological vulnerability and for the notion that individuals use a variety of rewarding behaviours to self-medicate their affective disturbances depending on the specific effects of each (Davis, 2001).
- Similar biological mechanisms account for the compulsively progressive nature of both disorders (Davis, 2001).
- Individuals require more of the behaviour to produce the same reinforcing effect (Berridge and Robinson, 1995).
- Relief of excessive anxiety serves to compensate for and counteract feelings of incompleteness, self-disgust and anger (Dunne et al., 1991).
- Preoccupation with the behaviour.
- Secrecy, use of rituals, engaging in compulsive behaviours.

- Both addictive behaviours and eating disorders may produce mood-altering effects in the individual.
- Both are chronic diseases/disorders with high rates of relapse (Strober et al., 1999).

Although there are similarities between addictive behaviours and eating disorders, it is argued that eating disorders do not validate as addictive behaviours. Wilson (2000) suggested that neither tolerance nor withdrawal reactions to food have been demonstrated and there is a lack of evidence for 'carbohydrate craving'. Other characteristics such as a loss of control over eating or preoccupation with food have bio-behavioural explanations that do not invoke addiction.

Aetiology of eating disorders

Despite extensive research exploring the aetiology of eating disorders there appears to be limited advancement in understanding the disorders. Much of the aetiology of eating disorders remains contentious but there is a general consensus that the causes of eating disorders are multi-factorial encompassing genetic, neurochemical, psychological, socio-cultural and environmental factors. Traditionally, eating disorders been regarded as a disorder with social and cultural explanations, rather than as a developmental or biological disorder (Nasser et al., 2000). It is argued that the cultivation of the ideal body and promotion of thinness values in fashion, media and the diet industry accounts for the increased prevalence of eating disorders (Nasser, 2009). However, there is the suggestion that eating disorders among young Asian women living in the UK may be the product of a culture clash rather than acculturation (McCourt and Waller, 1996).

However, current socio-cultural explanations include worldwide cultural dynamics, such as adopting 'westernization' and confused gender identities (Collier and Treasure, 2004). A number of global cultural forces have been implicated in the spread of eating disorders in non-Western cultures including the power of the media, market economy and urbanization (Nasser, 2006). The move away from socio-cultural explanations of eating disorders came into force when evidence from twin and family studies showed that they have a genetic component (Kay, 1999; Bulik et al., 2000). Chromosome harbouring genes has also been identified for anorexia nervosa in multiple affected families and in bulimia nervosa (Grice et al., 2002; Bulik et al., 2003).

Personality traits also appear to be significant in the development of eating disorders. High harm avoidance, novel-seeking behaviours, rigidity and impulsive behaviour are all enduring personality traits that appear to be linked to specific types of eating behaviours, whereas others are more general (Karwautz et al.,

Table 11.1 Factors in the development of eating disorders

Factors	Features
Genetic	Genetic influence – family and twin studies.
Biological	Neurochemical imbalances involving serotonin, and melanocortin.
Psychological	Low self-esteem, lack of social skills, depression, anxiety, anger, emptiness, loneliness, obsessive-compulsive personality traits, childhood rigidity, impulsive behaviours.
Socio-Cultural	Cultural pressure, cultural norms, media messages, acculturation, westernization.
Risk Factors	Difficulty expressing feelings and emotions, family disharmony, troubled interpersonal relationships, a history of sexual and/or physical abuse, unrealistic family expectations for achievement, a tendency to comply with other people's demands. Unusual familial interest in food, weight and shape.

2002; Vervaet et al., 2004). Studies on the relationships between neurochemical and personality factors have also been indicative of the influence of serotonin across the eating disorder spectrum (Steiger, 2004). Other risk factors include moving to a new neighbourhood, difficulty expressing feelings and emotions, family disharmony, troubled interpersonal relationships, a history of sexual and/or physical abuse, unrealistic family expectations for achievement, a tendency to comply with unrealistic demands and unusual familial interest in food, weight and shape. Childhood perfectionism appears to be a particularly strong antecedent risk factor (Anderluh et al., 2003).

Despite research to date, the study of gene-environment interaction has barely been touched and many questions remain to be answered regarding the aetiology of eating disorders (Collier and Treasure, 2004). Table 11.1 presents a summary of the key factors in the development of eating disorders.

Anorexia nervosa

Anorexia usually develops over time and most commonly starts in the mid-teens. In the UK, it is estimated that in teenagers and young adults, the condition affects about one in 250 females and one in 2,000 males (CKS, 2005). Anorexia is a serious psychiatric disorder that encompasses all the bio-psychosocial aspects of an individual's life and their family and significant others. Anorexia nervosa is characterized by emaciation beyond the point of slimness and unwillingness to maintain a normal or healthy weight. In addition, there is an endless pursuit of thinness by restricting what they eat and sometimes compulsively over-exercising. There is an obsession with eating, food and weight control.

Some people with anorexia lose weight by dieting and exercising excessively; others lose weight by self-induced vomiting, or misusing laxatives, diuretics or enemas. There is constant compulsion with obtaining weight measurements as the sufferer typically weighs herself or himself repeatedly.

People with anorexia nervosa usually find it very difficult to recognize their condition. They are often in a state of denial about the amount of weight loss and its physical and psychological consequences and are reluctant to seek treatment. There are also attempts by sufferers to conceal their condition and their eating behaviours from their family and significant others. If left untreated, it may be difficult to live with sufferers of anorexia nervosa because of their anxiety and frequent, unpredictable fluctuations in temperament, mood and behaviour. Anorexia nervosa is a relapsing condition and some people will have the chronic form of anorexia, in which their health deteriorates over many years. The most common complications that lead to death amongst people with anorexia are cardiac arrest, electrolyte and fluid imbalances and suicide. People with anorexia also have coexisting psychiatric and physical illnesses, including depression, anxiety, obsessive behaviour, cardiovascular and neurological complications, substance misuse and impaired physical development. Some common features observed in people with anorexia are presented in Table 11.2.

Table 11.2 Features observed in people suffering from anorexia nervosa

Symptoms

- Severe weight loss.
- Abdominal pain, constipation.
- Amenorrhoea.
- Bradycardia.
- Thinning of the bones (osteopenia or osteoporosis).
- Brittle hair and nails.
- Dry and yellowish skin.
- Growth of fine hair over body (e.g. lanugo).
- Drop in internal body temperature, causing a person to feel cold all the time.
- Excessive exercising.
- Self-induced vomiting and purging.
- Lethargy.
- Lack of concern about low body weight.
- Fatigue and decreased energy.
- Headaches.

- Mild anaemia, and muscle weakness and loss.
- Severe constipation.
- Low blood pressure, slowed breathing and pulse.
- Sleep disturbance, difficulty in sleeping.
- Irritability and anxious energy.
- Isolation and loss of friends.
- Distorted body image, misconception about body weight and size.
- Personality changes.
- Reduced libido.
- Perfectionism.
- Depression.

Bulimia nervosa

There are many similarities in both disorders, the most common being the aetiology. Psychological, cultural and biological factors all seem to play a role in the development of bulimia. People may have low self-esteem, difficult family and social relationships, may be lonely or depressed and have had traumatic life experiences (Institute of Psychiatry, 2009). There seems to be a common occurrence of sexual and/or physical and emotional abuse in direct relation to eating disorders (though not all people living with eating disorders are survivors of abuse). The roots of bulimia nervosa are quite distinct to those of anorexia nervosa. According to Lacey and Evans (1988), bulimia nervosa may even manifest as a proneness to being driven by impulses that cannot be controlled. As Gordon (1999) indicates, a differential pattern is apparent in people with bulimia nervosa. The experience of bulimia nervosa is likely to have involved poor emotional regulation, along with marked ambivalence and a chaotic lifestyle. According to Lacey (1992), the prevalence rate of bulimia nervosa is three per cent of females aged 15–40 years.

Bulimia nervosa shares various resemblance to anorexia nervosa but it also has very distinct features. In both eating disorders there is the obsession to lose weight, the fear of fatness and, 'the relentless pursuit of thinness' (Bruch, 1978). In contrast to anorexia nervosa, people with bulimia nervosa secretly over-eat and then purge to prevent weight gain by either vomiting or use of laxatives. However, despite the pursuit of trying to lose weight, there is much less likelihood of weight loss. One feature of bulimia nervosa is the nature of bingeing which provides an explanation for the absence of severe weight loss. It is the vicious cycle of bingeing and purging that is the main distinction between people with bulimia and anorexia. People with bulimia not only use laxatives or self-induced vomiting but are also involved in excessive jogging or aerobics. It is usually that after an episode of bingeing that people with bulimia may attempt to abstain from food. In addition, in order to lose weight, people with bulimia will use various diet medications and diuretics for losing weight. It is not uncommon for sufferers of bulimia to hide food for later secretive binges.

Men and women suffering from bulimia have usually an insight that they have an eating disorder. However, the disorder may go undetected for a long time, due largely to the disorder being concealed by sufferers. Some of the behavioural warning signs that can indicate that the someone is suffering from bulimia include: recurrent episodes of binge eating followed by purging (laxatives or self-induced vomiting); a feeling of guilt, a feeling of lacking control, over-eating behaviours, regularly engaging in stringent diet plans and exercise, fasting after a bingeing episode, the misuse of laxatives, diuretics, and or diet pills and a persistent concern with body image and shape. Some of the symptoms of bulimia nervosa are presented in Table 11.3.

Table 11.3 Symptoms of bulimia nervosa

Physical	Behavioural/Psychological
• Irregular heartbeat. • Bloodshot eyes. • Stomach pain and indigestion. • Fluid retention. • Dehydration. • Fluctuations in weight. • Weakness, tiredness and fatigue. • Constipation and diarrhoea. • Swollen glands in the face and neck. • Irregular menstrual cycle. • Fertility problems. • Stomach ulcers. • Malnutrition. • Epileptic fits. • Sore throat. • Damage to kidneys. • Dental cavities and erosion of tooth enamel (stomach acid when vomiting). • Heart attack.	• Binge eating. • Misuse of laxatives, diuretics, enemas or diet pills. • Fasting. • Excessive exercising. • Smell of vomiting in bathroom. • Wanting privacy constantly. • Social phobia. • Depression. • Anxiety. • Mood swings and irritability. • Low self-esteem. • Feeling a loss of control. • Obsession with weight shape, food, dieting and exercise. • Feelings of withdrawal.

Other eating disorders

Some other eating disorders include binge eating disorders, Body Dysmorphic Disorder, compulsive over-eating, compulsive exercising and Sleep Eating Disorder (SED-NOS).

Binge eating disorder is a little more common in women than in men. People with binge eating disorder regularly consume large amounts of food and feel their eating is out of control. Those with binge eating disorder also may eat much more quickly than usual during binge episodes and eat until they are uncomfortably full. They have a tendency to consume large amounts of food even when they are not really hungry, usually alone. Psychologically, they have low self-esteem and feel shame, disgusted, depressed, or guilty after over-eating.

People with Body Dysmorphic Disorder (BDD) are preoccupied or obsessed with real or imagined flaws – usually the skin, hair and nose. Psychologically, they experience a lot of anxiety and stress, often have low self-esteem and fear of rejection due to their perceived flaws. People with BDD spend a lot of time focusing on their perceived flaws and excessively checking their appearance in a mirror, or attempt to hide the imperfection or consider getting cosmetic surgery. There are two types of BDD: non-delusional and delusional (Institute of Psychiatry, 2009). The latter is when a person has hallucinations of a completely imagined defect, or grossly exaggerates a small defect. This is less common but more severe, and causes clinically significant distress and social impairment.

Compulsive over-eating is one of the eating disorders where the individual eats according to emotional cues rather than the physiological cues of hunger and satisfaction (Institute of Psychiatry, 2009). Psychologically, they compensate for their emotional problems by over-eating and feel terrible shame about their behaviour and also the real or imagined effect it has on their body size. The compulsive exercisers tend to have regular bouts of intense exercise beyond what is considered safe, with the main goal being to burn calories after eating, or to give the individual permission to eat afterwards (Institute of Psychiatry, 2009). Psychologically, it is another way of avoiding emotional issues and relieving guilt and stress. When people with this disorder cannot exercise, they feel guilty. Compulsive exercising is associated with a number of physical risks, including dehydration, stress fractures, osteoporosis, degenerative arthritis, amenorrhea and reproductive problems and heart problems (Institute of Psychiatry, 2009).

People with Sleep Eating Disorder (SED-NOS) binge on unusually large quantities of food, usually high in sugar or fat, while they are sleep walking. People with SED-NOS are characterized as being often anxious, tired, stressed and angry, and tend to be overweight. During the episodes of binge eating they are at risk from unintentional self-injury while sleep walking.

Eating disorders and substance misuse

Some people with eating disorders misuse psychoactive substances including tobacco, alcohol, amphetamines, cocaine, heroin and over-the-counter medications such as diuretics, emetics or laxatives. Self-medication is one approach to reduce the negative feelings and emotions that typically accompany such disorders. Individuals with eating disorders are up to five times likelier to abuse alcohol or illicit drugs and those who abuse alcohol or illicit drugs are up to 11 times likelier to have eating disorders (The National Center on Addiction and Substance Abuse at Columbia University, 2003). In addition, it is estimated that up to 35 per cent of alcohol or illicit drug misusers have an eating disorder compared with up to three per cent in the general population.

It is reported that people with eating disorders smoke cigarettes to suppress their appetite and provide themselves with an alternative oral activity to eating (The National Center on Addiction and Substance Abuse at Columbia University, 2003). Alcohol misuse is common to those suffering from bulimia nervosa. Bulimic women who are alcohol dependent report a higher rate of suicide attempts, anxiety disorders, personality disorders, conduct disorder and other substance dependence than bulimic women who are not alcohol dependent (The National Center on Addiction and Substance Abuse at Columbia University, 2003). Heroin and cocaine are used by bulimics to facilitate weight loss by suppressing appetite, increasing metabolism and purging.

Eating disorders and substance misuse have a number of characteristics in common. In binge eating, for example, there is a commonly held notion of urges or 'cravings' to consume food. Other features include loss of control, denial, secrecy, social isolation, obsession with a substance, and risk of suicide. The shared risk factors and characteristics are presented in Table 11.4.

There is significant evidence that many eating disorders meet the accepted clinical criteria for substance misuse. However, there are inherent difficulties in viewing eating disorders as analogous with substance misuse. It is argued that the physical dependence, withdrawal, craving and loss of control found in addictive disorders are not characteristic of binge eating and there is no evidence of craving in bulimia nervosa from any kind of chemical disturbance (Wilson, 1995). In bulimia nervosa, substance misuse is best viewed as a coping mechanism, in other words the self-medication hypothesis of dual diagnosis theory (Rassool, 2002).

Table 11.4 Eating disorders and substance misuse

Shared characteristics	*Shared risk factors*
• Common brain chemistry. • Common family history. • Occur in times of transition or stress. • History of sexual or physical abuse. • Low self-esteem, depression, anxiety, impulsivity. • Unhealthy parental behaviours. • Low monitoring of children's activities. • Unhealthy peer norms and social pressures. • Susceptibility to messages from advertising and entertainment mass media.	• Obsessive preoccupation. • Craving. • Compulsive behaviour. • Secretiveness. • Rituals. • Experience mood altering effects. Social isolation. • Suicide. • Difficult to treat, life-threatening. • Chronic diseases with high relapse rates. • Require intensive therapy.

Source: The National Center on Addiction and Substance Abuse at Columbia University (CASA) (2003) Food For Thought: Substance Abuse and Eating Disorders (New York, The National Center on Addiction and Substance Abuse at Columbia University). www.casacolumbia.org. Reproduced with kind permission.

Eating disorders with dual diagnosis

It has become increasingly recognized that there is a common co-occurrence of psychiatric disorders with eating disorders. Psychiatric disorders such as post-traumatic stress disorder, obsessive-compulsive disorder, mood disorders and personality disorders are found among those with eating disorders. It is estimated that psychiatric disorders among those with eating disorders range from 42 to 75 per cent (American Psychiatric Association, 2000; Rosenvinge et al., 2000).

Anorexia nervosa and bulimia nervosa are related to depression, bipolar disorder and other mood disorders (Wade et al., 2000). In about 50 per cent of women with anorexia nervosa and in about one-half to two-thirds of bulimic patients major depression has been reported (Bushnell et al., 1994). Those who seek treatment in the form of counselling usually present depressive symptoms rather than eating disorders (Schwartz and Cohn, 1996). Self-harm, suicidal thoughts and suicide itself are associated with eating disorders. The prevalence of self-harm among people with eating disorders is approximately 25 per cent, regardless of the type of eating disorder or the treatment setting. Prevalence rates are higher for bulimic individuals treated as outpatients (23 per cent) and inpatients (39 per cent). The highest rates of suicide attempts are reported among bulimic individuals who have co-morbid alcohol misuse (54 per cent) (Sansone and Levitt, 2002).

Obsessional personality traits and symptoms have been reported amongst people with anorexia nervosa. Up to 69 per cent of people with anorexia nervosa have a coexisting diagnosis of OCD and up to 33 per cent of patients with bulimia nervosa also have OCD (Von Ranson et al., 1999). Thornton and Russell (1997) found that 21 per cent of the eating disorder patients were found to have co-morbid obsessive-compulsive disorder (OCD) but even more significant was that 37 per cent of anorexia nervosa patients had co-morbid OCD. A review of the literature provides evidence that suggests that OCD co-occurs with eating disorders because of a shared etiological relationship (Altman and Shankman, 2009).

Patients with eating disorders frequently suffer from personality disorders such as histrionic, obsessive-compulsive, avoidant, dependent or borderline personality disorders (Tomotake and Ohmori, 2002). About 25 per cent of self-harming individuals with eating disorders appear to meet the criteria for borderline personality disorder (Levitt et al., 2003).

Assessment of eating disorders

Assessment of people with eating disorders should be comprehensive and include physical, psychological and social needs, and a comprehensive assessment of risk to self (NICE, 2004). As depression and self-harm are common among people with eating disorders, a risk assessment is part of the framework of assessment. The aim of risk assessment is to identify risk factors which can be used to determine the likelihood of 'harm' to self and others and then to use the information acquired to intervene as part of the care plan (Rassool and Winnington, 2006). Risk assessment should fully involve the individual being assessed but it is also important to seek information from other sources such as carers, or significant others as an individual may not disclose 'risky behaviours' or self-harm. The principal elements of risk assessment and management are (Rassool and Winnington, 2006):

- Suicide or self-harm – ideas, plans and intentions.
- Ideas, thoughts and actions of harming others.
- Self-neglect.
- Risk of unintentional harm to self, or exploitation.

This assessment should be conducted with a sensitive approach and in a non-judgemental manner despite the difficulties that the practitioners may face in asking about such 'risky behaviours' (Rassool and Winnington, 2006). In assessing whether a person has anorexia nervosa, attention should be paid to the overall clinical assessment (repeated over time), including rate of weight loss, growth rates in children, objective physical signs and appropriate laboratory tests (NICE, 2004).

Patients with eating disorders are sometimes managed in a shared care arrangement between primary and secondary care. In this case, there should be clear written agreement among individual health care professionals on the responsibility for monitoring patients with eating disorders.

Treatment interventions for eating disorders

Treatment interventions for eating disorders will vary according to the severity and type of eating disorder and the length of time it has continued, as well as the patient's individual choice of interventions. Early treatment is particularly important for those with, or at risk of, severe emaciation and such patients should be prioritized for treatment (NICE, 2004). Hospitalization may be necessary if the patient's physical health is in immediate danger. People with anorexia nervosa requiring inpatient treatment should be admitted to a setting that can provide the skilled implementation of refeeding with careful physical monitoring (particularly in the first few days of refeeding) in combination with psychosocial interventions (NICE, 2004).

Various pharmacological and non-pharmacological therapies are available, including cognitive analytic therapy (CAT), cognitive behaviour therapy

(CBT), interpersonal psychotherapy (IPT), focal psychodynamic therapy and family interventions focused explicitly on eating disorders and self-help groups. The aims of psychological treatment should be to reduce risk, to encourage weight gain and healthy eating, to reduce other symptoms related to an eating disorder, and to facilitate psychological and physical recovery (NICE, 2004). It is recommended that rigid inpatient behaviour modification programmes should not be used in the management of anorexia nervosa (NICE, 2004).

The different types of treatments for bulimia include therapy and medication. It is recommended that as a possible first step, patients with bulimia nervosa should be encouraged to follow an evidence-based self-help programme or offered a trial of an antidepressant drug (NICE, 2004). In addition to treating any weight gain and obesity-related health complications, it is important to address the underlying causes of binge eating disorder. Cognitive behaviour therapy for bulimia nervosa (CBT-BN), a specifically adapted form of CBT, should be offered to adults with bulimia nervosa (NICE, 2004). Treatment involves establishing a regular and balanced eating pattern and exploring, addressing and resolving underlying emotional problems. Adolescents with bulimia nervosa may be treated with CBT-BN, adapted as needed to suit their age, circumstances and level of development, and include the family as appropriate (NICE, 2004).

It is recommended that cognitive behaviour therapy for binge eating disorder (CBT-BED), a specifically adapted form of CBT, should be offered to adults with binge eating disorder. In addition, for all eating disorders, treatment interventions may include sharing of information, advice on behavioural management and facilitating communication (NICE, 2004). The NICE (2004) guidelines on managing eating disorders contains advice on the identification, treatment and management of the eating disorders anorexia nervosa, bulimia nervosa and related conditions, including the management of physical and psychological aspects of eating disorders.

Summary of key points

- Clinically, the addictive behaviours that define eating disorders and alcohol and drug misuse are very similar.
- The major eating disorders are anorexia nervosa and bulimia nervosa.
- Eating disorders are a range of complex syndromes with physical, psychological, behavioural and social features.
- It is estimated that about one million people in the UK live with an eating disorder regardless of their age, sex or cultural background.

- There is a consensus that the causes of eating disorders are multi-factorial encompassing genetic, neurochemical, psychological, socio-cultural and environmental factors.
- Anorexia nervosa is characterized by emaciation beyond the point of slimness and unwillingness to maintain a normal or healthy weight.
- The roots of bulimia nervosa are quite distinct to those of anorexia nervosa.
- People with bulimia nervosa secretly over-eat and then purge to prevent weight gain by either vomiting or the use of laxatives.
- People with eating disorders misuse psychoactive substances including tobacco, alcohol, amphetamines, cocaine, heroin and over-the-counter medications such as diuretics, emetics or laxatives.
- Psychiatric disorders such as post-traumatic stress disorder, obsessive-compulsive disorder, mood disorders and personality disorders are found among those with eating disorders.
- Assessment of people with eating disorders should be comprehensive and include physical, psychological and social needs, and a comprehensive assessment of risk to self.
- Various pharmacological and non-pharmacological therapies are available, including cognitive analytic therapy (CAT), cognitive behaviour therapy (CBT), interpersonal psychotherapy (IPT), focal psychodynamic therapy and family interventions focused explicitly on eating disorders and self-help groups.

Reflective activity 11.2

Case 1:

Julie, an attractive 15 year old, attended the local clinic with her mother. She was referred by the school because her teachers noticed she has been losing weight for the past three months and that she is having concentration problems during class. From an early age she prided herself on her figure. She watched her diet, exercised daily and maintained a regiment of self-discipline. She has done very well in her academic studies and has always been a high achiever. Julie has always been thin but has never been satisfied with her weight or appearance. She is 5' 6" and weighs 85 lbs/38.5 kg.

The mother says that her daughter has been eating alone in her room and refusing to have dinner with her family. Julie started regular menses at 11, but she has had no bleeding for the last two months. Julie is unaware of the fact that she is undernourished, therefore she sees no problem with her appearance or weight.

Case 2:

Margaret is a woman in her late twenties. She maintains a normal weight range but obsesses about food. Whenever she has had stress at work or feels lonely, she turns to food for comfort. At times, she starves herself then binges, when she has eaten too much she vomits. The food has been increasing in amount and the binges are coming more often as she spirals out of control. She usually eats chocolate cookies, cakes, ice cream, and bread products when bingeing.

For each case consider:

- What would be the immediate interventions required?
- What other physical symptoms or behavioural problems may be observed?
- What are the short-term goals for this patient?
- What are the long-term goals for this patient?
- What treatment interventions and/or strategies may be planned for this patient?
- Develop a treatment plan for an adolescent with an eating disorder.
- Devise health promotion strategies that address body image, dieting and eating disorders.

References

Altman, S.E. and Shankman, S.A. (2009) 'What is the Association Between Obsessive-compulsive Disorders and Eating Disorders?' *Clinical Psychology Review*, 29, 7, 638–46.

American Psychiatric Association (2000) 'Practice Guideline for the Treatment of Patients with Eating Disorders (revision)', *American Journal of Psychiatry*, 157 (Suppl. 1), 1–39.

Anderluh, M.B., Tchanturia, K., Rabe-Hesketh, S. and Treasure, J. (2003) 'Childhood Obsessive-compulsive Personality Traits in Adult Women With Eating Disorders: Defining a Broader Eating Disorder Phenotype', *American Journal of Psychiatry*, 160, 2, 242–47.

Berridge, K.C. and Robinson, T.E. (1995) 'The Mind of an Addicted Brain: Neural Sensitization of "Wanting" Versus "Liking"', *Current Directions Psychological Science* 4, 71–76.

Bruch, H. (1978) *The Golden Cage: The Enigma of Anorexia Nervosa* (Vintage: New York).

Bulik, C.M., Sullivan, P.F., Wade, T.D. and Kendler, K.S. (2000) 'Twin Studies of Eating Disorders: a Review', *International Journal of Eating Disorders*, 27, 1, 1–20.

Bulik, C.M., Devlin, B., Bacanu, S.A., Thornton, L., Klump, K.L., Fichter, M.M., Halmi, K.A., Kaplan, A.S., Strober, M., Woodside, D.B., Bergen, A.W. and

Bruch, H. (2003) 'Significant linkage on Chromosome 10p in Families with Bulimia Nervosa', *American Journal of Human Genetics*, 72, 200–207.

Bushnell, J.A., Wells, J.E., McKenzie, J.M., Hornblow, A.R., Oakley-Browne, M.A. and Joyce, P.R. (1994) 'Bulimia Comorbidity in the General Population and in the Clinic', *Psychological Medicine*, 24, 3, 605–11.

Collier D.A. and Treasure, J.L. (2004) 'The Aetiology of Eating Disorders', *The British Journal of Psychiatry* 185, 5, 363–65.

CKS (2005) *Eating Disorders* (Newcastle upon Tyne: Clinical Knowledge Summaries).

Davis, C. (2001) 'Addiction and the Eating Disorders', *Psychiatric Times*, 18, 2, www.psychiatrictimes.com/display/article/10168/54311, date accessed 30 November 2010.

Davis, C. and Claridge, G. (1998) 'The Eating Disorders as Addiction: a Psychobiological Perspective', *Addictive Behaviours* 23, 4, 463–75.

Davis, C., Katzman, D.K. and Kirsh, C. (1999) 'Compulsive Physical Activity in Adolescents With Anorexia Nervosa: a Psychobehavioral Spiral of Pathology', *Journal of Nervous and Mental Disease* 187, 6, 336–42.

Dunne, F.J., Feeney, S. and Schipperheijn, J. (1991) 'Eating Disorders and Alcohol Misuse: Features of an Addiction Spectrum', *Postgraduate Medicine Journal* 67, 784, 112–13.

Engs, R.C. (1996) *Alcohol and Other Drugs: Self Responsibility* (Bloomington: Tichenor Publishing Company).

Ganjei, J.K., Crow, S., Mitchell, J., Rotondo, A., Mauri, M., Cassano, G., Keel, P., Berrettini, W.H. and Kaye, W.H. (2003) 'Significant Linkage on Chromosome 10p in Families with Bulimia Nervosa', *American Journal of Human Genetics*, 72, 1, 200–07.

Gordon, R.A. (1999) *Eating Disorders: Anatomy of a Social Epidemic* (London: Blackwell).

Grice, D.E., Halmi, K.A., Fichter, M.M., Strober, M., Woodside, D.B., Treasure, J.T., Kaplan, A.S., Magistretti, P.J., Goldman, D., Bulik, C.M., Kaye, W.H. and Berrettini, W.H. (2002) 'Evidence for a Susceptibility Gene for Anorexia Nervosa on Chromosome 1', *American Journal of Human Genetics*, 70, 3, 787–92.

Institute of Psychiatry (2009) *Eating Disorders*. http://www.iop.kcl.ac.uk/sites/edu/?id=26, date accessed 15 November 2009.

Karwautz, A., Rabe-Hesketh, S., Collier, D.A. and Treasure, J.L. (2002) 'Pre-Morbid Psychiatric Morbidity, Comorbidity, and Personality in Patients with Anorexia Nervosa Compared with their Healthy Sisters', *European Eating Disorders Review*, 10, 4, 255–70.

Kay, W.H. (1999) 'The New Biology of Anorexia and Bulimia Nervosa: Implications for Advances in Treatment', *European Eating Disorders Review*, 7, 3, 157–61.

Keel, P.K., Fichter, M., Quadflieg, N., et al. (2004) 'Application of a Latent Class Analysis to Empirically Define Eating Disorder Phenotypes', *Archives of General Psychiatry*, 61, 2, 192–200.

Lacey, J.H. (1992) 'Homogamy: the Relationships and Sexual Partners of Normal-weight Bulimic Women', *The British Journal of Psychiatry* 161, 638–42.

Lacey, J.H. and Evans, C. (1986) 'The Impulsivist: a Multi-impulsive Personality Disorder', *British Journal of Addiction*, 81, 5, 715–23.

Lerner, M. (2006) Eating Disorders and Chemical Dependency. MyEDHelp.com. http://www.selfgrowth.com/articles/user/74255, date accessed 15 September 2010.

Levitt, J.L., Sansone, R.A. and Cohn, L. (2003) 'Eating Disorders and Self-Harm: A Chaotic Intersection', *Eating Disorder Review*, 14, 3, 1–2.

Marlatt, A.G. and Witkiewitz, K. (2008) *Addictive Behaviors: New Readings on Etiology, Prevention, and Treatment* (Washington: American Psychological Association).

McCourt, J. and Waller, G. (1996) 'The Influence of Sociocultural Factors on the Eating Psychopathology of Young Asian Women in British Society', *European Eating Disorders Review*, 4, 2, 73–83.

Nasser, M. (2006) 'Eating Disorders Across Cultures', *Psychiatry*, 5, 11, 392–95.

Nasser, M. (2009) 'Eating Disorders Across Cultures', *Psychiatry*, 8, 9, 347–350.

Nasser, M., Katzman, M. and Gordon, R. (2000) *Cultures in Transition: Eating Disorders as a Global Marker* (Hove: Brunner/Routledge).

National Institute for Clinical Excellence (NICE) (2004) *Core Interventions in the Treatment and Management of Anorexia Nervosa, Bulimia Nervosa, and Binge Eating Disorder* (London: British Psychological Society).

NIMH (2009) *Eating Disorders* (Bethesda: National Institute of Mental Health) http://www.nimh.nih.gov/health/publications/eating-disorders/complete-index.shtml, date accessed 12 January 2010.

Rassool, G.H. (2002) 'Substance Use and Dual Diagnosis: Concepts, Theories and Models', in Rassool, G.H. (ed.), *Dual Diagnosis: Substance Misuse and Psychiatric Disorders* (Oxford: Blackwell Publishing).

Rassool, G.H. and Winnington, J. (2006) 'A Framework for Multidimensional Assessment', in Rassool, G.H. (ed.), *Dual Diagnosis Nursing* (Oxford: Blackwell Publishing).

Rosenvinge, J.H., Martinussen, M. and Østensen, E. (2000) 'The Comorbidity of Eating Disorders and Personality Disorders: A Meta-analytic Review of Studies Published Between 1983 and 1998', *Eating Weight Disorders*, 5, 2, 52–61.

Sansone, R.A. and Levitt, J.L. (2002) 'Self-harm Behaviors Among Those With Eating Disorders: An Overview', *Eating Disorders Review*, 10, 205.

Schwartz, M.F. and Cohn, L. (1996) *Sexual Abuse and Eating Disorders: A Clinical Overview* (New York: Brunner/Mazel).

Steiger, H. (2004) 'Eating Disorders and the Serotonin Connection: State, Trait and Developmental Effects', *Journal of Psychiatry and Neuroscience*, 29, 1, 20.

Strober, M., Freeman, R. and Morrell, W. (1999) 'Atypical Anorexia Nervosa: Separation from Typical Cases in Course and Outcome in a Long-term Prospective Study', *International Journal of Eating Disorders* 25, 2, 135–42.

The National Center on Addiction and Substance Abuse at Columbia University (CASA) (2003) *Food For Thought: Substance Abuse and Eating Disorders* (New York, The National Center on Addiction and Substance Abuse at Columbia University). www.casacolumbia.org.

Thornton, C. and Russell, J. (1997) 'Obsessive Compulsive Comorbidity in the Dieting Disorders', *International* Journal of *Eating Disorders*, 21, 1, 83–87.

Tomotake, M. and Ohmori, T. (2002) 'Personality Profiles in Patients With Eating Disorders', *Journal of Medical Investigation*, 49, 3–4, 87–96.

Vervaet, M., van Heeringen, C. and Audenaert, K. (2004) 'Personality-related Characteristics in Restricting Versus Binging and Purging Eating Disordered Patients', *Comprehensive Psychiatry*, 45, 1, 37–43.

von Ranson, K.M., Kaye, W.H., Weltzin, T.E., Rao, R. and Matsunaga, H. (1999) 'Obsessive-compulsive Disorder Symptoms Before and After Recovery from Bulimia Nervosa', *American Journal of Psychiatry*, 156, 11, 1703–08.

Wade, T.D., Bulik, C.M., Neale, M. and Kendler, K.S. (2000) 'Anorexia Nervosa and Major Depression: Shared Genetic and Environmental Risk Factors', *American Journal of Psychiatry*, 157, 3, 469–71.

Wilson, G.T. (1995) 'Eating Disorders and Addictive Disorders', in Brownell, K.D. and Fairburn, C.G. (eds.), *Eating Disorders and Obesity. A Comprehensive Handbook* (New York: Guilford Press).

Wilson, G.T. (2000) 'Eating Disorders and Addiction', *Drugs and Society*, 8756–8233, 15, 1, 2000, 87–101.

Gambling Addiction **12**

Introduction

> ### Reflective activity 12.1
>
> Before reading this chapter, try to provide a true or false answer for each of the statements listed below. Think about some reasons as to why you chose a particular answer
>
> | Statements | True | False |
> |---|---|---|
> | Gambling is a form of behavioural addiction. | | |
> | Gambling is defined as 'the wagering of money or something of material value on an event with an uncertain outcome with the primary intent of winning additional money and or material goods' (Wikipedia). | | |
> | There is no such thing as socially responsible gambling. | | |
> | Problem gambling can develop into pathological behaviours and into the realm of psychiatric disorders. | | |
> | There are no withdrawal symptoms after ceasing problem gambling. | | |
> | Familial aggregation and genetics influence the development of behavioural addictions. | | |
> | Risk factors such as lack of coping strategies may contribute to the development of problem gambling. | | |
> | Problem gamblers do not have additional psychiatric disorders. | | |
> | High rates of suicidal tendencies have been reported in clinical populations of pathological gamblers. | | |
> | Problem gambling generally occurs in men aged 21 to 55, although the incidence is increasing among adolescents. | | |
> | Stress may have a significant influence on the development of problem gambling. | | |
> | Problem gambling does not impact on physical and mental health. | | |
> | The treatment interventions for problem gamblers focus on pharmacological therapies. | | |

When you have read this chapter, come back to this activity and consider your answers again. How many did you get right? For those you got wrong, think about the reasons for your original answer and compare this with what you know now.

Gambling, as a form of behavioural addiction, has become a growing concern in public health policy. During the last decade, there has been a rapid increase in the proliferation and accessibility of legalized gambling in the United Kingdom and other parts of the world. The prevalence rate of problem gambling in Britain is higher than that found in Norway, and similar to that of Canada, New Zealand, Sweden and Switzerland, and lower than Australia, South Africa, the US, and Singapore (Wardle et al., 2006). Gambling, according to the Merriam-Webster Online Dictionary (2010), is to play a game for money or property; to bet on an uncertain outcome; or to stake something on a contingency: or to take a chance. Problem gambling is characterized by many difficulties in limiting money and/or time spent on gambling which leads to adverse consequences for the gambler, others, or for the community (Gambling Research Australia, 2005).

Behavioural addictions are defined as the repetitive occurrence of impulsive behaviours without consideration of their potential negative consequences (Lobo and Kennedy, 2006). Thus, gambling addiction is considered to be an impulsive behaviour despite harmful negative consequences or a desire to stop.

Nature and extent of gambling and problem gambling

There are many different ways to gamble. The British Gambling Prevalence Survey (Wardle et al., 2006) list the following ways to gamble: National Lottery Draw, another lottery, scratchcards, football pools, bingo, slot machines, horse races, dog races, betting with a bookmaker (other than on horse or dog races), fixed odds betting terminals, online betting with a bookmaker on any event or sport, online gambling, table games in a casino, betting exchange, spread betting and private betting (e.g. with friends, colleagues).

In Britain, the British Gambling Prevalence Survey (Wardle et al., 2006) findings estimated that 68 per cent of the population, that is about 32 million adults, had participated in some form of gambling activity within the past year. The findings of the survey showed that the National Lottery Draw (57 per cent) was the most popular activity followed by scratch cards (20 per cent), betting on horse races (17 per cent), and playing slot machines (14 per cent). Only a small proportion of people (three per cent) gambled online (like playing poker or casino games etc.) or placed bets with a bookmaker using the Internet (four per cent), three per cent used fixed odds betting terminals

(FOBTs) and four per cent gambled in a casino. Overall, six per cent of the population used the Internet to gamble over the past year. More men (71 per cent) were likely to gamble than women (65 per cent), with the exception of bingo (four per cent of men compared with ten per cent of women). Respondents who described their ethnic origin as white were more likely to be past year gamblers (70 per cent) than those who classified themselves as black (39 per cent) or Asian (45 per cent).

Problem gambling was more prevalent among men than women, and tended to be more prevalent among younger age groups. The rates of problem gambling in the population were 0.6 per cent (using DSM-IV) (Wardle et al., 2006). A significant association was found between problem gambling and the following factors: being single, male and also regular parental gambling (particularly if a parent had a gambling problem), and poor health. In addition, according to the DSM-IV, problem gambling was significantly associated with being Asian/Asian British or Black/Black British, being separated/divorced, having fewer educational qualifications, and being younger than 55 years old (Wardle et al., 2006).

Policy on gambling

The Gambling Act 2005 was implemented on 1 September 2007. The Act established the Gambling Commission (Gambling Commission, 2008) to regulate gambling and made it responsible for 'protecting children and other vulnerable persons from being harmed or exploited' on the following basis: children shall not be allowed to gamble but shall still have access to low-prize gaming machines; vulnerable persons can become problem gamblers; socially responsible gambling incorporating education will prevent problem gambling; and the treatment will deal with those that, nevertheless, become problem gamblers. According to Moran (2009), the formulation is largely based on an attempt to present a socially aware image and the causes of harm from gambling are seen to reside mainly in the individual gambler rather than the gambling activity.

The Responsibility in Gambling Trust (RiGT) was set up by the gambling industry to arrange education about, and treatment for, problem gambling. Since the implementation of the Gambling Act, the Government with the support of the Gambling Commission has agreed on new casinos to begin operation, doubling high prize machines in bingo halls and proposed that public houses and seaside arcades, accessible by children, should have an increase in gaming machines and prizes (Department of Culture, 2008). It is suggested that it is vital that the Gambling Commission should ensure that the mistakes in alcohol public policy are not repeated in gambling (Moran, 2009).

Pathological gambling and problem gambling

Problem gambling can develop into pathological behaviours and into the realm of psychiatric disorders. Pathological gambling is now formally viewed as an impulse control disorder. Pathological gambling is recognized as a psychiatric disorder and is defined, according to the American Psychiatric Association [APA] Diagnostic and Statistic Manual, Revision IV – TR (APA, 2000), 'as persistent and recurrent maladaptive gambling behaviour that disrupts personal, family, or vocational pursuits'. This definition, although valuable in enabling clinical diagnosis and for planning public policy, does not take into account the cultural, social and environmental factors that have a significant influence on the gambling process. In addition, there is dispute as to whether a dichotomy exists between problem gambling and non-problem gambling; there is little evidence for underlying pathology; it does not serve the needs of those who are not diagnosed as problem gamblers and yet have gambling-related problems; and it does not serve the needs of service providers (Gambling Research Australia, 2005).

Pathological gambling is diagnosed if the individuals exhibit a minimum of five of the ten criteria as long as these behaviours are not better explained by a manic episode: Key elements for a clinical diagnosis of pathological gambling include: 'a continuous or periodic loss of control over gambling; a progression in gambling frequency and amounts wagered; a preoccupation with gambling and in obtaining monies with which to gamble; and a continuation of gambling involvement despite adverse consequences' (APA, 2000). The diagnostic criteria for pathological gambling are presented in Table 12.1.

The term problem gambling has been used both in the literature and clinical practice instead of pathological gambling. Gambling can be perceived as a 'continuum ranging from social or recreational gambling where there are no adverse impacts through to problem gambling where gambling leads to adverse consequences for the individual, his or her family, friends and colleagues, or for the community through to pathological gambling where the adverse consequences tend to be more severe (Gambling Research Australia, 2005). There are inherent problems associated in defining problem gambling in terms of a continuum because of the difficulties for diagnosis and objective measurement. More recently, problem gambling has been defined in terms of harm. Problem gambling, according to Dickerson et al. (1997) refers to 'the situation when a person's gambling activity gives rise to harm to the individual player, and/or to his or her family, and may extend into the community'. This definition distinguishes social gambling from problem gambling and refers both to individual behaviours and to the impact on others.

Table 12.1 Diagnostic criteria for pathological gambling

Key criteria	Examples
1. Preoccupation with gambling	• Frequent thoughts about gambling experiences.
2. Tolerance	• Need to gamble with increasing amounts of money to achieve the desired level of excitement.
3. Withdrawal	• Restlessness or irritability associated with attempts to stop or reduce gambling.
4. Escape	• Gambles as a way of escaping from problems or to relieve a dysphoric mood.
5. Lying	• Lies to others to conceal gambling.
6. Loss of control	• Repeated unsuccessful efforts to control, cut back, or stop.
7. Illegal acts	• Commits illegal acts to finance gambling.
8. Risked significant relationship	• The subject gambles despite risking or losing a relationship, job, or other significant opportunity.
9. Rescue or Bailout	• Relies on others to provide money to relieve a desperate financial situation caused by gambling.
10. Chasing	• Returns after losing money to get even. The subject tries to win back gambling losses with more gambling.

Source: Adapted from American Psychiatric Association (2000). DSM-IV-TR: Diagnostic and Statistical Manual of Mental Disorders (4th ed, text revision), (Washington, DC: Author).

Gambling as an addictive behaviour

Historically Freud, the founding father of psychoanalysis, associated the term addiction with gambling, believing that it was closely related to substance dependence (Freud, 1979/1921). The APA's classification of pathological gambling contains three criteria that are also found in the classification for alcohol and drug dependence. These common criteria include:

- Preoccupation with the behaviour;
- Tolerance; and
- Withdrawal.

Those who view pathological gambling as an addiction view problem gambling in the same frame as substance dependence introducing yet another non-clinically defined classification into the lexicon of pathological gambling (Moore and Jadlos, 2002). There has been a shift in the core feature of addiction so that it is the continued engagement in behaviour despite adverse consequences (Potenza et al., 2001; Holden, 2001). This key element is generally accompanied by diminished control over the behaviour and an anticipatory urge or craving state prior to the engagement in the behaviour (Holden, 2001; Potenza and Wilber, 2001). Using these criteria, pathological gambling can be considered as an addictive behaviour without exogenous substance use (Potenza et al., 2002).

The commonalities and differences in the natural histories of problem gambling and substance use disorders have been reported elsewhere (Hodgins et al., 2000; Hodgins, 2001). There are commonalities in terms of insight into the problem, the progression of substance misuse and problem gambling, amongst women in later life and classification of those with alcohol dependence and problem gambling.

Aetiology of problem gambling

There are several determinants of problem gambling: biological, psychological, socio-cultural and neurochemical. Problem gambling is thought to be influenced by neurobiological mechanisms. Norepinephrine, a hormone released in response to stress has been linked to arousal and risk-taking in compulsive gamblers. The role of the reward system in the nervous system plays a part in the aetiology of pathological gambling. Brain cells release dopamine as part of the reward system through which you learn to seek things that make you feel pleasure, such as food and sex. Dopamine plays a role in developing addiction. A study by Meyer et al., (2004) on the effect of casino gambling on the sympatho-adrenal system, the HPA-axis, and pituitary hormones found that heart rate and norepinephrine levels increased with the onset of blackjack and that the dopamine levels were significantly higher in problem gamblers. In some cases, certain traumatic head injuries such as those of the orbito-frontal cortex can alter brain function and can contribute to pathological gambling. This part of the brain is recognized to be involved in decision-making and in processing reward and punishment, including monetary gain and loss. Neuroimaging studies of the orbito-frontal cortex of problem gamblers maintain the notion that problem gambling has a biological basis.

There has been a growing body of evidence on the familial aggregation and genetic influences on the development of behavioural addictions and mainly on pathological gambling (Lobo and Kennedy, 2006). There is also evidence to suggest that children of pathological gamblers are more vulnerable in terms of developing dysfunctional behaviours (Jacobs, 1989). Other research findings showed the importance of the family environment in the development of a gambling habit and that adolescents who were diagnosed with pathological gambling were also more likely to report having parents with a gambling problem (Gupta and Derevensky, 1997; 1998). Although the sample sizes in these family studies are relatively small, the consistency of the reports provides fairly solid support for the importance of heritable factors in pathological gambling (Lobo and Kennedy, 2006).

Twin studies also provided light in the aetiology of problem gambling. Eisen et al. (1998) showed that inherited factors explained between 35 and 54 per cent of the liability for developing any symptom of pathological gambling. Monozygotic (MZ) twins are identical twins that share 100 per cent of the same DNA and twins are always the same gender. Dizygotic (DZ) twins share only 50 per cent of their DNA (fraternal twins). DZ twins can be the same gender or one male and one female. There is also evidence that the risk of pathological gambling was significantly higher among DZ and MZ co-twins of subjects with sub-clinical pathological gambling (Slutske et al., 2000).

In another twin study, Winters and Rich (1999) found that genetic factors were significantly responsible for 'high action' gambling, such as slot machines and roulette, in male twins. However, no significant genetic influence was found among males for 'low action' games (for example, betting on sports events or on games of skill), and no significant genetic influence among the female MZ and DZ twin pairs for both types of games. The findings from the brief review of studies on the aetiology of problem gambling should be taken with caution as the studies have important methodological limitations.

Psychological factors such as impulsive behaviour, coping strategies, anti-social behaviour and other risk factors may contribute to the development of problem gambling. Impulsive behaviour is a basic aspect of an individual's personality. According to Sinha (2004), the levels of impulsivity may influence development of an impulse control disorder such as pathological gambling or a substance use disorder (Sinha, 2004). As impulsive personality is an enduring trait, it is difficult to change the personality. McCormick and Taber (1988) have suggested that the inability to control impulses and to delay gratification are two major impulsivity-related symptoms of pathological gamblers. Impulsivity levels in both genders are important factors in the development of pathological gambling. Males and females differ in the factors contributing to the development of problem gambling. Males have a higher propensity than females to misuse psychoactive substances in conjunction with a gambling problem. However, in both genders, impulsivity was a strong predictor of a possible gambling problem (Nower, Derevensky, and Gupta, 2004).

Coping strategies are also contributory factors to the development of a gambling problem. There is evidence to suggest that there is a high positive correlation between ineffective coping strategies among the problem and pathological gamblers in their sample for both task and emotional coping in conjunction with high impulsivity (Lightsey and Hulsey, 2002). Antisocial behaviour has also been associated with problem gambling. Pathological gamblers have been known to also exhibit antisocial behaviour which is related to the impulse control disorder causing antisocial behaviour such as exhibited in antisocial personality disorder (Slutske et al., 2001).

The are other risk factors that may contribute to the development of problem gambling. Problem gambling generally occurs in men aged 21 to 55, although the incidence is increasing among adolescents. Although men tend to be much more likely than women to start out at a younger age and develop gambling problems, women who do gamble may become addicted more quickly. Men usually cite the need to win and the need for monetary sustenance whereas women cite negative emotions or situational problems (Hodgins and el-Guebaly, 2004). Stress may have a significant influence on the development of problem gambling. For persons low on impulsivity, outside factors such as stress may be more likely to contribute to gambling problems (Lightsey and Hulsey, 2002). Other factors include, accessibility of online gaming on the Internet and medications such as pramipexole (miraplex) used in the treatment of Parkinson's disease.

Problem gambling and co-morbidity

Some problem gamblers may have additional coexisting disorders such as substance misuse and psychiatric disorders. High rates of co-morbidity have been described between substance use and gambling disorders (Cunningham-Williams et al., 1998; Cunningham-Williams et al., 2001). There are high rates of substance use disorders in individuals with gambling problems. Pathological gambling has been reported from two to ten-fold more frequently in substance misusers than in the general adult population (Lesieur and Blume, 1991; Hall et al., 2000). The St. Louis ECA Study (Cunningham-Williams et al., 1998) also demonstrates a strong association between alcohol use and gambling. Individuals with both a substance use disorder and pathological gambling have been reported as having higher rates of unemployment and illegal behaviour, and links to the criminal justice system were observed in cocaine-dependent subjects with pathological gambling as compared to those without (Hall et al., 2000).

Increased rates of mental health disorders have been reported in problem and pathological gamblers such as major depression, schizophrenia, phobias, somatization syndrome, and antisocial personality disorders (Cunningham-Williams et al., 1998). High rates of suicidal tendencies have been reported in clinical populations of pathological gamblers, with estimates of attempted suicide in the range of 17 to 24 per cent (DeCaria et al., 1996).

Signs of problem gambling

Unlike alcohol or other drug misusers, problem gamblers usually do not exhibit easily recognizable signs. However, there are warning signs that may indicate someone is experiencing a gambling problem. Problems gamblers

Table 12.2   Signs of problem gambling

Behavioural signs	Psychological signs	Financial signs	Health signs
Stops doing things previously enjoyed. Changes patterns of sleep, eating or sex. Self-neglect, ignores work, school or family tasks. Conflicts with other people. Misuse of alcohol or other drugs. Failed in multiple attempts to reduce or stop gambling. Increasing marital problems. Is often late for work or school. Less willing to spend money on things other than gambling. Legal problems related to gambling. Less productive at work. Neglects personal responsibilities. Suicide attempts. Euphoria whilst gambling. Lying and secretive behaviour.	Insomnia. Uses gambling to escape stress, guilt, or depression. Becomes restless or irritable if prevented from gambling activity. Withdraws from family and friends. Complains of boredom or restlessness. Shows signs of depression. Feeling guilty about gambling or what happens while gambling.	Frequently borrows money or asks for salary advances. Takes a second job without a change in finances. Cashes in savings accounts, or insurance plans. Alternates between being broke and flashing money. Family members complain that valuables and appliances are disappearing, or money is missing from a bank account or wallet. Growing debts and unpaid bills. Needs financial help from others because of gambling. Commits illegal acts to finance gambling.	Headaches. Stomach and bowel problems. Insomnia. Over-eating or loss of appetite.

Source: Adapted from Centre for Addiction and Mental Health (CAMH) (2009) Signs of Problem Gambling (Ontario: CAMH). http://www.problemgambling.ca/EN/AboutGamblingandProblemGambling/ Pages/SignsOfProblemGambling.aspx, date accessed 20 January 2010.

often are in denial of their gambling problems – both to themselves and to their significant others. They tend to exhibit a sense of power and control and are highly competitive. Most people are recreational gamblers but when gambling becomes out of control it can cause people psychological, social and financial difficulties. The warning signs of problem gambling are presented in Table 12.2.

Screening and assessment

Problem gambling does impact on physical and mental health, although those who are directly affected often make no connection between their gambling behaviour and their health problems. The health care system may be the gambler's first point of contact. It is therefore important for health care professionals to recognize, refer and support someone who may be experiencing gambling problems. It should be routine work asking about a patient's alcohol and tobacco use and also their gambling behaviours. One of the challenges of identifying problem gambling is that gamblers are often highly skilled at being secretive and have no insight into their problems. Initially, it may be important to identify people who might have gambling problems and at a later stage to have the identification formally classified into a clinical diagnosis.

The most common instrument used to screen for problem gambling is the South Oaks Gambling Screen (SOGS) (Lesieur and Blume, 1987). The 20 item SOGS is based on DSM-III-R criteria and positive features of the SOGS include its ease of administration, availability of a cut-off score and breadth of items. It has good internal consistency, reliability, and concurrent validity, but classification rates are poorer in community samples (Gambling Research Australia, 2005). The Canadian Problem Gambling Index (CPGI) was specifically developed as a measure of community prevalence (Ferris and Wynne, 2001). Its positive features include its ease of administration and brevity, and availability to classify varying degrees of severity. Recent Canadian research suggests that the CPGI is possibly too similar in content to the SOGS and may therefore also give rise to false positives in community samples (Gambling Research Australia, 2005). The SOGS and DSM-IV have been subjected to much criticism. Sproston et al., (2000) conducted a cross-tabulation of the SOGS and DSM-IV and concluded that both instruments reflect false negatives and false positives. In addition, they suggested that this reveals why screening devices are inadequate to make a diagnostic or treatment decision for individual cases. A generic instrument is the Addiction Severity Index (ASI-G) (Lesieur and Blume, 1992) which is a modified version of the index used for other substance disorders. The psychometric properties of the instrument is adequate and it provides a quantitative index of problem severity based on the frequency and intensity of gambling.

Treatment interventions

Pharmacology

The treatment interventions for problem gamblers include both pharmaco-logical and psychological therapies. Pharmacological interventions in the treatment for pathological gambling include opioid antagonists, serotonin reuptake inhibitors (SRIs) and mood stabilizers. Naltrexone has been used with problem gamblers in reducing the frequency and intensity of urges to gamble, thoughts about gambling, and the behaviour itself when given in high doses (Kim and Grant, 2001; Kim et al., 2001). The efficacy of another opioid antagonist, nalmefene, in the treatment of pathological gambling has been demonstrated in a multi-centre study (Grant et al., 2006).

A review of the important findings showed that antidepressants may be effective in reducing the symptoms of pathological gambling; higher doses of antidepressants are required to treat pathological gambling; and for those with no or minimal symptoms of depression or anxiety, antidepressants were still effective in reducing gambling symptoms (Grant and Kim, 2006). Mood stabilizers such as lithium carbonate have also been used as pharmacological interventions. There has been only one randomized, placebo-controlled trial of a mood stabilizer tested on pathological gamblers. Ten weeks of lithium treatment was shown to be superior to a placebo in reducing gambling symp-toms among pathological gamblers with bipolar disorders (Hollander et al., 2005).

Behavioural therapies

Cognitive behavioural therapies for the treatment of problem gambling are beginning to be examined. Cognitive behavioural therapy, systematic desensiti-zation, and motivational enhancement have been shown to be effective in small to moderate sized controlled trials. It has been shown that pathological gamblers receiving cognitive behavioural therapy showing gains after six and 12 months following intervention and those receiving motivational enhancement showing gains at three and six months (Ladouceur et al., 2001; Hodgins et al., 2001).

Self-help group

Gamblers Anonymous (G.A.) is the main self-help group for those with problem gambling. GA is a fellowship of men and women who share their experi-ence, strength and hope with each other in order that they may solve their common problem and help others to recover from a gambling problem (www.gamblersanonymous.org).

Harm reduction

Problem gambling can be viewed as a public health problem and in recent years there has been a shift toward the concepts of harm reduction and responsible gambling. The adoption of a public health perspective on gambling offers a broad viewpoint on gambling in society – not solely a focus on problem and pathological gambling (Canadian Public Health Association, 2000). It is argued that by appreciating the health, social and economic dimensions of gambling, public health professionals can develop strategies that minimize gambling's negative impacts while recognizing its potential benefits.

In relation to problem gambling, 'harm reduction refers to a policy or program directed towards minimizing or decreasing the adverse health, social and economic consequences of gambling behaviour for individuals, families, communities and society. A harm reduction strategy does not require abstention from gambling' (Canadian Public Health Association, 2000). The concept of responsible gambling has now been introduced. Responsible gambling means that people can make choices based on all the facts, without pressure, and stay in control of how much time and money they spend on gambling activities for pleasure or for fun.

Summary of key points

- Gambling, as a form of behavioural addiction, has become a growing concern in public health policy.
- Gambling is defined as 'the wagering of money or something of material value on an event with an uncertain outcome with the primary intent of winning additional money and/or material goods' (Wikipedia).
- The British Gambling Prevalence Survey estimated that 68 per cent of the population; that is about 32 million adults, had participated in some form of gambling activity within the past year.
- Policy on gambling: Socially responsible gambling incorporating education will prevent problem gambling; and the treatment will deal with those that, nevertheless, become problem gamblers.
- Problem gambling can develop into pathological behaviours and into the realm of psychiatric disorders.
- Problem gambling includes: preoccupation with the gambling behaviour, tolerance and withdrawal.
- There are several determinants of problem gambling: biological, psychological, socio-cultural and neurochemical.
- Familial aggregation and genetic influences affect the development of behavioural addictions.

- Psychological factors such as impulsive behaviour, coping strategies, anti-social behaviour and other risk factors may contribute to the development of problem gambling.
- Problem gamblers have additional coexisting disorders such as substance misuse and psychiatric disorders.
- It should be routine work in asking about a patient's alcohol and tobacco use and also their gambling behaviour.
- The treatment interventions for problem gamblers include both pharmacological and psychological therapies.

Reflective activity 12.2

SW, a 34 year old accountant, had gambled recreationally for years. She had a history of depressive disorders and had brief contact with a local mental health service because of depression and marital problems. At age 30, she became hooked on casino slot machines. Her interest in gambling gradually escalated and, within a year, SW was gambling during most business days. To acquire funds to fuel her gambling, she embezzled her clients' funds but was eventually detected and arrested. She became severely depressed and suicidal in the wake of the arrest and public humiliation and attempted a drug overdose.

- What would be the immediate interventions required?
- What are the short-term goals for this patient?
- What are the long-term goals for this patient?
- What treatment interventions and/or strategies may be planned for this patient?

References

American Psychiatric Association (2000) *DSM-IV-TR: Diagnostic and Statistical Manual of Mental Disorders,* 4th edn, text revision (Washington, DC: Author).

Canadian Public Health Association (2000) Position Paper on Gambling Expansion in Canada: An Emerging Public Health Issue, 1–4, http://www.cpha.ca/uploads/resolutions/2000-1pp_e.pdf, date accessed 20 March 2010.

Cunningham-Williams, R.M., Cottler, L.B., Compton, W.M. and Spitznagel, E.L. (1998) 'Taking Chances: Problem Gamblers and Mental Health Disorders – Results from the St. Louis Epidemiologic Catchment Area Study', *American Journal of Public Health,* 88, 7, 1093–96.

Cunningham-Williams, R.M. and Cottler, L.B. (2001) 'The Epidemiology of Pathological Gambling', *Seminars in Clinical Neuropsychiatry*, 6, 3, 155–66.

DeCaria, C.M., Hollander, E., Grossman, R., Wong, C.M., Mosovich, S.A. and Cherkasky, S. (1996) 'Diagnosis, Neurobiology, and Treatment of Pathological Gambling', *Journal of Clinical Psychiatry*, 57, (suppl 8), 80–83.

Department of Culture (2008) Impact Assessment for The Draft Categories of Gaming Machine (Amendment) Regulations 2009 and The Draft Gambling Act 2005 (Limits on Prize Gaming) Regulations 2009. www.culture. gov.uk/images/consultations/IA-draftCatGamMac2009.pdf, date accessed 10 January 2010.

Dickerson, M., McMillen, J., Hallebone, E., Volberg, R. and Woolley, R. (1997) *Definition and Incidence of Pathological Gambling including the Socioeconomic Distribution* (Melbourne: Victorian Casino and Gaming Authority).

Eisen, S.A., Lin, N., Lyons, M.J., Scherrer, J., Griffith, K., True, W.R., Goldberg, J. and Tsuang, M.T. (1998) 'Familial Influences on Gambling Behavior: An Analysis of 3,359 Twin Pairs', *Addiction*, 93, 9, 1375–84.

Ferris, J. and Wynne, H.J. (2001) *The Canadian Problem Gambling Index Final Report* (Ottawa, Canada: Canadian Centre on Substance Abuse).

Freud, S. (1979) *Introductory Lectures on Psychoanalysis* (Strachey, J. ed. and Trans.) (New York: Norton). (Original work published in 1921).

Gambling Commission (2008) Licence Conditions and Codes of Practice, October. http://www.gamblingcommission.gov.uk/pdf/LCCP%20-%20Oct%202008. pdf, date accessed 12 January 2010.

Gambling Research Australia (2005) *Problem Gambling and Harm: Towards a National Definition* (Victoria Australia: Office of Gaming and Racing Victorian Government Department of Justice), also published on www.gamblin gresearch.org.au.

Grant, J.E., Potenza, M.N., Hollander, E., Cunningham-Williams, R., Nurminen, T., Smits, G. and Kallio, A. (2006) 'A Multicenter Investigation of the Opioid Antagonist Nalmefene in the Treatment of Pathological Gambling', *American Journal of Psychiatry*, 163, 12, 303–12.

Grant, J.E. and Kim S.W. (2006) 'Medication Management of Pathological Gambling', *Minnesota Medicine*, September, 89, 9, 44–48.

Gupta, R. and Derevensky, J.L. (1997) 'Familial and Social Influences on Juvenile Gambling Behavior', *Journal of Gambling Studies*, 13, 3, 179–92.

Gupta, R. and Derevensky, J.L. (1998) 'Adolescent Gambling Behavior: a Prevalence Study and Examination of the Correlates Associated With Problem Gambling', *Journal of Gambling Studies*, 14, 4, 319–45.

Hall, G.W., Carriero, N.J., Takushi, R.Y., Montoya, I.D., Preston, K.L. and Gorelick, D.A. (2000) 'Pathological Gambling Among Cocaine-Dependent Outpatients', *American Journal of Psychiatry*, 157, 7, 1127–33.

Hodgins, D.C. (2001) 'Processes of Changing Gambling Behaviour', *Addictive Behaviour*, 26, 1, 121–29.

Hodgins D.C. and el-Guebaly, N. (2000) 'Natural and Treatment-assisted Recovery from Gambling Problems: a Comparison of Resolved and Active Gamblers', *Addiction*, 95, 5, 777–89.

Hodgins, D.C. and el-Guebaly, N. (2004) 'Retrospective and Prospective Reports of Precipitants to Relapse in Pathological Gambling', *Journal of Consulting and Clinical Psychology*, 72, 1, 72–80.

Hodgins, D.C., Currie, S.R. and el-Guebaly, N. (2001) 'Motivational Enhancement and Self-help Treatments for Problem Gambling', *Journal of Clinical Consulting Psychology*, 69, 2, 50–57.

Holden, C. (2001) '"Behavioral" Addictions: Do they exist?' *Science,* 294, 5544, 980–82.

Hollander, E., Pallanti, S., Allen, A., Sood, E. and Baldini Rossi, N. (2005) 'Does Sustained-release Lithium Reduce Impulsive Gambling and Affective Instability Versus Placebo in Pathological Gamblers with Bipolar Spectrum Disorders?', *American Journal of Psychiatry*,162, 1, 137–45.

Jacobs, D.F. (1989) 'Children of Problem Gamblers', *Journal of Gambling Behavior*, 5, 4, 261–68.

Jacobs, D.F. (1993) 'Evidence Supporting a General Theory of Addiction', in Eadington, W.E. and Cornelius, J.A. (eds.), *Gambling Behavior and Problem Gambling* (University of Nevada, Reno: Institute for the Study of Gambling and Commercial Gaming) 287–94.

Kim, S.W. and Grant, J.E. (2001) 'An Open Naltrexone Treatment Study in Pathological Gambling Disorder', *International Clinical Psychopharmacology,* 16, 5, 285–89.

Kim, S.W., Grant. J.E., Adson, D.E. and Shin, Y.C. (2001) 'Double-blind Naltrexone and Placebo Comparison Study in the Treatment of Pathological Gambling', *Biological Psychiatry*, 49, 11, 914–21.

Ladouceur, R., Sylvain, C., Boutin, C., Lachance, S., Doucet, C. and Leblond, J. et al. (2001) 'Cognitive Treatment of Pathological Gambling', *Journal of Nervous Mental Disease*, 9, 9, 774–80.

Lesieur, H.R. and Blume, S.B. (1987) 'The South Oaks Gambling Screen (the SOGS): A New Instrument for the Identification of Pathological Gamblers', *American Journal of Psychiatry*, 144, 9, 1184–88.

Lesieur, H.R. and Blume, S.B. (1991) 'Evaluation of Patients Treated for Pathological Gambling in a Combined Alcohol, Substance Abuse and Pathological Gambling Treatment Unit Using the Addiction Severity Index', *British Journal of Addiction*, 86, 8, 1017–28.

Lesieur, H.R. and Blume, S.B. (1992) 'Modifying the Addiction Severity Index for Use with Pathological Gamblers', *American Journal of Addiction*, 1, 3, 240–47.

Lightsey, O.R. and Hulsey, C.D. (2002) 'Impulsivity, Coping, Stress, and Problem Gambling Among University Students', *Journal of Counselling Psychology*, 49, 9, 202–11.

Lobo, D.S. and Kennedy, J.L. (2006) 'The Genetics of Gambling and Behavioral Addictions', *CNS Spectrum* 11, 12, 931–39.

McCormick, R.A. and Taber, J.I. (1988) 'Attributional Style in Pathological Gamblers in Treatment', *Journal of Abnormal Psychology*, 97, 3, 368–70.

Merriam-Webster Online Dictionary. http://www.merriam-webster.com/dictionary/gambling, date accessed 15 September 2010.

Meyer, G., Schwertfeger, J., Exton, M.S., Janssen, O.E., Knapp, W., Stadler, M.A., Schedlowski, M. and Kruger, T.H.C. (2004) 'Neuroendocrine Response to Casino Gambling in Problem Gamblers', *Psychoneuroendocrinology*, 29, 10, 1272–80.

Moore, T. and Jadlos, T. (2002) *The Etiology of Pathological Gambling: a Study to Enhance Understanding of Causal Pathways as a Step Towards Improving Prevention and Treatment* (OR: Oregon: Wilsonville). This report is available at http://www.oregoncpg.com/.

Moran, E. (2009) 'UK Gambling Policy is a Recipe for the Growth of Problem Gambling', *Scan Bites* Spring 2009, 1, 1, 1–2. www.scan.uk.net.

Nower, L., Derevensky, J.L. and Gupta, R. (2004) 'The Relationship of Impulsivity, Sensation Seeking, Coping, and Substance Use in Youth Gamblers', *Psychology of Addictive Behaviors*, 18, 4, 49–55.

Potenza, M.N., Kosten, T.R. and Rounsaville, B.J. (2001) 'Pathological Gambling', *JAMA*, 286, 2, 141–44.

Potenza, M.N., Fiellin, D.A., Heninger, G.R., Rounsaville, B.J. and Mazure, C.M. (2002) 'Gambling: An Addictive Behavior with Health and Primary Care Implications', *Journal of General Internal Medicine*, 17, 9, 721–32.

Sinha, K. (2004) Factors Contributing to the Development of Pathological Gambling, http://www.personalityresearch.org/papers/sinha.html, date accessed 12 February 2010.

Slutske, W.S., Eisen, S., True, W.R., Lyons, M.J., Goldberg, J. and Tsuang, M. (2000) 'Common Genetic Vulnerability for Pathological Gambling and Alcohol Dependence in Men', *Archives of General Psychiatry*, 57, 7, 666–73.

Slutske, W.S., Eisen, S., Xian, H., True, W.R., Lyons, M.J., Goldberg, J., and Tsuang, M. (2001) 'A Twin Study of the Association Between Pathological Gambling and Antisocial Personality Disorder', *Journal of Abnormal Psychology*, 110, 2, 297–308.

Sproston, K., Erens, B. and Orford, J. (2000) *Gambling Behaviour in Britain: Results from the British Gambling Prevalence Survey* (London: National Centre for Social Research).

Wardle, H., Sproston, K., Orford, J., Erens, B., Griffiths, M., Constantine, R. and Pigott, S. (2007) *British Gambling Prevalence Survey 2007* (London: National Centre for Social Research).

Wikipedia, Definition of Gambling, http://en.wikipedia.org/wiki/Gambling, date accessed 1 December 2010.

Winters, K.C. and Rich, T. (1999) 'A Twin Study of Adult Gambling Behavior', *Journal of Gambling Studies*, 14, 3, 213–25.

13 Internet Addiction

Introduction

Statements	True	False
Both pharmacological and non-pharmacological therapies may be used in the treatment of IAD.		
Researchers have argued that more than 20 hours of personal internet use per week of internet use constitutes internet addiction.		

When you have read this chapter, come back to this activity and consider your answers again. How many did you get right? For those you got wrong, think about the reasons for your original answer and compare this with what you know now.

Addictive behaviours tend to be focused on pharmacological substances that have an effect on the nervous system that produce, in some cases, euphoria or 'highs'. However, this state of affairs is not restricted to pharmacological substances as an individual can also receive a similar kind of 'high' from using the Internet. This phenomenon has been termed Internet Addiction Disorder (IAD). This disorder, not formally recognized as a clinical/pathological disorder, is so serious that it is now regarded as a public health problem.

China and Korea has even declared internet addiction to be their top health concern. South Korea considers internet addiction to be one of its most serious public health issues (Ahn, 2007). In South Korea, it is estimated that approximately 210,000 South Korean children (2.1 per cent; ages 6–19) are afflicted and require treatment (Choi, 2007). In China, it is reported that 13.7 per cent of Chinese adolescent internet users (about ten million) meet internet addiction diagnostic criteria (cited in Block, 2008). Currently, there are no statistics of the prevalence of internet addiction in Europe and elsewhere.

There are a growing number of clinics for handling internet addiction popping up worldwide. Individuals with Internet Addiction Disorder can exhibit warning signs, symptoms, have relapses and have health and social consequences that are similar to individuals addicted to alcohol, drugs, gambling, and other compulsive behaviours. The best way to describe this disorder is that individuals suffering from IAD have been described as those who find the virtual environment to be more attractive than everyday reality (Chebbi et al., 2000). Like other addictions, the primary areas affected by internet addiction include school, family, work, marriage and relationships (Young, 1998; DeAngelis, 2000).

Internet addiction as a clinical disorder

The first mention of 'internet addiction' was in a 1996 paper by Drs O. Egger and M. Rauterberg of the Swiss Federal Institute of Technology in Lausanne

(Egger and Rauterberg, 1996). The diagnosis of obsession with internet use was coined as Internet Addiction Disorder (Grohol, 2005). The diagnosis consists of at least three subtypes: excessive gaming, sexual preoccupations, and e-mail/text messaging (Block, 2007). The three subtypes of Internet Addiction Disorder share the following four components (Beard and Wolf, 2001; Block, 2007):

- Excessive use, often associated with a loss of sense of time or a neglect of basic drives.
- Withdrawal, including feelings of anger, tension, and/or depression when the computer is inaccessible.
- Tolerance, including the need for better computer equipment, more software, or more hours of use.
- Negative repercussions, including arguments, lying, poor achievement, social isolation, and fatigue.

There is a consensus with those who acknowledge that the Internet is addictive that the disorder develops into a form of addiction for the individual as they experience tolerance and withdrawal effects (Ferris, 2003). In a study of 18,000 internet users, Greenfield (1999) found that 5.7 per cent of those who participated in the survey met his criteria for compulsive internet usage. He reported that those internet addicts experienced time distortion, accelerated intimacy and decreased inhibition and that the most affected areas seem to be marriages and relationships. This strain on marriages and relationships seems to have transpired from the compulsive use of pornography, cybersex and cyber affairs (Duran, 2003). The Internet can and does produce clear alterations in mood; nearly 30 per cent of internet users admit to using the Net to alter their mood so as to relieve a negative mood state, that is, they use the Internet like a drug (Greenfield, 1999). Due to the nature of Internet Addiction Disorder (failed impulse control without involving an intoxicant), of all other addictions, IAD is said to be closest to pathological gambling (Ferris, 2003). However, Bell (2007) argued that the Internet is a medium for communication rather than a true activity and therefore internet addiction is a fundamentally flawed idea. Furthermore, Bell believes that excessive computer and internet use results from the individual dealing with more underlying problems such as social anxiety or depression.

Internet addiction has been categories into different subtypes. Young (1998) categorized internet addiction into five types:

- Information overload (e.g. compulsive database searching)
- Computer addiction (excessive game-playing)
- Cyber sexual addiction

- Cyber relationship addiction
- Net compulsion (e.g. gambling or shopping on the Internet).

Davis (2001) subdivided problematic internet use into two types: specific (overuse of a particular function or application) and generalized ('multidimensional' overuse of the Internet). Internet addiction has been formally recognized as a disorder by the American Psychological Association.

Theories of internet addiction

There are many theories about why people become addicted to the Internet. Various behavioural, psychodynamic and personality, socio-cultural explanations, and biomedical explanations have been proposed to explain this phenomenon which involves rejecting the real world and adopting the Internet as a route of escape to a mood altering experience (DeAngelis, 2000).

According to a biomedical perspective, the aetiology of these disorders is based on hereditary and neurochemical factors. There may be an imbalance of neurotransmitters that regulate activity in the brain that produce the euphoric 'high'. This is similar to the temporary high produced by certain psychoactive substances or gambling. The psychodynamic and personality explanations for internet addiction focus on personality traits and childhood experiences. Ferris (2003) suggested that depending on the childhood events that affect the individuals and the personality's traits they have developed, they become predisposed to develop an addictive behaviour, or none whatsoever. According to Shotton (1991), introverted, educated, technologically sophisticated males are more prone to develop pathological internet use.

Socio-cultural explanations illustrate addicts according to their race, sex, age, economic status, religion, and country (Ferris, 2003). There are a consensus of opinions that suggest that those who have difficulty expressing themselves in personal relationships of a traditional nature find the Internet an attractive proposition to provide some form of social interactions and relationships. Those who have particular types of personality traits may be predisposed to stress according to the diathesis-stress model. This model focuses on the relationship between potential causes of addiction and the degree to which an individual may be vulnerable to react to these causes. It is postulated that an individual's diathesis must interact with stressful life events (social, psychological or biological in nature) in order to induce the onset of the disorder. However, there need to more robust findings among current internet users to validate these explanations.

The behavioural explanations are based on operant conditioning (Ferris, 2003). The learning theory emphasizes the positive reinforcing effects of internet use, which can induce feelings of well-being and euphoria in the user (Wallace,

1999). Based on the principle of operant conditioning, the individual is either rewarded positively, negatively, or punished for their behaviour or course of action – for example, an individual who has social anxiety in meeting new people and making social interactions and acquaintances. For this individual the Internet would represent the means to experience love, hate, satisfaction, and fulfilment without interacting face to face with another person (Ferris, 2003). This type of positive experience could become a reinforcement to repeat the behaviour again and again – that is repeated use of the Internet to get the reward.

Those who show symptoms of internet addiction are likely to engage proportionately more than the normal population in sites that serve as a replacement for real-life socializing (Morrison and Gore, 2010). Davis (2001) proposes a cognitive-behavioural theory of problematic internet use, which he views as arising from the development of a pattern of internet-related cognitions and behaviours. A summary of the theories of Internet Addiction Disorder is presented in Table 13.1.

Despite these theories or aetiological models, it is still not clear to what precisely internet abusers become addicted (Murali and George, 2007). Several factors have been suggested as among potential influences in the development of internet addiction. These factors are: specific applications, the process of typing, the role of the Internet as a medium for communication, the information gained, particular applications (e.g. email, gambling, video games,

Table 13.1 Theories of internet addiction disorder

Theories	Factors
Biomedical	• Hereditary. • Neurochemical (Neurotransmitters).
Behavioural	• Reinforcement – positive and negative. • Internet-related cognitions. • Peer behaviour. • Modelling.
Psychoanalytic/Personality	• Childhood traumas. • Low self-esteem. • Stress. • Personality and context. • Impulsivity.
Socio-cultural	• Sex. • Age. • Socio-economic status. • Ethnicity. • Religious belief. • Peer dynamics.

pornography and multi-user domains/dungeons – MUDs) and the anonymity afforded by the Internet (Young, 1998; Griffiths, 1998; Caplan, 2002).

Physical and psychosocial effects of internet addiction

Internet addiction can have wide-ranging physical and psychosocial consequences for the individual and significant others. There are several risk factors that have been identified in the development of internet addiction. Risk factors include psychological problems such as anxiety state, depression, social anxiety, addiction to psychoactive substances, other addictions such as gambling and sex, as well as the susceptibility of young people.

Some internet addicts also experience physical problems such as fatigue related to sleep deprivation, backache, and carpal and radial tunnel syndromes (Murali and George, 2007). Relationships, family life, 'cyberwidow' (neglected partner of internet addicts), social interactions and interests are often neglected. Internet addiction may lead to the impairment of occupational performances and academic performance. Psychosocial consequences include loneliness, frustration and depression (Kraut et al., 1998; Clark et al., 2004; Young and Rogers, 1998).

Some children and teens are more likely than their peers to become addicted to the Internet and this is more likely to happen if the children are depressed, hostile, or have attention deficit hyperactivity disorder (ADHD) or social phobia (Chih-Hung et al., 2009). The authors concluded that the results of their study suggest that ADHD, hostility, depression, and social phobia should be detected early on and intervention carried out to prevent internet addiction in adolescents. Also, sex differences in psychiatric co-morbidity should be taken into consideration when developing prevention and intervention strategies for internet addiction.

Psychologists in the UK have found that people addicted to the Internet are five times more likely to be depressed than non-addicted people (Morrison and Gore, 2010). The findings of the study also showed that there was a close relationship between internet addiction tendencies and depression, in that internet addiction respondents were more depressed. There were also significant differences between the sexes, with men showing more addictive tendencies than women. In addition, young people were significantly more likely to show addictive symptoms than older people.

Symptoms of internet addiction

The symptoms of internet addiction may vary from person to person and may include: excessive time devoted to internet use, apathy, irritability if deprived of access to the Internet, anger, insomnia, fatigue, poor academic performance, poor job performance, poor social interactions, withdrawal, losing track of time online, self-neglect, family neglect, isolation from family and friends, feeling guilty or defensive about your internet use, trembling, tremors, voluntary or involuntary typing movements of the fingers, obsessive thinking, fantasies, or dreams about the Internet and concealing from or lying to family members about the extent of internet use. In addition, other symptoms may include the use of internet engagement as a way of escaping problems or relieving feelings of guilt, helplessness, anxiety, or depression, and an inability to make unsuccessful efforts to quit or limit your computer use. Researchers in Taiwan have argued that more than 20 hours of personal internet use per week constitutes internet addiction (Lin and Tsai, 2002).

Screening and assessment

There are several screening and diagnostic instruments in the identification of internet addiction. Young (1998) developed the Internet Addiction Diagnostic Questionnaire (IADQ) to diagnose the disorder. This eight item screening instrument is based on the DSM-IV diagnostic criteria for pathological gambling and meeting five of the following symptoms are considered necessary to be diagnosed. The criteria are:

- Preoccupation with the Internet.
- Tolerance.
- Inability to cut back or stop internet use.
- Restless, moody, depressed or irritable when attempting to cut down or stop internet use.
- Spending more time online than intended.
- Adverse consequences in interpersonal, educational or vocational spheres of life.
- Lying to conceal the true extent of internet use.
- Use of the Internet as an attempt to escape from problems.

Another diagnostic instrument developed for a diagnosis of internet addiction is Beard and Wolf's questionnaire (Beard and Wolf, 2001). The individual must display all of five criteria (preoccupation, tolerance, inability to cut back, restlessness or moodiness when attempting to reduce use and spending more time online than intended) and at least one of a further three (adverse consequences, lying to conceal internet use and use of the Internet to escape from problems). Young (1998) also developed the Internet Addiction Test, a 20 question, self-report questionnaire to diagnose internet addiction. In addition, to enable the diagnosis of internet addiction, Young's questionnaire also helps determine the extent to which excessive internet use has affected the various aspects of the individual's life. The Generalized Problematic Internet Use Scale (Caplan, 2002) consists of 29 items, based on the Likert scale, and measures

Table 13.2   Assessment for internet addiction

Key components	
History-taking	• Onset, initiating factors. • Progression. • Diary of use – pattern, duration, at work/ at home, time of day, etc. • Maintaining factors. • Favourite applications (e.g. chatting, shopping, gambling, MUDs). • Symptoms of dependence (craving, tolerance, withdrawal, salience, etc.). • Attempts to cut back or stop, and outcome. • Previous attempts at treatment. • Reason for presentation now.
Obtain corroborative information where needed	• From significant others. • Past records. • Other addictive problems.
Assess applications used, emotions, cognitions and life events	• Applications used for chatting, shopping, gambling, social interactions, cybersex.
Assess the impact of internet use on interpersonal, social and vocational areas	• Identify consequences of internet addiction.
Assess the level of motivation to engage in treatment	• Application of process of change: pre-contemplation, contemplation, decision-making, action, maintenance, relapse. • Use of motivational interviewing.
Conduct a standard mental state examination	• Assess for mania, depression or psychosis, or psychosexual disorders.
Rule out psychiatric co-morbidity	• Assess for coexisting psychiatric disorders.
Combine clinical interview with other diagnostic/assessment instruments	• Use of diagnostic instruments.

Source: Adapted from Murali, V. and George, S. (2007) 'Lost Online: an Overview of Internet Addiction', *Advances in Psychiatric Treatment*, 13, 24–30. doi: 10.1192/apt.bp.106.002907.

cognitions, behaviours and negative outcomes associated with problematic internet use. The Internet Consequences Scale is a 38 item Likert-type scale used to assess the consequences of internet use (Clark et al., 2004). The diagnostic instruments have been subjected to criticism on the basis of their having different theoretical frameworks, lack of agreement on the dimensions of internet addiction, lack of identification of specific internet applications' and being self-reports (Beard, 2005).

Due to their limitations, a clinical assessment would be undertaken to complement the diagnostic instrument. It is important during the course of the clinical interview to assess the applications of internet use, emotions, cognition (e.g. low self-esteem and other depressive cognitions and life events (stressors) (Young, 1999). The key components in the assessment for internet addiction are presented in Table 13.2.

Treatment interventions for internet addiction

Since internet addiction disorder is a relatively new phenomenon, there is limited research on the effectiveness of treatment interventions. Applying the model of treatment interventions for gambling or alcohol and drug addiction, abstinence would one of the treatment options.

Learning how to use the Internet in moderation is often the main objective in therapy. Behavioural strategies that can be used to treat internet addiction include: practice the opposite; external stoppers; setting goals; reminder cards; personal inventory; and abstinence (Young, 1999). Cognitive psychological interventions may also help the person identify thoughts and feelings that trigger their use of the Internet. Cognitive behavioural therapy identifies maladaptive negative cognitions and faulty assumptions and reframes them to help the individual develop alternative, adaptive cognitions. Psychological therapy can also help to adopt healthier ways of coping with uncomfortable cognitions and emotions.

Psychological interventions may include interpersonal skills training, assertive and social skills training. Family and couple therapy may be indicated if the user is turning to the Internet to escape from family and marital problems. Marriage therapy can also help you to reconnect with your partner if you have been using the Internet for most of your social needs.

Pharmacological interventions such as an antidepressant or anti-anxiety medication may also be indicated if the internet addict has coexisting psychiatric disorders. Lapse and relapse is part of the process of addictive behaviours. Relapse prevention may be indicated as part of treatment interventions. Identifying situations that would trigger excessive internet use and generating ways to deal with these situations can greatly reduce the possibility of relapse.

There are some internet addiction support groups on the Internet. There are specific support groups that help people deal with their addiction to the Internet. One such support group is the Internet Addiction Support Group (http://health.groups.yahoo.com/group/Internet-Addiction). The support group provides education about internet addiction and advice on its management. However, there may be other self-help groups that may be helpful for those who wish to improve their social and coping skills.

Summary of key points

- Internet Addiction Disorder (IAD) is not formally recognized as a clinical/pathological disorder, but is now regarded as a public health problem.
- Individuals with Internet Addiction Disorder can exhibit warning signs, symptoms, have a relapse and have health and social consequences that are similar to individuals addicted to alcohol, drugs, gambling, and other compulsive behaviours.
- Internet addicts experience tolerance and withdrawal effects.
- Internet Addiction Disorder is said to be closest to pathological gambling.
- Various behavioural, psychodynamic and personality, socio-cultural, and biomedical explanations have been proposed to explain this phenomenon.
- Despite these theories or aetiological models, it is still not clear as to what precisely internet misusers become addicted.
- Risk factors include psychological problems such as anxiety states, depression, social anxiety, addiction to psychoactive substances, other addictions such as gambling and sex, and susceptibility of young people.
- People addicted to the Internet are five times more likely to be depressed than non-addicted people.
- Men show more addictive tendencies than women.
- Researchers have argued that more than 20 hours of personal internet use per week constitutes internet addiction.
- There are several screening and diagnostic instruments in the identification of internet addiction.
- A clinical assessment would be undertaken to complement the diagnostic instrument.
- There is limited research on the effectiveness of treatment interventions.
- Psychological and pharmacological interventions may be indicated for those with Internet Addiction Disorder.

Reflective activity 13.2

ME is a 14 year old male adolescent who reports that over the past two years, he has spent about 65 hours a week on his computer including 40 hours on the Internet. This includes two twelve hour sessions at the weekend. During the school holidays it increases even more, especially because he is on his own in the house whilst his mother is at work. As a consequence of his excessive internet use, the house telephone bills are large. His school work has also suffered recently as a result of the limited time he spent on his school work and activities. He rarely plays football during the week or at weekends and seems to have no friends outside of those he meets on the Internet. He has made many 'virtual' friends while playing games in multiple teams on the Internet.

He is an only child living with his mother in a suburban area. There appears to be few problems in ME's family life although his mother divorced his father about four years ago. There is no history of psychological and physical problems. However, he has been putting on weight in the last couple of years and has irregular sleeping patterns. He has tried to quit or reduce the number of hours he spends on the Internet but relapses into his old behavioural patterns. When he cannot get internet access, he gets withdrawal symptoms and becomes irritable, with mood swings and depression. He denies any kind of problem.

- Does ME appear to fit the stereotype of an internet 'addict'?
- What is his primary motivation to use the Internet?
- What message can you give to him about the dangers of internet addiction?
- What treatment interventions and/or strategies may be planned for ME?

References

Ahn, D.H. (2007) *Korean Policy on Treatment and Rehabilitation for Adolescents' Internet Addiction*, in 2007 International Symposium on the Counselling and Treatment of Youth Internet Addiction. Seoul, Korea, National Youth Commission, 49.

Beard, K.W. (2005) 'Internet Addiction: a Review of Current Assessment Techniques and Potential Assessment Questions', *Cyberpsychology and Behavior*, 8, 1, 7–14.

Beard, K.W. and Wolf, E.M. (2001) 'Modification in the Proposed Diagnostic Criteria for Internet Addiction', *Cyberpsychology and Behavior* 4, 3, 377–83.

Bell, V. (2007) 'Online Information, Extreme Communities, and Internet Therapy: Is the Internet Good for Our Mental Health?' *Journal of Mental Health*, 16, 4, 445–57.

Block, J.J. (2007) *Pathological Computer Use in the USA*, in 2007 International Symposium on the Counselling and Treatment of Youth Internet Addiction. Seoul, Korea, National Youth Commission, 433.

Block, J.J. (2008) 'Issues for DSM-V: Internet Addiction', *American Journal of Psychiatry*, 165, 3, 306–07.

Caplan, S.E. (2002) 'Problematic Internet Use and Psychosocial Well-being: Development of a Theory-based Cognitive–behavioral Measurement Instrument', *Computers in Human Behavior*, 18, 5, 553–75.

Chebbi, P., Koong, K.S. and Rottman, R. (2000) 'Some Observations On Internet Addiction Disorder Research', *Journal of Information Systems Education*, 11, 3–4, 97–99.

Chih-Hung, K., Ju-Yu, Y., Cheng-Sheng, C., Yi-Chun, Y. and Cheng-Fang, Y. (2009) 'Predictive Values of Psychiatric Symptoms for Internet Addiction in Adolescents – A 2-Year Prospective Study', *Archives of Pediatric and Adolescent Medicine*, 163, 10, 937–43.

Choi, Y.H. (2007) *Advancement of IT and Seriousness of Youth Internet Addiction*, in 2007 International Symposium on the Counseling and Treatment of Youth Internet Addiction. Seoul, Korea, National Youth Commission, 20.

Clark, D.J., Frith, K.H. and Demi, A.S. (2004) 'The Physical, Behavioural, and Psychosocial Consequences of Internet Use in College Students', *Computers, Informatics, Nursing*, 22, 3, 153–61.

Davis, R.A. (2001) 'A Cognitive–behavioural Model of Pathological Internet Use', *Computers in Human Behavior*, 17, 2, 187–95.

DeAngelis, T. (2000) 'Is Internet Addiction Real?' *Monitor on Psychology*, 31, 4, http://www.apa.org/monitor/apr00/addiction.aspx, date accessed 15 January 2010.

Duran, M.G. (2003) *Internet Addiction Disorder*. http://allpsych.com/journal/internetaddiction.html, date accessed 10 January 2010.

Egger, O. and Rauterberg, M. (1996) 'Internet Behavior and Addiction', Swiss Federal Institute of Technology, Zurich, http://www.idemployee.id.tue.nl/g.w.m.rauterberg/ibq/report.pdf, date accessed 10 February 2010.

Ferris, J.R. (2003) Internet Addiction Disorder: Cause, Symptoms, and Consequences, http://allpsych.com/journal/internetaddiction.html, date accessed 12 February 2010.

Greenfield, D.N. (1999) 'Psychological Characteristics of Compulsive Internet Use: A Preliminary Analysis', *Cyberpsychology and Behaviour*, 2, 5, 403–12. doi:10.1089/cpb.1999.2.403.

Griffiths, M.D. (1997) 'Psychology of Computer Use: Some Comments on "Addictive Use of the Internet"', *Psychological Reports*, 80, 1, 81–82.

Grohol, J.M. (2005) Dr. Grohol's Psych Central. Internet Addiction Guide. http://www.psychcentral.com/netaddiction, date accessed 15 February 2010.

Kraut, R., Patterson, M., Lundmark, V., Kiesler, S., Mukophadhyay, T. and Scherlis, W. (1996) 'Internet Paradox: A Social Technology that Reduces Social Involvement and Psychological Well-Being', *American Psychologist,* 53, 9, 1017–31.

Lin, S. and Tsai, C-C. (2002) 'Sensation Seeking and Internet Dependence of Taiwanese High School Adolescents', *Computers in Human Behavior*, 18, 4, 411–26.

Morrison, C.M. and Gore, H. (2010) 'The Relationship between Excessive Internet Use and Depression: A Questionnaire-Based Study of 1,319 Young People and Adults', *Psychopathology* 43, 2, 121–26. DOI: 10.1159/000277001.

Murali, V. and George, S. (2007) 'Lost Online: an Overview of Internet Addiction', *Advances in Psychiatric Treatment*, 13, 24–30. doi: 10.1192/apt.bp.106.002907.

Wallace, P. (1999) *The Psychology of the Internet* (Cambridge: Cambridge University Press).

Young, K.S. (1998) 'Internet Addiction: The Emergence of a New Disorder', *Cyberpsychology and Behavior*, 1, 3, 237–44.

Young, K.S. (1999) 'Internet Addiction: Symptoms, Evaluation and Treatment', in VandeCreek, L. and Jackson, T. (eds.), *Innovations in Clinical Practice: A Source Book* (Sarasota, FL: Professional Resource Press) 17, 19–31.

Young, K.S. and Rogers, R.C. (1998) 'The Relationship Between Depression and Internet Addiction', *Cyberpsychology Behaviour*, 1, 1, 25–28.

Sexual Addiction 14

Introduction

> ### Reflective activity 14.1
>
> Before reading this chapter, try to provide a true or false answer for each of the statements listed below. Think about some reasons as to why you chose a particular answer.
>
> | Statements | True | False |
> |---|---|---|
> | Sexual addiction is regarded as a major social problem. | | |
> | Both men and women are capable of having sexual addiction. | | |
> | Men and women use cybersex differently. | | |
> | Sex addiction may take various forms, including what many regard as 'normal' heterosexual behaviour. | | |
> | Neurochemical and psychosocial factors are potential determinants of sexual addiction. | | |
> | Sexual addicts are obsessive-compulsive and interpersonally sensitive. | | |
> | Sexual addiction is a form of self-medication. | | |
> | The roots of sex addiction are believed to be located during childhood and adolescence. | | |
> | Like other addicts, sexual addicts will sacrifice relationships, their own health, and jobs to pursue their compulsion. | | |
> | There may be some social, psychological, legal, physical, financial and spiritual consequences which may result from sexual addiction and indicate the existence of sexual addiction. | | |
> | Abstinence from sexual behaviour, though not a goal of treatment for sexual addiction, can on occasion be a helpful therapeutic technique. | | |

When you have read this chapter, come back to this activity and consider your answers again. How many did you get right? For those you got wrong, think about the reasons for your original answer and compare this with what you know now.

Sexual addiction is regarded as a major social problem with likeness to alcohol and drug addiction or problem gambling. Our society has licensed sexual provocation that has led to an increase in the number of individuals engaging in a variety of unusual or illicit sexual behaviours. Sexual addiction develops when any sexual behaviour and activity, which is not emotionally fulfilling, goes out of control. Individuals with sex addiction feel compelled to seek out and engage in obsessive sexual behaviour, in spite of the consequences to their personal, health, social and occupational lives.

The Diagnostic and Statistical Manual of Psychiatric Disorders, Volume Four (DSM-IV) (APA, 2004) describes sex addiction, under the category 'Sexual Disorders Not Otherwise Specified', as 'distress about a pattern of repeated sexual relationships involving a succession of lovers who are experienced by the individual only as things to be used'. According to the DSM-IV (APA, 2004), sex addiction also involves compulsive searching for multiple partners, compulsive fixation on an unattainable partner, compulsive masturbation, compulsive love relationships and compulsive sexuality in a relationship. The Society for the Advancement of Sexual Health (SASH) (www.ncsac.org) has defined sexual addiction as 'engaging in persistent and escalating patterns of sexual behaviour acted out despite increasing negative consequences to self and others'. Another definition of sexual addiction describes it as a condition in which some form of sexual behaviour is employed in a pattern that is characterized by two key features: 1) recurrent failure to control the sexual behaviour, and 2) continuation of the sexual behaviour despite significant harmful consequences (Goodman, 1998).

It is estimated that three to five per cent of the United States population could meet the criteria for sexual addiction and compulsivity (www.ncsac.org). However, these statistics may be an underestimate as more individuals may suffer from sex addiction than actually seek treatment. In *Illness as Metaphor* (Sontag, 2001), Sontag argues that the myths and metaphors surrounding disease can infuse shame and guilt in the sick, thus delaying them from seeking treatment. The same may be applicable to sex addiction.

Sexual addiction: Equal opportunity

Addictions to sexual behaviour are not gender-related. Both men and women are viewed as susceptible to sexual addiction. More men are diagnosed as having sexual addiction than women but this may be because women seek treatment for sex addiction less frequently. Sexual addiction can occur in people of any sexual orientation (heterosexuals, homosexuals and bisexuals).

In the United States, of the four million adults who admitted to having a sexual addiction problem, 680,000 are women. It is estimated that 17 per cent of all women struggle with porn addiction; one of three visitors to all adult websites are women and that 9.4 million women access adult websites every month (Simkus, 2009).

Men, influenced by traditional machismo ethic ideologies, have rendered them susceptible to becoming sexually addicted to practices, such as prostitution, pornography, extramarital sex, casual sex affairs, and co-dependence (Philaretou, 2006). The elements of sex addiction in women are the same as in any addiction: compulsion, continuation despite adverse consequences, and preoccupation or obsession. There is a fine line that exists between what may be considered acceptable sexual behaviour and what is sexually addictive. This is especially true for women in a society which discourages women from being direct in the expression of their sexual needs, thereby encouraging a less direct and potentially seductive or manipulative style (Goodman, 1998). Some women go beyond these culturally-sanctioned behaviours and use sex compulsively as a means of gaining power and love (Goodman, 1998).

Some sexual addictive behaviour patterns in women may include: excessive flirting, dancing, or personal grooming to be seductive; wearing provocative clothing whenever possible; changing one's appearance via excessive dieting, excessive exercise, and/or reconstructive surgery to be seductive; exposing oneself in a window or car; making sexual advances to younger siblings, clients, or others in subordinate power positions; seeking sexual partners in high risk locations; multiple extramarital affairs; disregard of appropriate sexual boundaries, e.g. considering a married person, one's boss, or one's personal medical doctor as appropriate objects of romantic involvement; trading sex for drugs, help, affection, money, social access, or power; having sex with someone they just met at a party, bar or on the Internet (forms of anonymous sex); compulsive masturbation; and exchanging sex for pain or pain for sex (Goodman, 1998).

Men and women use cybersex differently. Cooper, Delmonico and Burg (2000) found that females preferred chat rooms to other mediums whereas males preferred the Web. No female cybersex compulsives reported using newsgroups for sexual pursuits. Since newsgroups are primarily used for the exchange of erotic pictures, this supported the finding that women tend to desire cybersex in the context of a 'relationship' rather than simply viewing images or text (Cooper, Scherer et al., 1999).

Types of sex addiction

Sex addiction may take various forms, including what many regard as 'normal' heterosexual behaviour. The type and range of sexual behaviours make it difficult in defining what 'normal' sexual behaviour is as some individuals have a naturally stronger sex drive than others. What is significant is the negative impact on the self and on significant others and the inability to stop the compulsive sexual thoughts and acts.

Sexual addiction has many different forms: compulsive masturbation, sex with prostitutes, anonymous sex with multiple partners, multiple affairs outside a committed relationship, habitual exhibitionism, habitual voyeurism, inappropriate sexual touching, repeated sexual abuse of children, and episodes of rape (Book, 1997). Some individuals with sex addiction do not progress beyond compulsive masturbation or the extensive use of pornography or phone or cybersex. Others may be involved in illegal activities such as childhood sexual abuse or rape.

Potential determinants of sex addiction

There are various potential determinants of sex addiction including neurochemical and psychosocial factors. From a neurochemical perspective, it is the neurotransmitter endorphins that may be responsible for the mood changes that follow sexual release. Other neurotransmitters such as dopamine, serotonin and norepinephrine may play a vital role in sexual functioning and may cause sexual addiction. Any chemical that causes mood changes can be addictive, with repeated exposure altering brain chemistry to the point that more of the chemical is 'required' in order to feel 'normal' (Carnes, 1991). There are also disorders of the pituitary gland or irritation of the brain cortex by a tumour, arteriosclerosis or epilepsy and hormones such as androgens that have been associated with nymphomania in the female and satyriasis (excessive, often uncontrollable sexual desire in and behaviour by a man) in the male.

The roots of sex addiction are believed to be located during childhood and adolescence. The findings of a study showed that 60 per cent of sexual addicts were abused by someone in their childhood (Book, 1997). A deficiency in the development of emotional intelligence and a hostile, chaotic or neglectful home environment may be potential determinants. In this context, sex activity becomes a compensation to meet emotional needs, to escape boredom, to relieve anxiety or deal with insomnia. In some cases, the child was maybe introduced to sex in inappropriate ways by another adult or an older child. In these experiences, there often is a combination of natural curiosity, newfound pleasurable feelings and even the feelings of fear or shame (Carnes, 1991).

The findings of a major study of sexual addiction by Carnes (1991) showed that those who reported themselves to be sex addicts were typically unable to form close friendships, have feelings of shame and unworthiness, are lonely, and unable to accept real intimacy. In Carnes' survey, 97 per cent responded that their sexual activity led to loss of self-esteem; strong feelings of guilt or shame, 96 per cent; strong feelings of isolation and loneliness, 94 per cent; feelings of extreme hopelessness or despair, 91 per cent; acting against personal values and beliefs, 90 per cent; feeling like two people, 88 per cent; emotional exhaustion, 83 per cent; strong fears about their own future, 82 per cent; and emotional instability, 78 per cent. In addition to these psychological problems, 42 per cent of sex addicts in his sample also had a problem with either alcohol or drug dependence and 38 per cent had eating disorders.

A study by Raviv (1993) showed that the sexual addict group was significantly more anxious, depressed, obsessive-compulsive and interpersonally sensitive than the non-addict control group. The results supported the view that sexual addiction can be explained as a means of coping with anxiety, depression, obsessive-compulsiveness and interpersonal sensitivity.

Indicators of sexual addiction

Sexual addiction is a form of self-medication and a means of avoiding stress, emotional strain, boredom and anxiety. The sex addicts usually deny that they have problem and display increasingly secretive behaviour, deception, and withdrawal. Carnes (1991) suggests there are ten possible warning signs:

- Feeling that sexual behaviour and activity are out of control.
- Severe consequences resulting in the continuation of the behaviour or activity.
- A feeling of powerlessness or inability to stop.
- Using sexual fantasies as a way of coping with difficult feelings or situations.
- Needing more and more sexual activity in order to experience the same high.
- Experiencing intense mood swings around sexual activity.
- Time consumed planning sexual activity so that it interferes with other activities.
- Wanting to stop or control what you're doing and taking active steps to limit your activities.

- Spending an increasing amount of time planning, engaging in or regretting and recovering from sexual activities.
- Neglecting important social, occupational or recreational activities in favour of sexual behaviour.

Consequences of sexual addiction

There may be some social, psychological, legal, physical, financial and spiritual consequences which may result from sexual addiction and indicate the existence of sexual addiction. The consequences of sexual addiction are presented in Table 14.1.

In the Carnes survey (1991) of individuals in treatment, sexually transmitted diseases were contracted by 38 per cent of the men and 45 per cent of the women; 64 per cent reported that they continued their sexual behaviour despite the risk of disease or infection. Of the women, 70 per cent routinely

Table 14.1 Consequences of sexual addiction

Consequences	
Health	Genital trauma.
	Cervical cancer.
	HIV/AIDS.
	Herpes.
	Genital Warts.
	Other Sexually Transmitted Diseases.
	Problems related to alcohol or drug misuse.
Social	Sexual preoccupation.
	Loss of friendship.
	Damage to family relationships.
Psychological/ Emotional	Anxiety.
	Shame.
	Guilt.
	Boredom.
	Fatigue.
	Suicide.
	Coexisting psychiatric disorders.
Financial/ Occupational	Costs – use of prostitutes, cybersex, phone sex and multiple affairs.
	Costs of separation or divorce.
	Legal fees
	Job loss.
Spiritual	Self-pity; self-blame, guilt.
Legal	Violation of law due to illicit sexual activity.

risked unwanted pregnancy by not using birth control, and 42 per cent reported having unwanted pregnancies. Insomnia was reported by 65 per cent; they usually resulted from stress or shame connected with the sexual activity. Of the survey respondents, 56 per cent experienced severe financial difficulty because of their sexual activity. Loss of job productivity was reported by 80 per cent, and 11 per cent were actually demoted as a result. These consequences are progressive and predictable. Like other addicts, sexual addicts will sacrifice relationships, their own health, and jobs to pursue their compulsion.

Assessment and treatment interventions

Besides having a clinical assessment, there is a screening instrument that can be used in the diagnosis of sexual addiction. The Sexual Addiction Screening Test (SAST) is designed to assist in the assessment of sexually compulsive behaviour which may indicate the presence of sexual addiction. However, many sexual addicts live in denial of their addiction, and treating an addiction is dependent on the individual accepting and admitting that he or she has a problem.

Abstinence from sexual behaviour, though not a goal of treatment for sexual addiction, can on occasion be a helpful therapeutic technique. Treatment of sexual addiction focuses on controlling the addictive behaviour and helping the individual sufferer develop a healthy sexuality. Treatment interventions include education about healthy sexuality, individual counselling and marital and/or family therapy, psychotherapy, 12 step programmes and self-help groups. Couples or family therapy may be indicated for the treatment not for sexual addiction per se, but for the interpersonal issues and dysfunctional relationship patterns associated with sexual addiction. Relapse prevention can also be part of the whole treatment interventions package. This may also enhance the effectiveness of counselling, cognitive-behavioural therapies and psychotherapy. Self-help groups such as 12 step recovery programmes for individuals with sexual addictions such as Sex Addicts Anonymous, Sex and Love Addicts Anonymous, Sexaholics Anonymous, and Sexual Compulsives Anonymous. In some cases, pharmacological treatment may be used to control the compulsive nature of the sex addiction.

Summary of key points

- Sexual addiction is regarded as a major social problem.
- Sex addiction also involves compulsive searching for multiple partners, compulsive fixation on an unattainable partner, compulsive masturbation, compulsive love relationships and compulsive sexuality in a relationship.

- Addictions to sexual behaviour are not gender-related. Both men and women are viewed as having sexual addiction.
- Men and women use cybersex differently.
- Sex addiction may take various forms, including what many regard as 'normal' heterosexual behaviour.
- There are various potential determinants of sex addiction including neurochemical and psychosocial factors.
- Sexual addicts are significantly more anxious, depressed, obsessive-compulsive and interpersonally sensitive.
- Sexual addiction is a form of self-medication as a means of avoiding stress, emotional strain, boredom and anxiety.

Reflective activity 14.2

J works as a psychiatric nurse and is in her early 40s and is sexually involved with two men. She is married to P and loves her partner, Ed and cannot stand the thought of leaving him. She trusts Ed and feels that he understands her. Ed knows of J's recurrent pattern of intense infatuation with a new man, resisting and then giving in to overpowering sexual attraction, and then becoming bored. When J is not sexually involved with at least one man outside her marriage, she feels desperate, panicky, and empty. Typically, she begins a new involvement as soon as she senses that she is getting bored with her current extramarital affair. She reported that she has tried many times not to be involved in extramarital affairs. J recounts that her behaviour has cost her two serious relationships and her children, and she has gone through emotional turmoil. Currently J feels overwhelmed about her relationships and she is experiencing symptoms of major depression and panic disorder.

- Does J meet the criteria for sexual addiction?
- What would be the immediate interventions required?
- What other withdrawal symptoms or behavioural problems may be observed?
- What are the short-term goals for this patient?
- What are the long-term goals for this patient?
- What treatment interventions and/or strategies may be planned for this patient?

Source: Adapted from Goodman, A. (2009) 'Sexual Addiction Update Assessment, Diagnosis, and Treatment', *Psychiatric Times*, 26, 6, 1–3. http://www.psychiatrictimes. com/display/article/10168/1416827?pageNumber=1.

- There may be some social, psychological, legal, physical, financial and spiritual consequences which may result from sexual addiction and indicate the existence of sexual addiction.
- The Sexual Addiction Screening Test (SAST) is designed to assist in the assessment of sexually compulsive behaviour which may indicate the presence of sexual addiction.
- Self-help groups offer 12 step recovery programmes for individuals with sexual addictions such as Sex Addicts Anonymous, Sex and Love Addicts Anonymous, Sexaholics Anonymous, and Sexual Compulsives Anonymous.

References

APA (2004) *Diagnostic and Statistical Manual of Mental Disorders*, 4th edn (DSM-IV) (American Psychiatric Association).

Book, P. (1997) *Sex and Love Addiction, Treatment & Recovery* (New York: Lucerne Publishing).

Carnes, P. (1991) *Don't Call It Love: Recovery from Sexual Addiction* (New York: Bantam) 22–23, 30–34.

Cooper, A., Scherer, C., Boies, S.C. and Gordon, B. (1999) 'Sexuality on the Internet: From Sexual Exploration to Pathological Expression', *Professional Psychology: Research and Practice*, 30, 2, 154–64.

Cooper, A., Delmonico, D. and Burg, R. (2000) 'Cybersex Users, Abusers, and Compulsives: New Findings and Implications', in Cooper, A. (ed.), *Cybersex: The Dark Side of the Force* (Philadelphia: Brunner Routledge) 5–29.

Goodman, A. (1998) *Sexual Addiction: An Integrated Approach* (Madison, Connecticut: International Universities Press).

Philaretou, A.G. (2006) *Learning About Sexual Addiction: Theory and Intervention*, Thirteenth International Conference on Learning – 2006 http://l06. cgpublisher.com/proposals/2/index_html, date accessed 19 January 2010.

Raviv, M. (1993) 'Personality Characteristics of Sexual Addicts and Pathological Gamblers', *Journal of Gambling Studies*, 9, 1, 17–30.

Simkus, K. (2009) *Addiction to Internet Pornography*, http://reliableanswers. com/med/porn_addiction.asp, date accessed 10 January 2010.

Sontag, S. (2001) *Illness as Metaphor and AIDS and Its Metaphors* (New York: Picador).

PART
3

Addiction in Context

Dual Diagnosis: Psychiatric Disorders and Addictive Behaviours

15

Introduction

Reflective activity 15.1

Before reading this chapter, try to provide a true or false answer for each of the statements listed below. Think about some reasons as to why you chose a particular answer.

Statements	True	False
• Drug use is a direct cause of long-term mental health problems.		
• Individuals with dual diagnosis bring on all their problems because of their substance misuse.		
• If they stopped using drugs then all their symptoms of mental disorder would remit.		
• Individuals have to 'hit rock-bottom' before they will change to remain drug free.		
• It is impossible to work with substance misusers therapeutically.		
• It is important for someone with dual diagnosis to accept that they are an addict before they can benefit from treatment.		
• Small amounts of cannabis will make little difference to someone with schizophrenia.		
• It is not possible to work therapeutically with people who are on prescribed medication for mental health problems.		

Source: Banerjee et al. (2002)

When you have read this chapter, come back to this activity and consider your answers again. How many did you get right? For those you got wrong, think about the reasons for your original answer and compare this with what you know now. Please read the Royal College of Psychiatrists' Research Unit (2002) *Co-existing Problems of Mental Disorder and Substance Misuse (Dual Diagnosis)* pages 14–16 for possible explanations of the above statements.

This chapter deals with a number of issues related to coexisting disorders and addictive behaviours. It focuses on the relationships between psychiatric disorders and substance misuse, alcohol and eating disorders. In addition, it examines the relationship between physical health and addiction. Many individuals with addictive behaviours have other coexisting psychiatric problems and this issue needs to be accorded as much attention as their addiction. The term dual diagnosis covers a broad spectrum of mental health and addictive behaviours – problems that an individual might experience concurrently.

Psychiatric disorders and addictive behaviours

There is a strong relationship between psychiatric disorders and addiction. New research reveals that this type of dual diagnosis may stem from a common cause: developmental changes in the amygdala, a walnut-shaped part of the brain linked to fear, anxiety and other emotions (American Psychological Association, 2007).

Individuals with coexisting substance misuse and psychiatric disorders (dual diagnosis) meet the DSM-IV criteria for both substance abuse or dependence and a coexisting psychiatric disorder. The Diagnostic and Statistical Manual of Mental Disorders (DSM-IV) (American Psychiatric Association, 1994), defines a mental disorder as 'a clinically significant behavioural or psychological syndrome or pattern that occurs in an individual and that is typically associated with present distress (a painful symptom) or disability (impairment in one or more areas of functioning)'. Substance misuse, according to DSM-IV (American Psychiatric Association, 1994), is the maladaptive pattern of use not meeting the criteria for dependence that has persisted for at least one month or has occurred repeatedly over a long period of time. The dual diagnosis patient meets the DSM-IV criteria for both substance abuse or dependence and a coexisting psychiatric disorder.

A more manageable and clinically relevant interrelationship between psychiatric disorders and substance misuse has been described in the 'Dual Diagnosis Good Practice Guide' (Department of Health, 2002). In relation to addictive behaviours, there are four possible relationships:

- A primary psychiatric illness precipitating or leading to addictive behaviours.
- Addictive behaviours worsening or altering the course of a psychiatric illness.
- Addictive behaviours leading to psychological symptoms.
- Addictive behaviours leading to psychiatric symptoms or illnesses.

The nature of the relationship between psychiatric disorders and addiction misuse is complex. Despite certain methodological difficulties especially with earlier studies there is now strong research evidence that the rate of substance misuse is substantially higher among those with psychiatric disorders compared with the general population (Rassool, 2006). The prevalence rate of substance use disorders among individuals with mental health problems range from 35 to 60 per cent (Mueser et al., 1995; Menezes, 1996). There is also evidence of psychiatric disorders among individuals with primary substance use disorders (Gossop et al., 1998).

In a study by Weaver et al., (2002) the findings showed that some 74.5 per cent of users of drug services and 85.5 per cent of users of alcohol services experienced mental health problems. In a study of adults of whom 90 per cent were opiate dependent (Marsden et al., 2000), anxiety, depression, paranoia and psychoticism were found with poly-drug use closely linked to psychiatric symptoms. There are increased risks of suicide with those with substance use problems. Some of this increased risk may be explained by the presence of co-morbid psychiatric conditions such as depression or personality disorders in substance misusers (Neeleman and Farrell, 1997).

The Epidemiological Catchment Area Survey (ECAS) (Regier et al., 1990) study found a 'severe substance misuse' rate of 83.6 per cent in persons diagnosed with antisocial personality disorder. It is suggested that there are a number of shared characteristics between substance misuse and personality disorders. These are lowered self-esteem, self-confidence, self-satisfaction, social confidence, assertiveness, personal control and self-efficacy (Phillips, 2006).

The aetiology of substance misuse and psychiatric disorders is complex. There are a variety of theories that hypothesize why individuals with mental health problems are vulnerable to the misuse of alcohol and drugs. These include the self-medication hypothesis, the alleviation of dysphoria model, the multiple risk factor model and the supersensitivity model. These theories or models are described in Rassool (2006). The rationale for the occurrence of substance misuse and psychiatric disorders are presented in Table 15.1.

There may be other explanations why individuals with psychiatric disorders may use certain psychoactive substances. With the advent of deinstitutionalization, more of the individuals with mental health problems may be finding themselves exposed to an increased availability of drugs in the community (Williams, 2001). As a result, they may experience downward drift to poor inner city areas (social drift hypothesis) where drug availability is increased. Equally, an increased availability of illicit drugs in psychiatric institutions may be a contributory factor (Williams and Cohen, 2000).

Psychoactive drugs and mental health

Psychiatric symptoms occur more commonly in drug-related problems and it is difficult to distinguish between the psychiatric symptoms and dual diagnosis.

Table 15.1 Why do substance misuse and psychiatric disorders commonly co-occur?

Factors	Explanations
Genetic vulnerabilities	• Genetic factors may predispose individuals to both psychiatric disorders and addiction. • Having a greater risk of the second disorder once the first appears.
Environmental triggers	• Stress, trauma (for example physical or sexual abuse). • Early exposure to drugs.
Involvement of similar brain regions	• Brain is affected by both drug misuse and psychiatric disorders. • Brain circuits linked to reward processing. • Implicated in the stress response.
Developmental disorders	• Disorders arise during adolescence or even childhood. • Early exposure to drugs of addiction can change the brain in ways that increase the risk of mental illness. • Early symptoms of a psychiatric disorder may increase vulnerability to alcohol and drug misuse.

Source: Adapted from NIDA (2007) Co-morbid Drug Abuse and Mental Illness A Research Update from the National Institute on Drug Abuse. Topics in Brief, NIDA http://www.drugabuse.gov/tib/comorbid.html.

Problem drug users may show symptoms such as mania, psychosis, depression, anxiety and personality disorder symptoms. This is dependent on the type of drug used, the quantity consumed and the route of administration. A summary of the relationship of drugs and psychiatric disorders is presented in Table 15.2.

Cannabis consumption can lead to the development of anxiety and panic attacks. The symptoms are usually brief in duration and may include restlessness, depersonalization, derealization, paranoia and transient mood disorders (Thomas, 1993). Acute toxic confusional state can be developed as a result of high doses or prolonged consumption of cannabis and it is difficult to differentiate whether these illnesses are in fact relapses in previously psychotic patients who use cannabis, precipitated in patients who are vulnerable or have actual reactions produced by ingestion of cannabis (Harrison and Abou-Saleh, 2001). There is no conclusive evidence that cannabis can cause long-term psychiatric disorders or is an independent risk factor for schizophrenia.

It has been reported that up to 80 per cent of regular cocaine users experience symptoms such as euphoria, grandiosity, impulsiveness, impaired judgment and marked psychomotor activity, usually subsiding within half an hour and which are indistinguishable from hypomania (Harrison and Abou-Saleh, 2001). A condition known as a toxic psychosis, also referred

Table 15.2 Relationship of drugs and psychiatric disorders

Category of substance	Type of substance	Common mental health problems
Stimulant	Amphetamine	Disordered thinking Hallucinations Paranoid ideas Production of random, pointless, repetitive behaviour (such as involuntary picking and scratching at the skin) Restlessness Sleep disturbances
Stimulant	Cocaine	Experience of hallucinations (visual, auditory and tactile) Paranoid feelings Irritability Toxic psychosis with persecutory delusions and hallucinations Loss of insight (condition which usually subsides within 24 hours) Depression Sleep disturbances
Hallucinogen	Cannabis	Anxiety and panic attacks Restlessness Depersonalization Derealization Paranoia Transient mood disorders Acute toxic confusional state
	LSD	Hallucinations Panic reactions Flashback (recurrence of symptoms)
Opiate	Heroin	Anxiety Depression Suicide Overdose Personality disorder

Source: Adapted from Rassool, G.H. (2009) *Alcohol and Drug Misuse. A Handbook for Student and Health Professionals* (London: Routledge).

to as drug induced psychosis, results from prolonged or high dose use of cocaine but may be indistinguishable from acute psychosis due to other causes. Hallucinations, both visual and auditory similar to those seen in schizophrenia, and tactile hallucinations are experienced by the cocaine user. Amphetamines may produce similar toxic reactions, although the psychosis may last longer than that produced by cocaine, but will usually resolve within a few days (Connell, 1958). This condition usually occurs in long-term users, but may start a day or two after use and consists of disordered thinking, hallucinations and paranoid ideas and repetitive behaviour such as involuntary picking and scratching at the skin.

Alcohol and psychiatric disorders

Alcohol use is a socially approved behaviour and it is actively promoted in many cultural, social and religious circumstances. However, despite its benefits, alcohol is responsible for causing significant physical or mental health consequences. The Alcohol Strategy for England (Prime Minister's Strategy Unit, 2004) clearly states that mental health and alcohol problems are of high concern, particularly in relation to suicide, vulnerability and mental wellbeing. Alcohol is linked with homelessness and physical health consequences to the individual.

There is a close relationship between alcohol problems and mental health. The links between alcohol and mental health can be extremely complex, however there are four broad characteristics used in dual diagnosis to explain relationships (Abdulrahim, 2001).

- Alcohol is used to medicate psychological distress/symptoms (self-medication).
- Alcohol use causes psychological distress/symptoms (side effects).
- Alcohol use that has no causal or preventative mechanism for psychological distress or symptoms.
- Underlying trauma resulting in alcohol use and mood disorders.

Anxiety disorders may be a risk factor in the development of substance misuse and anxiety symptoms are likely to be present during chronic intoxication and withdrawal. There is evidence to suggest that people who experience symptoms such as 'butterflies', rapid breathing, or an increased heart rate in the face of a stressful situation are described as having high anxiety sensitivity and they are more likely to 'sooth' their anxiety by drinking (MacDonald et al., 2000). Those who have feelings of anxiety may use alcohol consumption to relieve their anxieties but prolonged alcohol misuse often heightens anxiety. It is reported that alcohol can increase clinical anxiety; especially after prolonged drinking and during withdrawal, and thus anxiety disorders such as panic disorder and generalized anxiety disorder may be related to these situations rather than a primary psychiatric disorder in these individuals (Harrison and Abou-Saleh, 2001). The relationship between alcohol and anxiety may differ between genders. One study of hospitalized male and female depressive patients found that there was a strong association between anxiety and alcohol misuse for women and a weaker association for men (Fischer and Goethe, 1998).

A UK study (Barnett et al., 2007) found that the majority of patients presenting with first episode psychosis reported substance use. Cannabis and alcohol were the two most frequently reported forms of substance misuse. Common links between alcohol and mental health include: depression, suicidal behaviour, anxiety (social anxiety, claustrophobia, agoraphobia), obsessive-compulsive disorders, bipolar disorders, schizophrenia and personality disorders (Institute of Alcohol Studies, 2007). The condition most clearly associated with problem drinking and dependence is antisocial personality disorder (ASPD). Individuals with ASPD have 21 times the average population risk of experiencing alcohol abuse or dependence (Institute of Alcohol Studies, 2007). Other signs of a relationship between alcohol and psychiatric disorders include: alcoholic hallucinosis (persecutory auditory hallucinations), pathological jealousy, delirium tremens, Wernike's encephalopathy, and Korsakoff's psychosis.

Eating disorders and dual diagnosis

The coexisting psychiatric disorders are common in individuals with eating disorders. Psychiatric disorders such as affective disorders, obsessive-compulsive disorder, somatization disorder, and substance misuse must be considered when individuals with eating disorders present with such symptoms. Anxiety disorders, especially social phobia, and obsessive-compulsive disorder are also common among individuals with eating disorders (Herzog et al., 1996; Milos et al., 2002). Personality disorders (Axis II diagnoses) also are common, with co-morbidity rates reported at 21 to 97 per cent (Westen and Harnden-Fischer, 2001). Lack of control and impulsivity in eating disorders such as bulimia nervosa are closely associated with personality disorder.

Major depression is the most common coexisting condition among individuals with anorexia. A major cause of death in relation to co-morbidity is suicide, owing to depression being the most likely psychiatric disorder to accompany both anorexia nervosa and bulimia nervosa. Suicidal thoughts and suicide itself are associated with anorexia nervosa, bulimia nervosa and depression. Cooper (1995) indicates that about half of people with eating disorders have a lifetime history of affective disorders.

Physical health and addiction

People who misuse drugs, alcohol or have an addictive behaviour relating to substances can cause considerable harm to themselves and to society.

This includes physical, social, economic and psychological harms. There are many aspects of addictive behaviours that have an impact on patients' physical health. It is vital that this forms part of the assessment and management process.

In relation to alcohol and drug misuse, the physical health sequelae of substance misuse may be broadly classified into three main areas (source: http://coce.samhsa.gov/cod_resources/PDF/PhysicalHealthQuickFacts.pdf):

- Alcohol and drug misuse as a causal or contributing factor to illness, injury, or the transmission of infectious disease (e.g., cocaine-induced myocardial infarction, substance-related cardio and skeletal myopathy, alcohol induced bone loss, intentional and unintentional injury, poor fetal outcomes, tobacco-related cancers, HIV transmission among drug injectors).
- Alcohol and drug misuse as an exacerbating factor in a non-substance-related illness (e.g., abdominal pain, diabetes, epilepsy, essential hypertension).
- Alcohol and drug misuse as a complicating factor in treatment or patient compliance (e.g., asthma, diabetes, tuberculosis).

The findings in a study by Jones (2004) showed that 74 per cent of the study sample (N = 109) had been given a diagnosis of at least one chronic health problem, and 50 per cent (N = 73) had been given a diagnosis of two or more chronic health problems. Chronic pulmonary illness was the most prevalent (31 per cent incidence) and the most co-morbid. In a study of physical health problems among patients (n = 315) with alcohol use disorders at alcohol treatment agencies in six European cities, Gossop et al., (2007) found that 79 per cent of the sample had at least one problem, and 59 per cent had two or more problems. Gastrointestinal and liver disorders were the most common problems followed by cardiovascular or neurological problems. Older drinkers had more physical health problems although they were less severely alcohol dependent than their younger counterparts.

There are also physical problems associated with cannabis use. The Advisory Council on the Misuse of Drugs (ACMD, 2008) has reported that one of the major short-term risks to physical health posed by cannabis consumption is the impact on blood pressure and heart rate which is similar to that caused by exercise. This can be dangerous for people with coronary artery disease, irregular heart rhythms or high blood pressure, especially if they are not aware of it. When cannabis resin is inhaled with tobacco this increases the risk of bronchitis, emphysema and other respiratory problems (Taylor et al., 2000). Smoking cannabis is associated with an increased risk of chronic bronchitis, potential long-term risk of lung cancer and adverse effects on the reproductive system and reproduction (ACMD, 2008).

Stimulants such as cocaine and amphetamines can cause myocardial infarction, acute myocardial ischemia, arrhythmias, sudden death, and cardiomyopathy. Primarily from the use of needles, the presence of adulterants in the drug and poor nutrition are the problems associated with heroin use. Heroin causes a number of physical problems including arrhythmias, reduced cardiac output and infective endocarditis due to injecting drug use. Heroin use has been associated with both ischaemic (hypoxic and watershed area infarctions particularly) and haemorrhagic stroke, and small scattered lesions have been found in the brains of opiate dependent patients (Neiman et al., 2000). A summary of physical problems is presented in Table 15.3.

Injecting drug users are at high risk of acquiring blood-borne viruses such as HIV and the hepatitis C virus. There has been a rise in the incidence of the hepatitis C virus in England (Judd et al., 2005). Possible explanations for the rising incidence of hepatitis C include changes in patterns of injecting drug use, with greater injection of crack and injecting risk behaviour in newer injecting drug users increasing in the size of the population of injecting drug users over and above any increase in protective interventions.

Table 15.3 Physical problems and addiction

Addiction	Physical/Medical problems
Amphetamine	• Myocardial infarction, acute myocardial ischemia, arrhythmias, sudden death, and cardiomyopathy.
Cocaine	• Myocardial infarction, acute myocardial ischemia, arrhythmias, sudden death, and cardiomyopathy. Exacerbated with concomitant alcohol consumption; cardiomyopathy and arrhythmias can be caused by alcohol abuse alone.
Cannabis	• Risk of bronchitis, emphysema and other respiratory problems. • Low blood pressure. • Increased heart rate. • Adverse effects on reproductive system and reproduction.
Heroin	• Arrhythmias and reduced cardiac output. • Infective endocarditis (injecting drug use).
Alcohol	• Gastrointestinal disorders. • Liver disorders. • Cardiovascular. • Neurological.

Complex needs

Individuals with substance misuse and psychiatric disorders are a vulnerable group of people with complex needs. The national guidance on good practice in dual diagnosis focuses on the complex needs of patients with coexistence of substance misuse and mental health problems (Department of Health, 2002). In addition, to their medical, psychological and/or psychiatric conditions, they have problems relating to social, legal, housing, welfare and 'lifestyle' matters. They are more likely to have a worse prognosis with high levels of service use including emergency clinic and inpatient admissions (McCrone et al., 2000). In summary, the major problems associated with individuals with dual diagnosis are presented in Table 15.4.

In addition to these complex problems and needs, individuals with coexisting psychiatric disorders and addiction suffer from the compounded pressures of stigma, prejudice, institutional racism and ethnocentric intervention strategies. Dual diagnosis patients tend to place a heavy demand on service provision and have been associated with poor outcomes on most measures – housing status, employment status, social functioning and family relationships (Department of Health, 1999). A variety of problems are possible as a result of a dual diagnosis: the withdrawal from alcohol or drugs can mimic or give the appearance of some psychiatric disorders; psychiatric symptoms may be covered up or masked by alcohol or drug use; untreated alcohol and drug dependence can contribute to a reoccurrence of psychiatric

Table 15.4   Problems associated with dual diagnosis

- Increased likelihood of self-harm
- Increased risk of HIV infection
- Increased use of institutional services
- Poor compliance with medication/treatment
- Homelessness
- Increased risk of violence
- Increased risk of victimization/exploitation
- Higher recidivism
- Contact with the criminal justice system
- Family problems
- Poor social outcomes including impact on carers and family
- Denial of substance misuse
- Negative attitudes of health care professionals
- Social exclusion

---

symptoms; and untreated psychiatric disorders can contribute to an alcohol or drug lapse or relapse.

Assessment and management

The accurate assessment and treatment of individuals with dual diagnosis requires time, adequate resources and relevant experience. Drake et al., (1993) described nine principles in the treatment of drug misuse in individuals with dual diagnosis. These principles are applicable in most settings and within a shared care framework. An assessment of substance misuse should form an integral part of standard assessment procedures for mental health problems. Osher and Kofoed (1989) provide a useful framework for utilizing therapeutic interventions with individuals who have coexisting substance misuse and mental health problems. They identified four stages of intervention: engagement, motivation for change (persuasion), active treatment and relapse prevention. Inherent within the stages in the care and treatment of individuals with dual diagnosis are interventions including harm reduction, motivational interviewing, individual cognitive behavioural counselling, lifestyle change, relapse planning and prevention and family education. For a comprehensive account of the application of the four stages of interventions see Rassool (2006).

Engagement is concerned with the development and maintenance of a therapeutic alliance between staff and client. A good practice guideline to promote engagement is found in Rethink and Turning Point (2004). This stage draws upon the principles of Motivational Interviewing to effect change and is contingent upon regular contact and a working alliance between staff and client. In this context, its purpose is to empower the client to gain insight into their problems and to strengthen a client's motivation and commitment to change whilst avoiding confrontation and resistance. A variety of simple techniques (Department of Health, 2002) can be used for this purpose. This stage involves the persuasion of the client of the value and benefits of treatment although it may take a few months before a client is ready to receive active treatment interventions for their substance misuse. Given the relapsing nature of substance misuse it is important once a problem user has reduced their misuse, or become abstinent, to offer interventions aimed at the prevention and management of future relapses.

A number of interventions have been identified for the effective treatment of dual diagnosis but these lack specificity (Department of Health, 2002). The interventions are: integrated treatment, staged interventions, assertive outreach, motivational interventions, individual counselling, social support interventions and a long-term perspective.

Model of care and service provision

Dual diagnosis patients are a heterogeneous population and the demand they make on services poses huge challenges to the models of interventions and health care delivery system. Generally, four models of service provision have been described for the treatment of substance misuse and psychiatric disorders: the serial model, the parallel model, the integrated treatment model and the joint liaison/collaborative approach. The four models of service delivery and the potential problems and difficulties of each model are examined in Rassool (2002).

The National Treatment Agency (2002) suggested the need to work towards an integrated approach by all the relevant services, with one lead service co-ordinating the comprehensive care package. The involvement of service users, families and carers is central in the care planning and treatment process and must not be tokenistic or superficial. The involvement should take place at all stages: in treatment, in the planning, delivery and development of existing services and in the planning and commissioning of future services (Rethink and Turning Point, 2004). Attention also needs to be focused on special populations in relation to dual diagnosis such as black and minority ethnic groups, homelessness, older people (alcohol and tranquillizers), young people and women (Health Advisory Service, 2001). Dual diagnosis is similar to substance misuse in that it is not the sole responsibility of one discipline or specialist. It requires a multi-dimensional approach and involving inter-agency collaboration in the ownership of common goals in meeting the complex physical/medical, social, psychological and spiritual needs of the individual (Rassool, 2006).

Summary of key points

- The term dual diagnosis covers a broad spectrum of mental health and substance misuse problems that an individual might experience concurrently.
- Psychiatric symptoms occur more commonly in drug-related problems and it is difficult to distinguish between the psychiatric symptoms and dual diagnosis.
- The prevalence rate of substance use disorders among individuals with mental health problems ranges from 35 to 60 per cent.
- Anxiety disorders, especially social phobia, and obsessive-compulsive disorders are also common among individuals with eating disorders.
- Individuals with substance misuse and psychiatric disorders are a vulnerable group of people with complex needs and problems.

- Alcohol misusers may have affective disorders (depression), anxiety disorders and psychosis.
- Drug misusers may show symptoms such as mania, psychosis and depression.
- There are many aspects of alcohol and drug misuse that have an impact on patients' physical health.
- In relation to alcohol and drug misuse, the physical health sequelae of substance misuse may be broadly classified into three main areas.
- Gastrointestinal and liver disorders were the most common problems followed by cardiovascular or neurological problems.
- Frequency of drinking, duration of alcohol use disorder, and severity of alcohol dependence are associated with increased physical morbidity.
- A useful framework for utilizing therapeutic interventions identifies four stages of intervention: engagement, motivation for change (persuasion), active treatment and relapse prevention.
- Dual diagnosis, similar to substance misuse, requires a multi-dimensional approach involving inter-agency collaboration.

Reflective activity 15.2

B is a 23 year old, unemployed, female, born in England, but she has spent most of her life in Holland. She first tried smoking cannabis when she was 12 years old with her friends at weekends but she liked it straight away and started smoking every day. She attended school until the age of 12 and was subsequently expelled due to her cannabis use. She had many jobs in her younger days, in shops and catering. She lived with her mother but the relationship is characterized by frequent rows. B says her mum knew she was smoking the drug but she did not try to make her quit. She has a history of depression and has attempted suicide on two occasions. Recently she began to smoke a strong strain of cannabis (white widow). B began to worry when she realized how much the drug was affecting her mental health. She was admitted to an acute unit as a result of her depression and paranoia.

- What would be the immediate interventions required?
- What other withdrawal symptoms or behavioural problems may be observed?
- What are the short-term goals for this patient?
- What are the long-term goals for this patient?
- What treatment interventions and/or strategies may be planned for this patient?

References

Abdulrahim, D. (2001) *Substance Misuse and Mental Health Co-Morbidity (Dual Diagnosis)* (London: The Health Advisory Service).

American Psychiatric Association (APA) (1994) *Diagnostic and Statistical Manual of Mental Disorders*, 4th edn (Washington, DC: American Psychiatric Association).

American Psychological Association (2007) 'Mental Illness and Drug Addiction may Co-occur due to Disturbance in Part of the Brain', *ScienceDaily*, (3 December) date accessed 15 September, 2010, from http://www.sciencedaily.com/releases/2007/12/071203090143.htm.

Banerjee, S., Clancy, C. and Crome, I. (2002) *Co-existing Problems of Mental Disorder and Substance Misuse (Dual Diagnosis)* (London: Royal College of Psychiatrists' Research Unit).

Barnett, J.H, Werners, U., Secher, S. M., Hill, K.E., Brazil, R., Masson, K., Pernet, D.E., Kirkbridge, J.B., Murray, G.K., Bullmore, E.T. and Jones, P.B. (2007) 'Substance Use in a Population-based Clinic Sample of People with First-episode Psychosis', *British Journal of Psychiatry*, 190, 6, 515–20.

Carney, C.P. and Andersen, A.E. (1996) 'Eating Disorders. Guide to Medical Evaluation and Complications', *Psychiatric Clinics of North America*, 19, 4, 657–79.

Connell, P.H. (1958) *Amphetamine Psychosis*, Maudsley Monograph number 5, (London: Oxford University Press).

Cooper, P.J. (1995) 'Eating Disorders and Their Relationship to Mood and Anxiety Disorders', in Brownell, K.D. and Fairburn, C.G. (eds.), *Eating Disorders and Obesity. A Comprehensive Handbook* (New York: Guilford Press) 159–64.

Department of Health (1999) *Effective Care Co-ordination in Mental Health Services: Modernising the Care Programme Approach – A Policy Document* (London: Department of Health).

Department of Health (2002) *Mental Health Policy Implementation Guide Dual Diagnosis Good Practice Guide* (London: Department of Health).

Drake, R.E., Bartels, S.J., Teague, G.B., Noordsy, D.L. and Clark, R.E. (1993) 'Treatment of Substance Abuse in Severely Mentally Ill Patients', *Journal of Nervous and Mental Disease*, 181, 10, 606–11.

Fischer, E.H. and Goethe, J.W. (1998) 'Anxiety and Alcohol Abuse in Patients in Treatment for Depression', *American Journal of Alcohol Abuse* 24, 3, 453–63.

Gossop, M., Mardsen, J. and Steward, D. (1998) *NTORS at One Year: The National Treatment Outcome and Research Study* (London: Department of Health).

Gossop, M., Neto, D., Rasovanovic, M., Batra, A., Toteva, S., Musalek, M., Skutle, A. and Goos, G. (2007) 'Physical Health Problems Among Patients

Seeking Treatment for Alcohol Use Disorders: a Study in Six European Cities', *Addiction Biology*, 12, 2, 190–96. DOI: 10.1111/j.1369-1600.2007.00066.

Harrison, C.A. and Abou Saleh, M.T. (2001) 'Psychiatric Disorders and Substance Misuse: Psychopathology', in Rassool, G.H. (ed.), *Dual Diagnosis: Substance Misuse and Psychiatric Disorders* (Oxford: Blackwell Publications).

Health Advisory Service (2001) *Substance Misuse and Mental Health Co-Morbidity (Dual Diagnosis). Standards for Mental Health Services* (London: Health Advisory Service).

Institute of Alcohol Studies (2007) *Alcohol and Mental Health* (St Ives, Cambs: IAS), http://www.ias.org.uk.

Jones, D.R., Macias, C., Barreira, P.J., Fisher, W.H., Hargreaves, W.A. and Harding, C.M. (2004) 'Prevalence, Severity, and Co-occurrence of Chronic Physical Health Problems of Persons with Serious Mental Illness', *Psychiatric Services*, 55, 11, 1250–57.

Judd, A., Hickman, M., Jones, S., McDonald, T., Parry, J.V., Stimson, G.V. and Hall, A. (2005) 'Incidence of Hepatitis C Virus and HIV Among New Injecting Drug Users in London: Prospective Cohort Study', *British Medical Journal*, 330, 7841, 24–25. Doi: 10.1136/bmj.38286.841227.7C.

MacDonald, A.B., Baker, J.M., Stewart, S.H. and Skinner, M. (2000) 'Effects of Alcohol on the Response to Hyperventilation of Participants High and Low in Anxiety Sensitivity', *Alcoholism: Clinical and Experimental Research* 24, 11, 1656–65.

Mccrone, P., Menezes, P.R., Johnson, S., Scott, H., Thornicroft, G., Marshall, J., Bebbington, P. and Kuipers, E. (2000) 'Service Use and Costs of People with Dual Diagnosis in South London', *Acta Psychiatrica Scandinavica*, 101, 6, 464–72.

Menezes, P., Johnson, S., Thornicroft, G., Marshall, J., Prosser, D., Bebbington, P. and Kuipers, E. (1996) 'Drug and Alcohol Problems Among Individuals with Severe Mental Illnesses in South London', *British Journal of Psychiatry*, 168, 5, 612–19.

Milos, G., Spindler, A., Ruggiero, G., Klaghofer, R. and Schnyder, U. (2002) 'Comorbidity of Obsessive-compulsive Disorders and Duration of Eating Disorders', *International Journal of Eating Disorders*, 31, 3, 284–89.

Mueser, K., Bennett, M. and Kushner, M. (1995) *'Epidemiology of Substance Use Disorders Among Persons with Chronic Mental Illness'* in Lehman, A. and Dixon, L. (eds.), *Double Jeopardy: Chronic mental illness and Substance Use Disorders* (Chur, Switzerland: Harwood Academic).

National Treatment Agency (2002) *Models of Care for Treatment of Adult Drug Users* (London: NTA).

Neeleman, J. and Farrell, M. (1997) 'Suicide and Substance Misuse', *British Journal of Psychiatry*, 175, 303–04.

Neiman, J., Haapaniwmi, H.M. and Hillbom, M. (2000) 'Neurological Complications of Drug Abuse: Pathophysiological Mechanisms', *European Journal of Neurology*, 7, 6, 595–606.

Osher, F.C. and Kofoed, L.L. (1989) 'Treatment of Patients with Psychiatric and Psychoactive Substance Abuse Disorders', *Hospital and Community Psychiatry* 4, 10, 1025–30.

Phillips, P. (2006) 'Problem Drug Use and Personality Disorders', in Rassool, G.H. (ed.), *Dual Diagnosis Nursing* (Blackwell Publishing: Oxford).

Rassool G.H. (2002) *Dual Diagnosis: Substance Misuse and Psychiatric Disorders* (Oxford: Blackwell Publishing).

Rassool, G.H. (2006) 'Understanding Dual Diagnosis', in Rassool, G.H. (ed.), *Dual Diagnosis Nursing* (Blackwell Publishing: Oxford).

Rethink and Turning Point (2004) *Dual Diagnosis Toolkit: Mental Health and Substance Misuse: A Practical Guide for Professionals and Practitioners* (London: Rethink and Turning Point).

Thomas, H. (1993) 'Psychiatric Symptoms in Cannabis Users', *British Journal of Psychiatry* 163, 2, 141–49.

Westen, D. and Harnden-Fischer, J. (2001) 'Personality Profiles in Eating Disorders: Rethinking the Distinction between Axis I and Axis II', *American Journal of Psychiatry*, 158, 4, 547–62.

Williams, H. (2002) 'Dual Diagnosis–An Overview: Fact or Fiction?' in Rassool, G.H. (ed.), *Dual Diagnosis: Substance Misuse and Psychiatric Disorders* (Oxford: Blackwell Publishing).

Williams, R. and Cohen, J. (2000) 'Substance Use and Misuse in Psychiatric Wards: a Model Task for Clinical Governance?' *Psychiatric Bulletin*, 24, 2, 43–46.

Addiction and Harm Reduction

16

Introduction

Reflective activity 16.1

Before reading this chapter, try to provide a true or false answer for each of the statements listed below. Think about some reasons as to why you chose a particular answer.

Statements	True	False
The prevention of alcohol and drug misuse is intended to delay or avoid the onset of substance misuse.		
Primary prevention programmes are aimed mainly at individuals who have been treated for addictive behaviours.		
Secondary prevention programmes are aimed mainly at individuals who are currently being treated for addictive behaviours.		
A tertiary level of prevention seeks to limit and reduce further complications.		
Universal prevention activities may include schools based prevention programmes and selective prevention programmes.		
Rational use of psychoactive substances means that the right drug is taken by the right patient and the right dose is taken for the right duration.		
The goal of health education programmes is to modify addictive behaviours.		
Harm reduction cannot work alongside approaches that aim for reductions in drugs, alcohol and other addictive behaviours.		
Harm reduction approaches aim to encourage those who have addictive behaviour problems to engage in prevention and treatment programmes.		
Engagement in treatment can provide a window of opportunity to minimize harms caused by addictive behaviours.		

Statements	True	False
A comprehensive alcohol policy needs population-level interventions focusing on the availability and accessibility of alcohol and alcohol harm reduction interventions.		
Abstinence-oriented treatment such as nicotine replacement therapy may be a viable option for most smokers.		
There is evidence that needle exchange programmes increased either the number of people using drugs or the frequency of injecting drug use.		
There are online treatment programmes that deal with reducing the harms caused by gambling and internet addiction.		

When you have read this chapter, come back to this activity and consider your answers again. How many did you get right? For those you got wrong, think about the reasons for your original answer and compare this with what you know now.

Public health policies in relation to the increasing trend in addictive behaviours are gaining ground in many countries, as for example, with internet addiction. Prevention and harm reduction increasingly form part of public health policy and are now considered a priority. Various approaches and strategies have been used to prevent addictive activities and addictive behaviours. These approaches include awareness raising programmes, law enforcement approaches (demand and supply prevention), media campaigns, community based health information, school based education, and harm reduction.

Global and national strategy

Globally, the World Health Organization has proposed a universal strategy to promote and support local, regional and global actions to prevent and reduce the harmful use of alcohol (WHO, 2009). The WHO's vision is relevant to all forms of addictive behaviours and activities in the improvement of health and social outcomes for individuals, families and communities. The guiding principles suggested by WHO are also applicable to addictive behaviours in general:

- Prevent and reduce addictive behaviours or activity-related harm (public policies and interventions).
- Policies should be equitable and sensitive to national, religious and cultural contexts.
- Public health should be given proper deference in relation to competing interests and approaches.

- Protection of populations at high risk of harm and economic costs.
- Affordable and effective prevention and care services.

Policies and strategies have been set out in relation to prevention and harm reduction approaches. In England, the government alcohol strategy (Department of Health, 2007) sets out clear goals and actions to promote sensible drinking and reduce the harm that alcohol can cause. It specifically focuses on the minority of drinkers who cause the most harm to themselves, their communities and their families.

The Department of Health and the National Treatment Agency for Substance Misusers report, *Reducing Drug-related Harm: an Action Plan* (2007) sets out the actions to be taken in England to enhance harm reduction activities within the drug treatment sector. The aim is to progressively reduce the number of drug misusers either dying through a drug-related death or contracting blood-borne virus infections. The plan focuses on three key areas: increased surveillance and monitoring; improved needle exchange and drug treatment delivery; and public health campaigns focused upon those most at risk.

The rising prevalence of sexually transmitted infections and of HIV in England has prompted the development of a national strategy on sexual health and HIV for 'better prevention, better services, better sexual health' (Department of Health, 2001). The broad sexual health strategy covers a wider sexual health agenda, including HIV, sexually transmitted infections (STIs) and unintended pregnancies in the areas of prevention, testing, treatment and care, stigma and discrimination.

In relation to gambling, the legislative aims have the same general theme around the world; that is to keep gambling crime free, to protect the vulnerable and to ensure gambling is fair and honest (Department of Social Development, 2010).

Framework and approaches to prevention

A framework of classifying prevention initiatives is based on the universal, selective and indicated prevention programmes. According to this framework, the approaches used in any prevention strategy will depend on the specific aims and intended audience or targeted behaviour/contexts (Mrazek and Haggerty, 1994). That is the strategies are tailor-made and focused on different sectors of the population and the type of prevention activities delivered depend on the specific group.

Activities in the universal prevention domain may include schools based prevention programmes or mass media campaigns, or the target audience may be whole communities, or parents and families but focusing on children and young people. Selective prevention programmes target groups or subsets of the population who may have already started to use drugs or are at an increased risk of developing substance use problems compared to the general population, or both (Edmonds et al., 2005). The prevention programmes are aimed at reducing the influence of the 'risk factors', developing resilience (the protective factors) and preventing addictive behaviours. Indicated prevention programmes (harm reduction) target those exhibiting problematic addictive behaviours which require specialist interventions.

From a public health perspective, prevention activities have been viewed as existing on three levels: (a) primary, (b) secondary and (c) tertiary prevention. Primary prevention is a process that includes efforts to reduce the demand and stop the occurrence of illegal drug use, any drinking behaviour or tobacco smoking (Rassool, 2009a). This may also include preventing vulnerable individuals from developing into problem gamblers or developing internet addiction or eating disorders. The goal of primary prevention stategy is to prevent or delay the onset of addictive behaviours and reduce their associated harms. In addition, it reduces susceptibility and exposure to risk factors by promoting factors such as resilience. It is targeted towards the non-using population but also towards experimental, recreational, dependent and high risk users. For example, the findings of a primary prevention programme to prevent and reduce the use of psychoactive substances and related problems among young people showed that positive outcomes manifested across the evaluation sites regarding psychoactive substance use-related issues among young people (WHO, 2007).

Secondary prevention is the prevention of the harm caused as a consequence of the addictive activities. It identifies risks, reduces harms and treats problems in the early stages of their development. The harm reduction approach has been widely implemented as a response to the threat presented, for example, by blood-borne viruses such as HIV and hepatitis infections. Examples include the rational use of prescribed medication, health information on safer alcohol and drug use, safer sexual practices, controlled social gambling, appropriate use of the Internet or video gaming. The aim of the tertiary level of prevention is to restore the individual to an optimal level of functioning and prevent relapse. In particular, tertiary prevention involves actual treatment and is conducted primarily by specialist services (residential and community facilities).

What is harm reduction?

Harm reduction approaches recognize that many of those with addictive behaviours lack the readiness to change, to remain abstinent or to be free from the substance or activity but nonetheless could benefit from harm reduction. Harm reduction is a humanistic approach to diminishing the individual and social

Table 16.1   Benefits and limitations of the harm reduction approach

Advantages	Disadvantages
• Addiction free society is unrealistic.	• Provides a disguise for pro-legalization efforts.
• Is a pragmatic public health approach.	• Encourages illegal use of psychoactive substances.
• Complements approaches that aim for reductions in drug, alcohol and tobacco consumption and other addictive behaviours.	• Encourages addictive behaviours.
• Engages people and motivates them to make contact with services.	• Discourages addicts from attaining abstinence.
• Reduces harm caused by addiction.	• Undercuts abstinence-oriented treatment programmes.
• Promotes controlled use of addiction behaviours and activities.	
• Avoids moralistic, stigmatizing and judgmental statements.	
• Reduces accidental death and overdose and saves lives (alcohol, drug, tobacco use).	
• Reduces the transmission of blood-borne infections.	

harms associated with drug use, especially the risk of HIV infection (OSI, 2001). Harm reduction means trying to reduce the harm that people do to themselves, or other people, from their addictive behaviours. It can be contrasted with primary prevention which tries to stop people using alcohol/drug or involvement in addictive behaviours in the first place or to stop their addictive activities if they have already started. A more comprehensive definition, in relation to drug misuse, refers to an approach aimed directly at reducing the number of drug-related deaths and blood-borne virus infections, with wider goals of preventing drug misuse and of encouraging stabilization in treatment and support for abstinence (Department of Health/NTA, 2007). The benefits and limitations of harm reduction approaches are presented in Table 16.1.

Principles of harm reduction

The principles of harm reduction (Harm Reduction Coalition) have been modified to include the following:

• The understanding and acceptance that addiction to substance and activities is a part of our society;

- Addictive behaviours are a complex and multi-faceted phenomenon that encompasses a continuum of behaviours;
- Focusing on the harmful effects of addiction rather than ignoring or condemning them;
- Affirms that those with addictive behaviours are themselves the primary agents of reducing the harms of their addiction;
- Approach those who are addicted with a non-judgmental approach and provide a non-coercive provision of services;
- Recognizes that the realities of poverty, class, racism, social isolation, past trauma, sex-based discrimination and other social inequalities affect both people's vulnerability to, and capacity for effectively dealing with, substance-related harm.
- The principles also include an awareness of the harms and dangers associated with addiction.

An important aspect of harm reduction is its focus on public health, which has improved co-operation between the health, social, criminal justice system and law enforcement agencies (Rassool, 2009b). Harm reduction must be carried out in a public health framework and one in which the health, human rights and social needs of drug users, their families and communities are met (Cabinet Office, 2005).

Good practice in harm reduction

Harm reduction uses a range of service provision and delivery to achieve its goals. The service provisions should be accessible and flexible in meeting the needs of the patients with addictive problems. A range of interventions include assessment, health care, counselling, psychosocial interventions, relapse prevention, pharmacological interventions, needle exchange, blood-borne virus testing and treatment pathways. In relation to reducing drug-related harm, needle exchanges and methadone substitution therapy treatment are two of the most effective interventions.

In order to develop good practice in harm reduction, Hando et al., (1999) suggests the following key principles should be adopted:

- Comprehensive – considering the full range of social influences and institutions on use.
- Sustainable.
- Clearly targeted, particularly regarding age and stage of drug use.
- Developmentally appropriate and culturally sensitive.
- Based on research knowledge and use of sound methods.

- Clear objectives.
- Reduce risk factors and increase protective factors.
- Evaluated for both positive and negative effects.

A study by the National Treatment Agency (NTA, 2008) highlights the good practice in harm reduction by identifying good practice in interventions to reduce drug-related harm related to blood-borne viruses and overdose. One of the key factors influencing good practice in harm reduction is that harm reduction is embedded in the service provision and delivery. The findings also showed that prompt and flexible access to good drug treatment was essential to harm reduction, which in turn forms an integral part of a client's care plan. Implicit in the delivery of this service is the involvement of service users in the planning, delivery and development of harm reduction services. The findings also stress that the delivery of a range of interventions in pharmacies, including: distributing injecting equipment and other injecting paraphernalia; pharmacy staff referring clients to appropriate specialist harm reduction services; and drug workers working in pharmacies to provide brief harm reduction interventions. In addition, the service provisions also have a strategy for reducing drug-related overdose deaths, usually as part of the harm reduction strategy and the development of competent staff.

Public health interventions

Public health interventions, in the context of addictive behaviours, include screening, outreach, case-finding, referral and follow-up, case management, health teaching, counselling, advocacy and social marketing.

On an individual basis, health promotion materials may be used to assist in reducing demand for psychoactive substances through the promotion of healthy lifestyles and suitable alternatives. In order to complement health promotion materials, provision of advice and brief interventions have been found to be effective. However, in terms of media campaigns, successful techniques used by commercial marketers, termed 'social marketing' are being introduced. Rather than dictating the way that information is to be conveyed from the top-down, public health professionals are learning to listen to the needs and desires of the target audience themselves, and work on building the program from there (Weinreich, 2006).

Kotler et al., (1971) define social marketing as 'differing from other areas of marketing only with respect to the objectives of the marketer and his or her organization. Social marketing seeks to influence social behaviours not to benefit the marketer, but to benefit the target audience and the general society'. Social marketing utilizes commercial marketing principles and technologies designed to influence the knowledge, attitudes, values, beliefs, behaviours, and lifestyles of the general population and those who are at risk of developing addictive behaviours. The guidance for helping people to change their health-related knowledge, attitudes and behaviour at population and community levels has been published by the National Institute of Clinical Excellence (NICE, 2007).

Sexual behaviour is a major factor determining the transmission of HIV and the prevention of poor sexual health depends on everyone having the information, skills and services that they need in order to make informed choices. Some 'higher risk' groups include young people (in or out of care), black and minority ethnic groups, gay and bisexual men, injecting drug misusers, adults and children living with HIV, sex workers and people in prisons and youth offending establishments who need targeted sexual health information and HIV/STI prevention. In relation to hepatitis, the goals of prevention are to lower the incidence of acute hepatitis C and reduce the disease burden from chronic hepatitis infection. These are achieved by the education of health care professionals and the public at large on the dangers of hepatitis C. There is also a need to focus on those who are at risk, for example, injecting drug users by the provision of health information, harm reduction and counseling.

However, a workable strategy means implementing prevention strategies that include educating young people about the harmful effects of drugs, blood-borne viruses and sexual health education, involving the community in recreational activities, educating the community in stress reduction and coping skills, outreach programmes, harm reduction initiatives and mass media campaigns.

Harm reduction: alcohol

The updated government alcohol strategy (Department of Health, 2007) sets out clear goals and actions to promote sensible drinking and reduce the harm that alcohol can cause. It specifically focuses on the minority of drinkers who cause the most harm to themselves, their communities and their families.

Alcohol harm reduction can be broadly defined as targeted measures that aim to reduce the negative consequences of drinking rather than focusing on the overall consumption of alcohol (IHRA, 2007). It is a strategy that has the aim of reducing the negative consequences of problem drinking or binge drinking. A comprehensive alcohol policy needs population-level interventions, which focus on the availability and accessibility of alcohol (such as taxation and restricted licensing hours) and alcohol harm reduction interventions (IHRA, 2007).

Harm reduction offers a pragmatic approach to alcohol consumption and alcohol-related problems based on three core objectives (Marlatt and Witkiewitz, 2002):

- To reduce harmful consequences associated with alcohol use.
- To provide an alternative to zero-tolerance approaches by incorporating drinking goals (abstinence or moderation) that are compatible with the needs of the individual.
- To promote access to services by offering low-threshold alternatives to traditional alcohol prevention and treatment.

The focus of harm reduction strategies are on reducing high risk behaviours such as drinking and driving, binge drinking and the use of alcohol in pregnancy. These approaches have broadened the sphere of interest in alcohol-related harms to include social nuisance and public order problems (IHRA, 2007).

Examples of alcohol harm reduction in practice include (IHRA, 2007):

- 'Designated driver' schemes to reduce drinking and driving.
- Improving public transport in the evenings to reduce drinking and driving.
- Serving alcohol in shatterproof glass or plastic in order to prevent injuries.
- Training bar staff to serve alcohol responsibly.
- Promoting the safer design of drinking environments (such as bars).
- Brief interventions advising people on moderate or controlled drinking.
- Providing shelters for homeless drinkers (known as 'Wet Centres').
- Providing shelters for heavily intoxicated individuals (known as 'Sobering-Up Centres').

The key to the prevention and minimization of harm related to high risk alcohol use is the provision of health education and promotion. There is ample evidence to suggest that harm reduction approaches to alcohol problems are at least as effective as abstinence-oriented approaches at reducing alcohol consumption and alcohol-related consequences (Marlatt and Witkiewitz, 2002). Based on these findings, the authors suggested that harm reduction efforts seek to meet the individual where he or she is at and assist that person in the direction of positive behaviour change, whether that change involves abstinence, moderate drinking, or the reduction of alcohol-related harm.

Harm reduction: drugs

Harm reduction programmes in relation to drug misuse include information about safer drug use and safer sex, needle exchanges schemes (pharmacy-based needle exchange or other forms of needle exchange), programmes to reduce the risk associated with HIV and hepatitis and the supervision of the consumption of methadone or other opiate substitutes.

The harm reduction advice about safer drug use concerns safer places and methods of taking drugs, the prevention of risks and hygiene associated with injecting and the mixing of drugs with alcohol and other psychoactive substances. The harm reduction advice about safer drug use is presented in Table 16.2.

Table 16.2 Safer drug use

Safer places to use drugs	• Taking drugs with friends is safer than doing it alone. • Avoid using drugs in isolated places (e.g. toilets, derelict buildings, canal banks, railway lines).
Safer methods of taking drugs	• Swallowing, smoking or inhaling drugs is safer than injecting.
Injecting drugs is more risky because of	• Overdose • Infection • Abscesses • Blood Clots (Thromboses) • Blood Poisoning (Septicaemia) • Gangrene • Death.
If you intend to inject drugs	• Help and advice is available from your local needle and syringe exchange. • It is safer not to inject. • It is more dangerous to inject in big veins like the groin or neck.
Sharing needles, syringes, filters, spoons and water should always be avoided to reduce the risk of HIV, hepatitis B and C transmission.	• Ask your GP about hepatitis B vaccination. • Do not use other people's 'wash outs'. • It is not just the needle that's dangerous, it is everything used for injecting that could pass on the virus.
Hygiene	• It is very important when injecting drugs – always remember to use clean, preferably new, equipment and make sure your hands and the injection site are clean.
Mixing drugs	• Avoid cocktails of drugs – mixing drugs makes it more difficult to predict what will happen and for how long.
Combining alcohol and drugs	• Can lead to respiratory depression. • May choke on your vomit. • Accidental overdoses and deaths.

Source: Adapted from 'Problem Drug Use: a Guide to Management in General Practice' Nottingham Alcohol and Drug Team, The Wells Road Centre, Nottingham, NG3 3AA.

Table 16.3   Harm reduction and injecting drug users

Safer injecting use	Method of cleaning injecting equipment
• Always inject with the blood flow. • Rotate injection sites. • Use sterile new injecting equipment, with the smallest-bore needle possible. • Avoid neck, groin, breast, feet and hand veins. • Mix powders with sterile water and filter solution before injecting. • Always dispose of equipment safely (either in a bin provided or by placing the needle inside the syringe and placing both inside a drink can). • Avoid injecting into infected areas. • Do not inject into swollen limbs, even if the veins appear to be distended. • Poor veins indicate a poor technique. Try to see what is going wrong. • Do not inject on your own. • Learn basic principles of first aid and cardiopulmonary resuscitation in order that you may help friends at times of crisis.	1. Pour bleach into one cup (or bottle) and water into another. 2. Draw bleach up with the dirty needle and syringe. 3. Expel bleach into sink. 4. Repeat steps 2 and 3. 5. Draw water up through needle and syringe. 6. Expel water into sink. 7. Repeat steps 5 and 6 at least two or three times.

Source: Department of Health (1999) Drug Misuse and Dependence – Guidelines on Clinical Management (London: HMSO).

The focus of harm reduction involves drawing attention to technique-specific hazards (related to the technology of injecting and sharing of equipment) (Rassool, 2009b). The procedure of safer injecting and methods of cleaning injecting equipment are presented in Table 16.3.

Reducing drug overdose

The high prevalence of mortality amongst substance misusers from overdose and blood-borne viruses led to a number of harm reduction strategies. The aim of the report *Reducing Drug-Related Harm: An Action Plan* (Department of Health and National Treatment Agency for Substance Misuse) (2007) is to limit the number of drug misusers dying from drug-related causes or contracting blood-borne virus infections. Drug-related deaths are defined as 'Deaths where the underlying cause is poisoning, drug abuse, or drug dependence and where any of the substances are controlled under the Misuse of Drugs Act (1971)' (ONS, 2003). The Advisory Council on the Misuse of Drugs (ACMD, 2000, xi, 6), report on *Reducing Drug-Related Deaths* highlighted their concern about this issue and acknowledged that the prevention of drug-related deaths is a matter of pressing urgency.

An overdose is 'an event in which a person intentionally or accidentally ingests one or more psychoactive substances at unsafe levels, leading to physical trauma, which may require immediate medical care to reverse and manage symptoms and other complications' (NTA, 2002). In a prospective study of mortality among drug misusers, Gossop et al., (2002) found that the majority of deaths (68 per cent) were associated with drug overdoses. Opiates were the drugs most commonly detected during post-mortem examinations. In the majority of cases, more than one drug was detected. Poly-drug use and, specifically, heavy drinking, and the use of benzodiazepines and amphetamines, were identified as risk factors for mortality. The use of antidepressants amongst polysubstance users has also been found to heighten the risk of fatality (Oyefeso et al., 2000).

There are several risk factors that are reported to be associated with an increased likelihood of overdose. The multiple risk factors include: administration by injection; concomitant use of other depressant drugs; loss of tolerance after a period of abstinence; injecting in public places (which may be associated with the use of untested drugs) or solitary drug use; a long history of opiate dependence; older age; and possibly unexpected changes in purity (EMCDDA, 2003). Drug overdose is the most common method of suicide amongst substance misusers and the likelihood of overdose is increased when drugs are taken by injection and fatal overdose (immediate death) is particularly associated with injecting opioid users (Oyefeso et al., 1999).

Substance misusers are at higher risk of suicide than the general population, and prescribed drugs, notably antidepressants and methadone, heighten that risk. The misuse of a combination of psychoactive substances such as benzodiazepines and alcohol with opiates or combining heroin with cocaine as a 'speedball' can increase the chances of an overdose. There are some general principles concerning interventions for individuals who take a drug overdose and in any settings, emergency treatment should begin immediately. The priority is treating life-threatening problems such as respiratory depression, airway obstruction, cardiovascular collapse and convulsions (epileptic-form seizures) alongside specific measures to treat the overdose.

Rational use of psychoactive substances

According by the World Health Organization (WHO, 2004a), irrational use is the use of psychoactive substances that does not conform to good clinical practice. Irrational prescribing may be regarded as 'pathological' prescribing, where the criteria in the process of prescribing are not fulfilled. For example, extravagant prescribing, over-prescribing, incorrect prescribing, multiple prescribing, indiscriminate uses of injections and under-prescribing of medication of hypno-sedative drugs and antibiotics.

The over-prescribing and irrational use of psychoactive substances has led to an increasing consumption of psychoactive substances resulting in both psychological and physical dependence. Many of the prescribed psychoactive drugs such as hypnotics, sedatives and tranquillizers are frequently the subject of irresponsible prescribing and widespread misuse. Many medications contain alcohol, hallucinogenic compounds and narcotics such as codeine which can be addictive. The availability and accessibility of medications over the Internet has highlighted the need to be vigilant in public health education about the use of psychoactive substances and other drugs (Rassool, 2005). In the context of this chapter, the term rational use means that the right drug is taken by the right patient, in the right dose and for the right duration of therapy, and that the risks of therapy are acceptable (WHO, 1989).

The process of rational prescribing and the rational use of drugs includes assessing the health care needs of the patient (making a diagnosis); planning and setting goals for care; administering and monitoring the effects of medications; providing patient education and discharge planning; interdisciplinary collaboration; evaluating desired and adverse effects of medications and documenting the process (Rassool, 2005). Harm reduction interventions include counselling, relaxation and other therapies which may be an alternative to medication of psychoactive substances.

Harm reduction: tobacco

Tobacco harm reduction describes actions taken to lower the health risks associated with using tobacco or nicotine. A very important part of tobacco harm reduction is simply educating people about the risks of different sources of nicotine (tobaccoharmreduction.org). Tobacco harm reduction is a policy or strategy for tobacco users who cannot or will not stop which explicitly includes the continued use of tobacco or nicotine and is designed to reduce the detrimental health effects of tobacco use (IHRA, 2006). According to IHRA (2006), examples of harm reduction interventions could include using potentially reduced-exposure products (PREPs), reducing consumption, switching to long-term nicotine replacement therapy (NRT), switching to smokeless tobacco products, and using replacement products for temporary abstinence.

The technological innovation has produced electronic cigarettes. Some electronic cigarettes (or e-cigarettes) look exactly like regular cigarettes or cigars; others look more like pens (tobaccoharmreduction.org). Electronic cigarettes are battery powered, and create their effect by vaporizing nicotine which is dissolved in a solution of water and propylene glycol (minus the nicotine). The result is something that feels somewhat like smoke in the mouth and lungs but without involving any real smoke, tobacco or combustion. This e-cigarette fog (or vapour) dissipates rapidly, and leaves little scent in the air or on clothing (tobaccoharmreduction.org).

Harm reduction: gambling and internet addiction

Currently, there are limited harm reduction approaches in the management of addictive behaviours such as gambling and internet addiction. However, there are online programmes that deal with reducing the harms caused by these addictive behaviours. The same framework used for alcohol and drug misuse can be adapted in reducing the harms caused. The harm reduction model would be based on particular addictive activity and tailored for a particular individual. This may include psychosocial interventions such as individual, group, family therapy and counselling. For example, adult gamblers or those with internet addiction learn to develop skills, insight, and goals for the real world. In addition, they are taught coping skills such as how to regain control of their behaviours, set appropriate limits and improve their relationships with their family or significant others. In fact, the whole immediate family is educated about the nature of gaming or internet addiction and the difficulties faced when addicted gamers or internet abusers go through withdrawal and then struggle to learn how to live well in the real world. Relationship building is the primary focus of the intervention strategy.

Controlled gambling programmes are intended for individuals who are at mild or moderate risk of developing gambling problems. They are not generally targeted towards problem or pathological gamblers. Controlled gambling programmes provide information and practical strategies to help participants moderate their gambling behaviour (i.e., in terms of time and money spent on gambling activities), offering them a choice that includes, but is not limited to, abstinence (Robson et al., 2006).

Harm reduction: HIV and blood-borne infections

In the context of HIV and other blood-borne diseases, harm reduction strategies aim to reduce the health and social harms of drug injecting and prevent HIV transmission among injecting drug users (IDUs). Among injecting drug users, cocaine use is strongly associated with more frequent needle sharing, increased sexual risk-taking and a higher HIV sero-prevalence. In contrast, rates of needle sharing amongst methamphetamine users appear comparable to those seen amongst opioid injectors. The ability of psycho-stimulant drugs to increase libido enhances the risk of sexual disease transmission among this group.

A core package of interventions including exchange syringe schemes, methadone maintenance, hepatitis vaccination, safer sexual practice, sexual health, access to drug and HIV services. Prevention of HIV transmission among injecting drug users (IDUs) can best be achieved by implementing a core package of interventions including exchange syringe schemes, methadone maintenance, hepatitis vaccination, safer sexual practice, sexual health, access to drug and HIV treatment and clinical and home-based care (Cabinet Office, 2005). A comprehensive list of interventions in the prevention of HIV is provided in Table 16.4.

Patients entering harm reduction or drug treatment services are offered tests for hepatitis A, B and C, HIV, or sexually transmitted infections if appropriate or required. The issues of blood-borne viruses are usually raised by staff at the initial assessment, or as soon as possible afterwards and the offer of pre-test and post-test counselling (NTA, 2008). For the actual testing, the services reported a mixture of oral swab testing and blood testing for hepatitis and offering hepatitis A and B vaccinations. Some services have developed hepatitis support groups, not specifically for drug users with hepatitis C, but that would be of great benefit to all patients going through hepatitis treatment, enabling them to discuss a range of issues, including difficulties (such as depression) they are experiencing with the treatment (NTA, 2008).

Table 16.4   Prevention of HIV among IDUs: core package
of interventions

• Availability of and referral to a variety of drug treatment options.	• Prevention and treatment of other sexually transmitted infections (STIs).
• Substitution therapy such as methadone maintenance therapy.	• Voluntary confidential counselling and HIV testing (VCT).
• Sterile needle and syringe access and disposal programmes.	• Access to AIDS treatment for injecting drug users.
• Outreach programmes and community-based interventions.	• Provision of information, advice and education about HIV, other diseases, and sexual and reproductive health.
• Primary health care, such as hepatitis B vaccinations, abscess and vein care.	• Access to affordable clinical and home-based care, essential legal and social services, psychosocial support and counselling services.
• Prevention of sexual transmission among drug users and their partners, including access to condoms.	

Source: Adapted from Cabinet Office (2005).

Needle exchange schemes

The World Health Organization (2004b) report stated there is evidence to suggest that providing access to and encouraging utilization of sterile needles and syringes for people who inject drugs is now generally considered to be a fundamental component of any comprehensive and effective HIV prevention programme. Other studies have also found that increasing injecting equipment supply through syringe 'exchange' and other means:

- Reduces hepatitis B and C viruses and other blood-borne pathogens among injecting drug users (Hagan et al., 1995).
- Reduces the number of used needles discarded in the community (Doherty et al., 2000).
- Does not encourage injecting drug use; does not increase the duration or frequency of injecting; and does not decrease motivation to reduce drug use (Stimson et al., 1998).
- Are cost effective and deliver substantial savings in HIV treatment (cited in UK Harm Reduction Alliance).
- Are often the only contact injecting drug users have with health and social service providers (cited in UK Harm Reduction Alliance).

In order to prevent continuing blood-borne viral spread, and in particular the risk of a widespread HIV epidemic amongst injectors, users must have access to a full range of injecting equipment and items of paraphernalia (UK Harm Reduction Alliance). Syringe exchange schemes provide paraphernalia (syringe, citric and vitamin C sachets, water ampoules, stericups, and sterifilts), educational resources (for example, safer drug use, safer sexual practice, overdose, first aid) and health interventions to enable injecting drug users to protect themselves and their communities through safer injection practices and harm reduction methods. In some countries, there is the provision of syringe dispensing machines and mobile vans as part of the needle exchange schemes. A more recent technological innovation is the 'Nevershare syringe' designed for injecting drug users with plungers in a range of colours to reduce accidental sharing, and syringes with retracting needles.

Summary of key points

- Promoting and educating about health issues has emerged as an integral part of public health policy.
- Prevention activities have been viewed as existing on three levels: primary, secondary and tertiary prevention.

- Harm reduction means trying to reduce the harm that people do to themselves, or other people, from their addictive behaviours.
- One of the key factors influencing good practice in harm reduction is that harm reduction is embedded in service provision and delivery.
- The harm reduction approach to drugs is based on a strong commitment to public health and human rights.
- Harm reduction focuses on safer drug use and safer sexual practice.
- Harm reduction programmes include supervised consumption of methadone or other opiate substitutes and needle exchange schemes (pharmacy-based needle exchange or other forms of needle exchange).
- Public health interventions, in the context of addictive behaviours, include screening, outreach, case-finding, referral and follow-up, case management, health teaching, counselling, advocacy and social marketing.
- A comprehensive alcohol policy needs population-level interventions, which focus on the availability and accessibility of alcohol and alcohol harm reduction interventions.
- Currently, tobacco harm reduction strategy is based on supply and demand reduction strategies.
- In the context of HIV and other blood-borne diseases, harm reduction strategies aim to reduce the health and social harms of drug injecting.
- Harm reduction approaches also focus on controlled gambling and internet use.

Reflective activity 16.2

- What should a harm reduction programme for addictive substances include?
- What are the principles of harm reduction?
- Discuss the advantages and limitations of harm reduction for non-pharmacological addictive behaviours.
- Identify the hierarchy of goals for addictive substances.

References

ACMD (Advisory Council on the Misuse of Drugs) (2000) *Reducing Drugs-related Deaths*. A report by the Advisory Council on the Misuse of Drugs (London: The Stationery Office).

Cabinet Office (2005) *Harm Reduction Tackling Drug Use and HIV in the Developing World* (London: Department for International Development).

Department of Health (2007) *Safe. Sensible. Social. The Next Steps in the National Alcohol Strategy* (London: Department of Health).

Department of Health and National Treatment Agency for Substance Misuse (2007) *Reducing Drug-related Harm: An Action Plan* (London: Department of Health).

Department of Social Development (2010) Gambling Review Northern Ireland: Review of the Literature on Gambling Legislation in Great Britain, Ireland (North and South) and Other National Jurisdictions with Additional Reference to Economic and Social Factors. www.dsdni.gov.uk, date accessed 16 September 2010.

Doherty, M.C., Junge, B., Rathouz, P., Garfein, R.S., Riley, E. and Vlahov, D. (2000) 'The Effect of a Needle Exchange Program on Numbers of Discarded Needles: A 2-year Follow-up', *American Journal of Public Health* 90, 6, 936–39.

Edmonds, K., Sumnall, H., McVeigh, J. and Bellis, M.A. (2005) *Drug Prevention Among Vulnerable Young People* (Liverpool: The National Collaborating Centre for Drug Prevention [NCCDP]).

European Monitoring Centre for Drugs and Drug Addiction (2003) *Annual Report 2003: The State of the Drugs Problem in the European Union and Norway* (Lisbon: EMCCDA).

Gambling Commission (2008) Licence Conditions and Codes of Practice, October. www.gamblingcommission.gov.uk, date accessed 12 January 2010.

Hagan, H., Des Jarlais, D.C., Friedman, S.R., Purchase, D. and Alter, M.J. (1995) 'Reduced Risk of Hepatitis B and Hepatitis C Among Injection Drug Users in the Tacoma Syringe Exchange Program', *American Journal of Public Health*, 85, 11, 1531–37.

Hando, J., Hall, W., Rutter, S. and Dolan, K. (1999) *Current State of Research on Illicit Drugs in Australia* (Canberra: NH and MRC).

Harm Reduction Coalition. *Principles of Harm Reduction*, http://www.harmreduction.org/section.php?id = 62, date accessed 20 February 2010.

IHRA (2006) Tobacco Harm Reduction. http://www.ihra.net/, date accessed 24 March 2010.

IHRA (2007) *What is Alcohol Harm Reduction*. www.ihra.net, date accessed 13 March 2010.

Kotler, P. and Zaltman, G. (1971) 'Social Marketing: An Approach to Planned Social Change', *Journal of Marketing*, 35, 3–12.

Marlatt, G.A. and Witkiewitz, K. (2002) 'Harm Reduction Approaches to Alcohol Use: Health Promotion, Prevention, and Treatment', *Addictive Behaviors* 27, 8, 867–86.

Mrazek, P.J. and Haggerty, R.J. (1994) *Reducing Risks for Mental Disorders: Frontiers for Preventive Intervention Research* (Washington DC: National Academy Press).

National Institute of Clinical Excellence (NICE) (2007) *Behaviour Change*, (London: NICE). www.nice.org.uk/PH006/, date accessed 10 December 2009.

NTA (2008) *Good Practice in Harm Reduction* (London: National Treatment Agency).

Office for National Statistics (2003) 'Deaths Related to Drug Poisoning: Results for England and Wales, 1993 to 2001', *Health Statistics Quarterly* (Spring).

OSI (2001) *What is Harm Reduction?* http://www.soros.org/initiatives/health/focus/ihrd/articles_publications/articles/what_20010101, date accessed 15 April 2010.

Oyefeso, A., Ghodse, A.H., Clancy, C. and Corkery, J.M. (1999) 'Suicide Among Drug Addicts in the UK', *British Journal of Psychiatry*, 175, 277–82.

Oyefeso, A., Valmana, A., Clancy, C., Ghodse, A.H. and Williams, H. (2000) 'Fatal Antidepressant Overdose Among Drug Abusers and Non-drug Abusers', *Acta Psychiatrica Scandinavia*, 102, 4, 295–99.

Rassool, G.H. (2005) 'Nursing Prescription: The Rational Use of Psychoactive Substances', *Nursing Standard* 19, 21, 45–51.

Rassool, G.H. (2009a) 'Prevention and Health Education Approaches to Substance Misuse', in Rassool, G.H. (ed.), *Alcohol and Drug Misuse: A Handbook for Students and Health Professionals* (Oxford: Routledge).

Rassool, G.H. (2009b) 'Harm Reduction Approach', in Rassool, G.H. (ed.), *Alcohol and Drug Misuse: A Handbook for Students and Health Professionals* (Oxford: Routledge).

Robson, E., Edwards, J., Smith, G. and Newman, S. (November 2006) Investigating the Efficacy of the Gambling Decisions Program in Three Alberta Communities. Report of the one-year community trial (Edmonton, AB: Capital Health, Public Health).

Stimson, G.V., Alldritt, L.J., Dolan, K.A., Donoghoe, M.C. and Lart, R.A (1998) Injecting Equipment Exchange Schemes Final Report. Monitoring Research Group, University of London, Goldsmiths College.

Tobaccoharmreduction.org (2010) Harm reduction: concepts and practices. http://www.tobaccoharmreduction.org/faq/harmreduction.htm, date accessed 15 April 2010.

UK Harm Reduction Alliance (2010) (Reducing Injecting Related Harm: Consensus Statement on Best Practice. http://www.ukhra.org/Resources/best_practice_v1.pdf, date accessed 20 March 2010.

Weinreich, N.K. (2006) *What is Social Marketing?* http://www.social-marketing.com/Whatis.html, date accessed 10 March 2010.

World Health Organization (1989) *Report of the WHO Meeting on Nursing/Midwifery Education in the Rational Use of Psychoactive Drugs.* DMP/PND/89.5, (Geneva, WHO).

World Health Organization (2004a) *Promoting Rational Drug Use*. A CD–Rom Training Programme in collaboration with Boston University School of Public and International Health, (Geneva: WHO).

World Health Organization (2004b) *Effectiveness of Sterile Needle and Syringe Programming in Reducing HIV/AIDS Among Injecting Drug Users*, Geneva: WHO. http://www.who.int/hiv/pub/prev_care/en/effectivenesssterileneedle. pdf, date accessed 26 March 2009.

WHO Mental Health: Evidence and Research Team and Management of Substance Abuse Team Department of Mental Health and Substance Abuse (2007) *Outcome Evaluation Summary Report: WHO/UNODC Global Initiative (1999–2003) on Primary Prevention of Substance Abuse* (Geneva: WHO).

WHO (2009) *Strategies to Reduce the Harmful Use of Alcohol: Draft Global Strategy*, Report by the Secretariat, EXECUTIVE BOARD EB126/13, 126th Session, Provisional agenda item 4.10, http://apps.who.int/gb/ebwha/pdf_files/ EB126/B126_13-en.pdf, date accessed 10 March 2010.

Special Populations and Diversity **17**

Introduction

Reflective activity 17.1

Before reading this chapter, try to provide a true or false answer for each of the statements listed below. Think about some reasons as to why you chose a particular answer.

Statements	True	False
The psychoactive substances misused by Black and minority ethnic groups are different from those used by the white population.		
Drug misuse is increasingly being reported amongst young Black and minority ethnic women.		
South Asians do not use opiates and cocaine.		
Injecting drug use behaviour is largely uncommon among Black and minority ethnic groups.		
People from Black and minority ethnic groups are more likely to be diagnosed with mental health problems.		
Women's alcohol consumption, particularly in younger and older women has been increasing over the last few decades.		
The most serious outcome of maternal drinking during pregnancy are fetal alcohol spectrum disorders (FASD).		
Smoking during pregnancy not only harms a woman's health, but can lead to pregnancy complications and serious health problems in newborns.		
The blood-borne viruses such as HIV, hepatitis B and C are transmitted from mother to baby.		
Women who misuse alcohol or drugs face a variety of barriers including barriers to treatment entry, to engagement in treatment and long-term rehabilitation.		

Statements	True	False
Substance misuse in young people should be considered in the context of 'normal' adolescent risk-taking behaviours and experimentation.		
Alcohol and drug misuse in elderly people are a common but under-recognized problem.		
Recent research has highlighted that the over-60s are drinking more alcohol than other age groups.		
Benzodiazepine dependence can be more problematic among elderly persons.		
Levels of use of cannabis, amphetamine and ecstasy are high amongst homeless people.		

When you have read this chapter, come back to this activity and consider your answers again. How many did you get right? For those you got wrong, think about the reasons for your original answer and compare this with what you know now.

This chapter addresses the contemporary issues of those with special needs and the needs of the diverse populations. Given the growing diversity within the UK population, health, social care and criminal justice agencies will need to evolve culturally competent systems if they are to meet the needs of the population in integrated service delivery systems. In the context of this chapter, those with special needs include groups such as ethnic minorities, young people, women, elderly and the homeless who have addictive behaviour problems. In addition carers and families are increasingly being recognized as a significant factor in addressing challenging social and behavioural problems. The carers and family members need to be supported. The order of presentation in no way reflects the priorities that should be accorded to any individual group.

Black and ethnic minority communities

Black and ethnic minorities are a heterogeneous population within a diverse cultural entity, with a wide variation in lifestyle, health behaviour, religion and language. In England people from minority ethnic groups made up nine per cent of the total population compared with only two per cent in both Scotland and Wales. Much of the impetus for current government policy that impacts on Black and ethnic minority communities comes from the need to provide accessible substance misuse services (Rassool, 2009). There is wide recognition of the failure of Black and ethnic minority drug users to utilize the range of available treatment services. The National Treatment Agency for Substance Misuse (NTA, 2002) has identified diversity as one of its key strategic objectives, recognizing the need to ensure equal access to service provision regardless of age, gender, sexuality, disability and ethnicity. The *Mental Health Policy Implementation Guide: Dual Diagnosis Good Practice Guide* (Department of Health, 2002) pointed out that ethnicity is associated with poor access to services and that service provision must therefore be congruent with and sensitive to the needs of each minority ethnic group.

Ethnic minorities: alcohol and drug misuse

The psychoactive substances misused by Black and minority ethnic groups are not clearly different from those used by the white population. However, there seem to be preferences for a certain class or classes of substances and mode of consumption by different ethnic groups which are linked with the historical and cultural characteristics of each ethnic group (Oyefeso et al., 2000).

However, there are clear indications that drug misuse is increasingly being reported amongst young Black and minority ethnic women (National Treatment Agency, 2003). In the Needs Assessment Project (Bashford et al., 2003), cannabis is the most widely reported drug used (51 per cent) followed by cocaine (19 per cent) and khat (18 per cent). Heroin use is reported by 10 per cent. Cannabis is the most widely-used illicit drug amongst the younger members of Black and minority ethnic communities and presentations to drug services by Black Caribbeans are more likely to focus on crack cocaine than other ethnic groups (including white groups) (Sangster et al., 2002). Heroin is also the first drug used (Patel et al., 2001) and reported to be used by South Asian, Iranian, Vietnamese and Chinese people (Sangster et al., 2002). Black Caribbean drug consumption is characterized by the use of crack, amphetamine and ecstasy (Bashford et al., 2003). Crack cocaine has been reported to be used along with cocaine use by young Bangladeshis and Kashmiris (Sheikh et al., 2001).

The contention that injecting drug use behaviour is largely uncommon among Black and minority ethnic groups has been rejected. South Asians have been reported to be injecting heroin by Patel et al., (2001); Sangster et al., (2002); and Sheikh et al., (2001). Studies have also reported young South Asian males injecting steroids (Sheikh et al., 2001). There is great concern that dangerous injecting practices are occurring, particularly amongst South Asian female drug-injecting sex workers (Hall, 1999). Other psychoactive substances such as stimulants, ecstasy, hallucinogens, LSD and ice (a smokeable form of amphetamine) have been reported to be used by South Asians (Bola and Walpole, 1999). Khat was found to be used by the Somali community, Yemeni communities,

Ethiopians and amongst Arabs from the Middle East (Mohammed, 2000; Fountain et al., 2002).

A survey from Alcohol Concern (2001) found that whilst most Pakistani and Bengali men and women, and Sikh and Hindu women were non-drinkers, among Afro-Caribbean men and women and Sikh men, alcohol was used by most people. The Health Survey of minority ethnic groups for England 2004 (The Information Centre, 2004) reported that Pakistani adults (89 per cent of men and 95 per cent of women) and Bangladeshi adults (97 per cent of men and 98 per cent of women) were the most likely to be non-drinkers. Amongst Black and ethnic minority communities, the main ethnic group exceeding the daily recommended limit were Irish but lower levels of drinking were found among Black Caribbean, Indian, Chinese, Black African, Pakistani and Bangladeshi participants. For more comprehensive literature on alcohol in Black and minority ethnic groups see Alcohol Concern (2001).

Smoking patterns have been shown to vary between different Black and minority ethnic groups. The rates of tobacco smoking are: Bangladeshi (40 per cent), Irish (30 per cent), Pakistani (29 per cent), Black Caribbean (25 per cent), Black African and Chinese (21 per cent), and Indian (20 per cent) populations (The Information Centre, 2004). Among ethnic minority groups, many types of smokeless tobacco are used, particularly among the South Asian population. The survey (The Information Centre, 2004) found that Bangladeshis (both men and women) were more likely than other South Asian groups to report chewing tobacco. Tobacco is often consumed in combination with other products such as paan (a leaf preparation stuffed with betel nut and/or with tobacco or other ingredients). Ready-made mixtures of snuff are known as Gutka or paan masala which are chewed either on their own or in betel quid.

Complex needs

Patients from different cultural and ethnic backgrounds may present a special challenge to health and social care professionals. Language barriers; cultural differences in pain response; sick-role behaviour; denial due to stigma attached to alcohol or drug misuse in some ethnic groups; cultural and religious diversity; and attitude of professionals towards members of ethnic minorities may act as barriers in meeting the complex needs of the Black and ethnic minorities.

In general, people from Black and minority ethnic groups living in the United Kingdom (Mental Health Foundation, 2010) are: more likely to be diagnosed with mental health problems and admitted to hospital; more likely to experience a poor outcome from treatment; and more likely to disengage from mainstream mental health services, leading to social exclusion and a deterioration in their mental health. In addition, young Asian women have been reported to have higher rates of attempted suicide and suicide than the national average (Ineichen, 2008).

Black and ethnic minority communities in the UK, especially Black Africans and Afro-Caribbeans are disproportionately affected by HIV. The rate of new HIV diagnoses amongst the African community in the UK continues to rise, and is one of the most serious challenges posed by the HIV/AIDS epidemic in Britain. The document *Testing Times – HIV and other Sexually Transmitted Infections in the United Kingdom* (Health Protection Agency, 2007) reports that almost half of all new HIV diagnoses in 2006 were among Black Africans and 3.2 per cent were among Black Caribbeans. An increasing number of Black Africans and Black Caribbeans are being infected heterosexually in the UK. The HIV/AIDS epidemic has compounded the stigmatization, discrimination and racism faced by Black and ethnic minority communities and this has a direct impact on equal access to health services. HIV/AIDS related stigma and discrimination linked to race and ethnicity, increases vulnerability to HIV infection in the following ways (Ukblackout, 2005).

The issue of health status of ethnic minorities is of particular significance in the assessment and planning of equitable and culturally sensitive interventions (Rassool, 1995). The low rates of early presentation of health problems to services by ethnic minorities may be a challenge to health care providers. This may be due to a multitude of factors such as the use of traditional medicine instead of conventional medicine; cultural dissonance, education and literacy, previous experience of persecution, communication difficulties, religio-cultural prescriptions and discrimination. In order to be culturally sensitive to the health care needs of ethnic minority clients, some of the above issues need to be addressed at all levels of the professional disciplines.

Women: Alcohol and drugs

Research indicates that women with substance use problems are more likely to be younger, have a partner with a substance use problem; fewer resources; dependent children; live with a drug-using partner; have more severe problems at the beginning of treatment; trauma related to physical and sexual abuse; or concurrent psychiatric disorders (UNODC, 2004). The numbers of young women who are binge drinking has risen dramatically in a decade as the proportion of people who exceeded the daily limits for regular drinking on at least one day during the previous week was 34 per cent for women (Office of National Statistics, 2009). In 2007, 20 per cent of women smoked and there has been a steady decline in cigarette smoking since the start of the decade. Women are most likely to have drunk at home (60 per cent) or in someone else's home (11 per cent), whilst only 17 per cent of women drinkers had been in a pub or bar and 6.9 per cent of women reported taking illicit drugs for the year 2006/2007 (The Information Centre, 2008).

Issues related to alcohol and drug misuse

The consequences of problem drinking for women are more severe than men. Women develop alcohol-related problems faster than men and have an increased risk of developing alcohol hepatitis, heart disease, liver disease, ulcers, reproductive problems, osteoporosis, pancreatitis, brain damage, breast cancer, memory loss, and other illnesses caused by alcohol and drug misuse.

Smoking during pregnancy can lead to pregnancy complications and serious health problems in newborns. Maternal alcohol use during pregnancy contributes to a wide range of disorders in the offspring including social, emotional and cognitive development, learning deficits, hyperactivity and attention problems. The most serious outcome of maternal drinking during pregnancy is fetal alcohol spectrum disorders (FASD). Alcohol can adversely impact on the reproductive process in a number of ways, including: infertility, higher rates of menstrual disorders, a decreased chance of becoming pregnant, miscarriage, major structural malformations of the fetus, pre-term deliveries and stillbirth (British Medical Association, 2007). The findings of a study by Aiken et al., (2010) found that women who drink to excess are 1.8 times more likely to have taken emergency contraception such as the morning after pill at least once over the past year, and 1.4 times more likely to have had at least one abortion over the past 18 months.

A mother taking illegal drugs during pregnancy increases her risk of anaemia, blood and heart infections, skin infections, hepatitis, and other infectious diseases. Use of heroin, cocaine, and other psychoactive substances can cause withdrawal in the newborn as well as growth retardation in the unborn baby. The blood-borne viruses such as HIV, hepatitis B and C are transmitted from mother to baby. There is a high risk that an infected mother will transmit HIV on to her unborn baby either during pregnancy, birth or while breast-feeding. The Department of Health in England and Wales has recommended that all pregnant women should be offered antenatal screening for blood-borne viruses and antenatal tests – see *Immunisation Against Infectious Disease* (Department of Health, 2008). Child care issues also have an effect on many pregnant substance misusers who are reluctant to contact health and social care agencies fearing that the child or existing children may be taken into care. It is asserted that a parent who misuses psychoactive substances should be treated in the same way as other parents whose personal difficulties interfere with or lessen their ability to provide good parenting (ACPC's, 2006).

Women who misuse alcohol or drugs face a variety of barriers including barriers to treatment entry, to engagement in treatment and long-term rehabilitation. Research indicates that women with substance use problems are more likely than men to have: a partner with a substance use problem; more severe problems at the beginning of treatment; trauma related to physical and sexual abuse; and concurrent psychiatric disorders (UNDOC, 2004). These complex factors give some indications as to why women have been reluctant to engage in treatment programmes. The availability of female-oriented services, a supportive therapeutic environment and non-coercive treatment approaches have been found to be important in attracting and retaining women in treatment.

Young people and substance misuse

Young people will experiment with alcohol and/or illegal drugs and use a range of readily available and legal substances such as tobacco, alcohol and volatile substances through to more uncommon and illegal substances such as ecstasy, cannabis, cocaine or heroin. The misuse of illicit psychoactive substances gives rise to public concern but only for a small minority of young people will the use of alcohol and/or illegal drugs escalate into addiction. A central aim of the Government's Updated National Drug Strategy (DfES, 2005) is to reduce drug use by young people, particularly the most vulnerable. Cannabis remains the

Table 17.1   Presenting features of substance misuse in young people: physical, social and psychological

Physical	Social	Psychological
• Respiratory symptoms caused by smoking. • Peri-oral and peri-nasal lesions caused by inhalation or snorting. • Physical injuries incurred during intoxication. • Agitation after poly-drug or prolonged use. • Needle tracks, thrombosis or abscesses owing to intravenous use. • Withdrawal syndromes.	• Deteriorating educational performance. • Family conflict. • Crime: petty associated with intoxication; theft to provide funds; 'dealing' as part of more serious association with drug culture.	• Mood changes. • Confusion. • Depression on withdrawal of stimulants. • Irritability as part of withdrawal syndrome. • Deliberate self-harm or suicide attempt. • Psychosis.

Source: World Health Organization (2003–2004).

drug most likely to be used by young people, followed by cocaine powder, and ketamine. Currently, 20,000 young people are receiving specialist substance misuse treatment. Five per cent are experiencing problems with dependency on Class A drugs, while 90 per cent are experiencing problems with cannabis and/or alcohol use (NTA, 2007). The features of substance misuse in young people are presented in Table 17.1.

It is recognized that there are multiple risk factors which contribute to young people's decision to use alcohol or drugs. There is evidence to suggest that the number of risk factors that a person is exposed to is a predictor of drug use, regardless of what those particular risk factors are; the more risk factors there are, the greater the likelihood of drug use (Home Office, 2007). The task of recognition and accurate diagnosis of alcohol and drug misuse in young people are made more difficult because of the increasing trend of multiple drug use. Young vulnerable people who use substances, be it drugs and/or alcohol, are heterogeneous and it would be excluding to ignore their diversity (Epling and McGregor, 2006).

Alcohol, drugs and the elderly

Alcohol and drug misuse in elderly people are a common but under-recognized problem with a significant negative impact on their physical and psychological health and quality of life. The over-55s in Britain are more likely than their European counterparts to be regular drinkers (20 per cent) and Britain is the only country in Europe to have a statistically significant number of over-55s drinking more than six units per day (one per cent) (Alcohol Concern, 2007).

Table 17.2   Risk factors for alcohol problems in the elderly

Psychosocial problems	Medical problems	Practical problems
• Bereavement • Decreased social activity • Loss of friends • Loss of social status • Loss of occupational role • Impaired ability • Family conflict • Reduced self-esteem • Reduced self-efficacy • Depression	• Physical disabilities • Chronic pain • Insomnia • Sensory deficits • Reduced mobility • Cognitive impairment	• Impaired self-care • Reduced coping skills • Altered financial circumstances

Source: Adapted from DAR (2006).

Recent research has highlighted that the over-60s are drinking more alcohol (Foundation66, 2009). Alcohol use disorders in elderly people can cause a wide range of physical and psychosocial problems. The risk factors, signs and symptoms associated with alcohol problems in the elderly are presented in Table 17.2.

The prevalence of drug dependence in Great Britain was four per 1000 population for tranquillizers within the 65–69 age group, and in the 70–74 age group four per 1000 population for cannabis, and one per 1000 for tranquillizers (McGrath et al., 2005). Psychotropic drugs such as anxiolytics, hypno-sedatives, tranquillizers and antidepressants are frequently prescribed to elderly individuals and many individuals frequently use over-the-counter medications. Benzodiazepine dependence in general can be more problematic among elderly persons, because tolerance to alcohol and benzodiazepine decrease with age (Bogunovic and Greenfield, 2004). Tobacco is the most commonly used psychoactive substance amongst the elderly and many elderly people have chronic disease including cardiovascular diseases, lung cancer, bladder cancer and chronic obstructive pulmonary disease.

There is limited research on the coexistence of alcohol misuse and psychiatric disorders in later life. Older people were more likely to have the triple diagnosis of alcoholism, depression and personality disorder (Speer and Bates, 1992), increased risk of suicide (Waern, 2005), and schizophrenia may coexist with alcohol problems (Dar, 2006). It has been reported that there is increased occurrence of all types of dementia except Alzheimer's disease in elderly people with alcohol use disorders (Thomas and Rockwood, 2001). In addition, dementia, depression and suicide have been associated with substance misuse in the elderly.

Homelessness and substance misuse

Homelessness is an increasing problem in the United Kingdom. The findings of research studies have showed that drug misusers are seven times more likely to be homeless than the general population, three quarters of homeless people have a history of problematic substance misuse and more than 2/5 of homeless people cite drug use as the main reason for homelessness (Homelessness Directorate, 2002; Fountain et al., 2002; Kemp et al., 2006). It is estimated that 95 per cent of homeless young people have used drugs and their experimentation with illicit psychoactive substances started as early as 14 years of age (Wincup et al., 2003). Levels of use of cannabis, amphetamine and ecstasy were particularly high, but a substantial minority had used heroin and crack cocaine.

The relationship of homelessness and substance misuse is complex as trends in homelessness are clearly affected by changing social, political and economic factors (Rassool, 2006). In a Home Office study, 70 per cent of the homeless had been diagnosed with depression or other mental health problems, or had concerns about their mental health (Wincup et al., 2003). Health complications associated with alcohol misuse may consist of gastric/digestive problems, gastrointestinal bleeding, skin ulcers and sores, hypertension, cardiac problems, memory loss, accidental injury, epileptic fits linked with heavy drinking or temporary unavailability of alcohol due to shortage of money, loss of consciousness, and alcohol-related psychosis.

Risky behaviours such as poly-drug use and unsafe injecting are common practices. The lack of hygiene, security and personal organization that are part of a transient lifestyle increases the tendency towards, and exposure to, risky drug use behaviours with implications for both the drug user and the wider community (Rowe, 2005). Recently, there has been a rise in the incidence of tuberculosis (TB), and this is magnified in the homeless due to poor living conditions and diet.

Caring for carers

People with addictive behaviours will have networks of families, significant others and carers who will feel the impact of the problems of addictions. Families are increasingly being recognized as a significant factor in addressing challenging social and behavioural problems (UKDPC, 2009). It is estimated that nearly 1.5 million adults are affected by a relative's drug use; over 250,000 are seriously affected by a relative's problematic use of opiates or crack; nearly 130,000 have a relative who shows signs of dependence on cocaine powder; and over one million have a relative who shows signs of dependence on cannabis; about 575,000 of those affected are spouses, 610,000 are parents and 250,000 are other family members, such as grandparents or siblings; and there are over 140,000 family members living with someone who is receiving treatment for illicit drug use (UKDPC, 2009).

Hence, in addictive behaviours, carers may play an important role within a person's addictive behaviour career and treatment journey, especially in the maintenance of recovery and changing lifestyle behaviours. According to the UKDPC (2009), carers or families can play a critical role in two essential ways: by providing a bedrock of support for those using and recovering from problematic substance use or other addictive behaviours; and as a resource to help prevent use and misuse of drugs or addictive behaviours among children and young people.

The range of types of services and interventions needed to support carers or families includes the following (UKDPC, 2009):

- Advice and information provided through non-specialist settings, such as NHS Direct, Carers Direct etc.
- Dedicated family and carer support services providing help and support to family members in their own right.

- Proper assessment of family relationships at the point when a drug user enters a treatment programme.
- Providing support and recognizing the contribution of family members within treatment programmes for drug users, including residential recovery programmes. This could typically include the provision of information and education about drug misuse, the identification of sources of stress, handling relapses and the promotion of coping skills.
- For some people there will be a need for more intensive and specialist support, provided through such interventions as intensive family-based therapy, behavioural couples therapy, multidimensional family therapy and social network approaches.

There are now a number of self-help groups which offer a range of services for families and carers who want to find out more about addictions and to those having to cope with problems related to someone else's addictive behaviours. The services include: advice, support and information, referrals to other services, outreach support, and courses in basic and intermediate counselling, first aid and overdose training, drug and alcohol basic awareness training and self-assertiveness training.

Summary of key points

- Black and minority ethnic communities in the UK are a heterogeneous group.
- Cannabis is the most widely-used illicit drug amongst the younger members of Black and minority ethnic communities.
- Cocaine was reported as a main drug of use by Black Caribbean, African and 'other' ethnicities than either South Asian or white drug users.
- Women's alcohol consumption, particularly in younger and older women has been increasing over the last few decades.
- The most serious outcome of maternal drinking during pregnancy are fetal alcohol spectrum disorders (FASD).
- Smoking during pregnancy not only harms a woman's health, but can lead to pregnancy complications and serious health problems in newborns.
- The blood-borne viruses such as HIV, hepatitis B and C are transmitted from mother to baby.
- Women who misuse alcohol or drugs face a variety of barriers including barriers to treatment entry, to engagement in treatment and long-term rehabilitation.
- Substance misuse in young people should be considered in the context of 'normal' adolescent risk-taking behaviours and experimentation.

- There is not a single factor that predisposes young people to substance misuse rather there are multiple risk factors which act together on any one individual and contribute to their decision to use alcohol or drugs.
- Alcohol and drug misuse in elderly people is common but may be largely under-diagnosed and under-treated.
- Alcohol use disorders in elderly people can cause a wide range of physical and psychosocial problems.
- Carers may play an important role within a person's addictive behaviour career and treatment journey, especially in the maintenance of recovery and changing lifestyle behaviours.

Reflective activity 17.2

- Discuss the failure of service provision in meeting the needs of Black and ethnic minority communities.
- Discuss the barriers to service utilization by Black and ethnic minority communities.
- Discuss the relationship between homelessness and addictive substances.
- Discuss the factors and motivations for young people not to use addictive substances.
- Identify the type of illicit addictive substances and prescribed psychoactive drugs among the elderly.
- Discuss the special treatment needs of women with addictive behaviours.
- Discuss the problems associated with addictive substances in pregnancy.

References

Aicken, C.R., Nardone, A. and Mercer, C.H. (2010) 'Alcohol Misuse, Sexual Risk Behaviour and Adverse Sexual Health Outcomes: Evidence from Britain's National Probability Sexual Behaviour Surveys', *Journal of Public Health*, Published online 12 August 2010, doi:10.1093/pubmed/fdq056.

Alcohol Concern (2007) *Alcohol and the Elderly*, Fact Sheet (London: Alcohol Concern).

Area Child Protection Committees (2006) *Regional Policy and Procedures*, Department of Health, Social Services and Public Safety, Northern Ireland. www.dhsspsni.gov.uk/index/hss/child_care/child_protection/child_protection_guidance.htm, date accessed 13 December 2009.

Bashford, J., Buffin, J. and Patel, K. (2003) *The Department of Health's Black and Minority Ethnic Drug Misuse Needs Assessment Project. Part 2 The Findings*. The Centre for Ethnicity and Health, Faculty of Health, University of

Central Lancashire. https://www.uclan.ac.uk/schools/iscri/files/Report_2_The_Findings.pdf, date accessed 10 December 2009.

Bogunovic, O.J. and Greenfield, S.F. (2004) 'Practical Geriatrics: Use of Benzodiazepines Among Elderly Patients', *Psychiatric Services* 55, 3, 233–35.

Bola, M. and Walpole, T. (1999) *Drugs Information and Communication Needs Among South Asians in Crawley.* Executive summary (Crawley: Youth Action Crawley).

British Medical Association (2007) *Fetal Alcohol Spectrum Disorders. A Guide for Health Professionals* (London: BMA Board of Science).

Dar, K. (2006) 'Alcohol Use Disorders in Elderly People: Fact or Fiction?' *Advances in Psychiatric Treatment* 12, 173–81.

Department of Health (2002) *The Mental Health Policy Implementation Guidance; Dual Diagnosis Good Practice Guide* (London: Department of Health).

Department of Health (2008) *Immunisation Against Infectious Disease 2006* (London: Department of Health).

DfES (2005) *Every Child Matters Young People and Drugs. Department of Education and Skills* (Nottingham: DfES) Publications. http://www.dcsf.gov.uk/everychildmatters/about/background/background/.

Epling, M. and McGregor, J. (2006) 'Vulnerable Young People and Substance Misuse', in Rassool, G.H. (ed.), *Dual Diagnosis Nursing* (Oxford: Blackwell Publications).

Foundation66 (2009) Press Release: *Foundation66 Highlights Epidemic of Late-onset Drinking.* 14 July 2009. http://www.foundation66.org.uk/news.php/5/press-release-foundation66-highlights-epidemic-of-late-onset-drinking, date accessed 22 November 2009.

Fountain, J., Bashford, J., Underwood, S., Khurana, J., Winters, M., Patel, K. and Carpentier, C. (2002) *Update and Complete the Analysis of Drug Use, Consequences and Correlates Amongst Minorities.* Cited in: National Treatment Agency (2003) Black and Minority Ethnic Communities: a Review of the Literature on Drug Use and Related Service Provision (London: NTA).

Hall, C. (1999) *Drug Use and HIV Infection in South Asian and Middle Eastern Communities in the UK: A Literature Review* (London: Naz Project).

Health Protection Agency (2007) *Testing Times – HIV and Other Sexually-transmitted Infections in the United Kingdom, 2007 Annual Report* (London: Health Protection Agency). http://www.hpa.org.uk/.

Home Office (2007) Identifying and Exploring Young People's Experiences of Risk, Protective Factors and Resilience to Drug Use. Home Office Development and Practice Reports (London: Home Office).

Homelessness Directorate (2002) Drug Services for Homeless People (London: Office of the Deputy Prime Minister).

Ineichen, B. (2008) 'Suicide and Attempted Suicide Among South Asians in England: Who is at Risk?' *Mental Health in Family Medicine,* 5, 3, 135–38.

Kemp, P., Neale, J. and Robertson, M. (2006) 'Homelessness Amongst Problem Drug Users: Prevalence, Risk Factors and Trigger Events', *Health and Social Care in the Community* 14, 4, 319–28.

McGrath, A., Crome, P. and Crome, I.B. (2005) 'Substance Misuse in the Older Population', *Postgraduate Medical Journal* 81, 954, 228–31.

Mental Health Foundation (2010) *Black and Minority Ethnic Communities and Mental Health* http://www.mentalhealth.org.uk/information/mental-health-a-z/black-minority-ethnic-communities/, date accessed 3 April 2010.

Mohammed, S. (2000) *A Gob Full of Khat: a Study of Contemporary Khat Use in Toxteth, Liverpool* (Liverpool: Liverpool Avaanca Publications).

National Treatment Agency (NTA) (2002) *Models of Care for Treatment of Adult Drug Misusers, Part 2* (London: NTA). www.nta.nhs.uk.

National Treatment Agency (NTA) (2003) *Black and Minority Ethnic Communities: A Review of the Literature on Drug Use and Related Service Provision* (London: NTA). www.nta.nhs.uk.

National Treatment Agency (NTA) (2007) New Era for Young People's Substance Misuse Treatment. Media release: 31 July 2007 (London: NTA).

Office of National Statistics (2009) *Smoking and Drinking Among Adults 2007 and Drinking: Adults' Behaviour and Knowledge in 2008.* www.statistics.gov.uk/pdfdir/ghs0109.pdf, date accessed 19 October 2010.

Oyefeso, A., Ghodse, H., Keating, A., Annan, J., Phillips, T., Pollard, M. and Nash, P. (2000) *Drug Treatment Needs of Black and Minority Ethnic Residents of the London Borough of Merton.* Addictions Resource Agency for Commissioners (ARAC) Monograph Series on Ethnic Minority Issues, (London: ARAC).

Patel, K. (1993) 'Ethnic Minority Access to Services' in Harrison, L. (ed.), *Race, Culture and Substance Problems,* Department of Social Policy and Professional Studies (Hull: University of Hull).

Rassool, G.H. (1995) 'The Health Status and Health Care of Ethno-Cultural Minorities in the United Kingdom: An Agenda for Action. Editorial', *Journal of Advanced Nursing* 21, 2, 199–201.

Rassool, G.H. (2009) *Alcohol and Drug Misuse: A Handbook for Student and Health Professionals* (Oxford: Routledge).

Rowe, J. (2005) 'Laying the Foundations: Addressing Heroin Use Among the "Street Homeless"', *Drugs: Education, Prevention and Policy* 12, 1, 47–59.

Sangster, D., Shiner, M., Sheikh, N. and Patel, K. (2002) *Delivering Drug Services to Black and Minority Ethnic Communities,* DPAS/P16, (London: Home Office Drug Prevention and Advisory Service (DPAS)) Also available on www.drugs.gov.uk.

Sheikh, N., Fountain, J., Bashford, J. and Patel, K. (2001) *A Review of Current Drug Service Provision for Black and Minority Ethnic Communities in Bedfordshire*. Final Report to Bedfordshire Drug Action Team, August 2001 (Preston: Centre for Ethnicity and Health, Faculty of Health, University of Central Lancashire).

Speer, D.C. and Bates, K. (1992) 'Comorbid Mental and Substance Disorders Among Older Psychiatric Patients', *Journal of the American Geriatric Society* 40, 9, 886–90.

The Information Centre (2004) *Health Survey for England 2004. The Health of Minority Ethnic Groups* (Leeds: The Information Centre).

The Information Centre (2008) *Statistics on Drug Misuse: England, 2008*. www.ic.nhs.uk/webfiles/publications/Drugmisuse08/Statistics%20on%20 Drug%20Misuse%202008%20final%20format%20v12.pdf, date accessed 20 November 2009.

Thomas, V.S. and Rockwood, K.J. (2001) 'Alcohol Abuse, Cognitive Impairment and Mortality Among Older People', *Journal of the American Geriatric Society* 49, 4, 415–20.

Ukblackout (2005) http://www.ukblackout.com/index.php, date accessed 5 January 2010.

UKDCP (2009) *Supporting the Supporters: Families of Drug Misusers: Prevalence, Social Cost, Resource Savings and Treatment Responses*. www.ukdpc.org.uk/ reports.shtml, date accessed 3 April 2010.

UNDOC (2004) *Substance Abuse Treatment and Care for Women* (Vienna: United Nations Office on Drugs and Crime), http://www.unodc.org/docs/ treatment/Case_Studies_E.pdf.

Waern, M. (2005) 'Alcohol Dependence and Misuse in Elderly Suicides', *Postgraduate Medical Journal* 81, 228–31.

Wincup, E., Buckland, G. and Bayliss, R. (2003) *Youth Homelessness and Substance Use, Report to the Drugs and Alcohol Research Unit*, Home Office Research Study 258, (London: Home Office Research, Development and Statistics Directorate).

World Health Organization (2003–4) *Substance Misuse in Young People*. World Health Organization – UK Collaborating Centre. www.library.nhs.uk/ SpecialistLibrarySearch/download.aspx?resID=79797. NHS National Library for Health, date accessed 25 October 2009.

18 Service Provision and Interventions

Introduction

The changing nature and pattern of addictive behaviours and the emergence of eco-smart psychoactive substances require a flexible service provision and delivery in responding to the needs of the addicted person. The report of the *Task Force to Review Services for Drug Misusers* (1996) has advocated a co-ordinated response to tackling drug misuse, with a variety of different treatments and facilities available. Models of Care for treatment of adult drug misusers (MoCDM) (NTA, 2002; 2006a) and alcohol misusers (MoCAM) (Department of Health/NTA, 2007) set out a national framework, in England, for the commissioning of adult treatment for alcohol and drug misuse to meet the needs of diverse local populations.

The Models of Care for drug and alcohol misusers advocate a whole system approach to meeting the multiple needs of substance misusers. The challenge is the integration of addiction services with other generic health, social and criminal justice services including throughcare and aftercare. This chapter outlines the more common provision of services, statutory, non-statutory and voluntary services for addictive behaviours. Both specialist and generic services are presented.

Alcohol: models of care

Models of Care for Alcohol Misusers (MoCAM) identify four main categories of alcohol misusers who may benefit from some kind of intervention or treatment: hazardous drinkers; harmful drinkers; moderately dependent drinkers and severely dependent drinkers (see Chapter 3). Key points of the four-tiered framework are presented in Table 18.1.

In Tier 1, there is a wide range of agencies in a range of settings, the main focus of which is not alcohol treatment. For example: primary health care services; acute hospitals, A&E departments; psychiatric services; social services departments; homelessness services; antenatal clinics; general hospital wards; police settings, e.g. custody cells; probation services; the prison service;

Table 18.1 Alcohol: model of care

Tier	Settings	Specialist settings	Intervention strategies
1	Primary health care services. Acute hospitals, e.g. A&E departments. Psychiatric services. Social services departments. Homelessness services. Antenatal clinics. General hospital wards. Police settings, e.g. custody cells. Probation services. Prison service. Education and vocational services. Occupational health services.	Specialist Liver disease units. Specialist psychiatric wards. Forensic units. Residential provision for the homeless Domestic abuse services.	Interventions include identification of hazardous, harmful and dependent drinkers. Information on sensible drinking with simple brief interventions to reduce alcohol-related harm. Referral of those with alcohol dependence or alcohol-related harm for more intensive interventions.
2	Primary health care services. Acute hospitals, e.g. A&E departments. Psychiatric services. Social services departments. Homelessness services. Antenatal clinics. General hospital wards. Police settings, e.g. custody cells. Probation services. Prison service. Education and vocational services. Occupational health services.	Alcohol Services	Alcohol-specific information, advice and support. Extended brief interventions and brief treatment to reduce alcohol-related harm. Alcohol-specific assessment and referral of those requiring more structured alcohol treatment. Partnership or 'shared care' with staff from Tier 3 and Tier 4 Provision, or joint care of individuals attending other services providing Tier 1 Interventions. Mutual aid groups, e.g. Alcoholics Anonymous Triage assessment, which may be provided as part of locally agreed arrangements.

(Continued)

Table 18.1 Continued

Tier	Settings	Specialist settings	Intervention strategies
3	Primary care settings (shared care schemes. GP-led prescribing services. The work in community settings can be delivered by statutory, voluntary or independent services providing care-planned, structured alcohol treatment.	Community-based, structured, care-planned alcohol treatment.	Comprehensive substance misuse assessment. Care planning. Case management. Community detoxification. Prescribing interventions to reduce risk of relapse. Psychosocial therapies and support. Interventions to address coexisting conditions. Day programmes. Liaison services, e.g. for acute medical and psychiatric health services (such as pregnancy, mental health or hepatitis services). Social care services (such as child care and housing services and other generic services).
4	Inpatient provision in the context of general psychiatric wards. Hospital services for pregnancy, liver problems, etc. with specialized alcohol liaison support.	Alcohol specialist inpatient treatment and residential rehabilitation.	Comprehensive substance misuse assessment. Care planning and review. Prescribing interventions. Alcohol detoxification. Prescribing interventions to reduce risk of relapse. Psychosocial therapies and support. Provision of information, advice and training and 'shared care' to others.

Source: Adapted from Models of Care for Alcohol Misusers (NTA, 2006).

education and vocational services; and occupational health services. Tier 1 interventions include provision of information on sensible drinking; simple brief interventions to reduce alcohol-related harm; and referral of those with alcohol dependence. Such interventions can also be provided in highly specialist non-alcohol specific residential or inpatient services.

Tier 2 provision may be delivered by the following agencies: specialist alcohol services; primary health care services; acute hospitals, psychiatric services; social services; domestic abuse agencies; homelessness services; antenatal clinics; probation services; the prison service; and occupational health services. Tier 2 interventions include provision of alcohol-specific advice, information and support; extended brief interventions; and assessment and referral of those with more serious alcohol-related problems for planned care treatment.

Tier 3 interventions are delivered in specialized alcohol treatment services (inpatient unit), in the community or by outreach services. Some of the Tier 3 work is based in primary care settings (shared care schemes and General Practitioner (GP)-led prescribing services. The work in community settings can be delivered by statutory, voluntary or independent services providing care-planned, structured alcohol treatment. Tier 3 interventions include provision of community-based specialized alcohol misuse assessment that is care co-ordinated and care-planned.

In Tier 4, there are specialized statutory, independent or voluntary sector inpatient facilities. Specialized inpatient alcohol units are ideal for inpatient alcohol assessment, medically assisted alcohol withdrawal (detoxification) and stabilization. Tier 4 interventions include provision of residential, specialized alcohol treatments which are care-planned and co-ordinated to ensure continuity of care and aftercare.

Drugs: models of care

The Models of Care (NTA, 2002; 2006a) introduced a four tier system of Models of Care. A summary of the key points is presented in Table 18.2. The Models includes the key tenets of care planning and co-ordination of care and the development of integrated care pathways. The focus of service provisions and interventions include harm reduction approaches in reducing the risk of immediate death due to overdose and risks of morbidity and mortality due to blood-borne viruses and other infections.

Tier 1 services are generic (non-substance misuse specific as are that of the alcohol models of care) services providing screening and referral to local drug and alcohol treatment services in Tiers 2 and 3. The aim of the treatment in Tier 2 is to engage substance misusers in drug treatment and reduce

Table 18.2 Drugs: models of care

Tier	Settings	Professionals	Intervention strategies
1.	Primary health care services. Acute hospitals, e.g. A&E departments. Psychiatric services. Social services departments. Homelessness services. Antenatal clinics. General hospital wards. Police settings, e.g. custody cells. Probation services. Prison service. Education and vocational services. Occupational health services. Hepathology services.	Primary Care. General medical services. Social workers. Community pharmacists. Probation officers. Housing officers. Homeless persons units.	Drug and alcohol screening. Referral to alcohol and drug services. Assessment. Information to reduce drug-related harm. Liaison with drug and alcohol services. General medical care. Housing support. Hepatitis B vaccination.
2.	Drug advice and information centres. Drop-in services. Pharmacy. Outreach services. Self-Referrals. Referral from a variety of other sources.	Specialist drug and alcohol workers. Specialist social workers.	Drug and alcohol screening and assessment. Care planning and management. Criminal justice screening and referral. Motivation and brief interventions Drug and alcohol information services. Needle exchange. Ad hoc support (no care planning). Social work advice. Child care/parenting assessment. Assessment of social care needs. Low-threshold prescribing programme. Outreach work.

3.	Community-based specialist drug and alcohol services. Structured community-based services for stimulant users, young people, black and minority ethnic groups, women, HIV and Aids, dual diagnosis. Self-referrals. Referral from a variety of sources.	Specialist drug and alcohol workers. Dual diagnosis workers. Specialist social workers.	Drug assessment. Care plan. Care-co-ordinator. Shared-care prescribing. Testing order drug treatment. Cognitive behaviour therapy. Motivational interventions. Counselling. Methadone maintenance programmes. Community detoxification. Day care. After-care programme.
4a.	Inpatient drug and alcohol detoxification services. Drug and alcohol residential rehabilitation units. Residential drug crisis intervention centres. Referral from Tiers 2 or 3 services.	Specialist drug and alcohol workers. Counsellors/therapists. Specialist liaison services to tiers 1–4a services.	Provision of holistic care: physical, psychological, social and spiritual care. Pharmacotherapy. Psychological interventions. Social interventions. Educational interventions.
4b.	Non-substance misuse specific:	Specialist liver disease units. HIV clinics & genito-urinary clinics. Eating disorder units. Forensic services. Personality disorder units. Terminal care services.	

Source: Adapted from Models of Care for Adult Misusers (NTA, 2002; 2006)

drug-related harm. This tier includes services such as needle exchange, drug and alcohol advice and information services, low-threshold prescribing programmes, and ad hoc support not delivered in the context of a care plan.

Tier 3 services are specialist services provided solely for drug and alcohol misusers in structured programmes of care. Tier 3 services require the drug and alcohol misusers to receive a drug assessment and to have a care plan and a whole gamut of pharmacotherapy and psychosocial interventions. Tier 3 services and mental health services should work closely together to meet the needs of drug misusers with dual diagnosis. Tier 4 services are aimed at individuals with complex needs and include inpatient drug and alcohol units, residential rehabilitation units and crisis intervention centres.

Drug Dependence Units (DDUs)

Inpatient or Drug Dependence Units (DDUs) are specialist units which in the past have dealt primarily with opiate addiction. Currently, many units see a variety of clients with alcohol, cocaine, heroin and hypno-sedative dependence as many of the patients attending treatment or rehabilitation are usually poly-drug users. The inpatient treatment units can also include stabilization on substitute medication, emergency medical care for substance misusers in crisis, and in some cases treatment for stimulant users. In addition, these units provide help with alcohol problems, harm reduction and treatment for blood-borne viruses. The intervention strategies include detoxification, individual and group psychotherapy, health education, social skills training, stress management and relapse prevention. In some units, there are day programmes with various activities. Programmes often include group work, counselling, education and life skills, and creative activities and can be set individually for patients according to their needs.

Community Drug Teams (CDTs)

Community Drug Teams (CDTs) have been in existence since the mid 1980s and are strategically placed in community locations offering a variety of structured and semi-structured interventions to individuals affected by illicit drug use. CDTs are more likely to encounter patients with a variety of substance misuse issues for whom a community-based approach to interventions are more likely to be appropriate. Community Drug Teams provide a range of free and confidential services and the types of interventions are dependent on the needs of the individual, but will include a comprehensive assessment and a jointly negotiated Plan of Care. CDTs are staffed by nurse specialists, medical practitioners and social workers and/or psychologists.

Community Alcohol Teams (CATs)

Community Alcohol Teams have been in existence since 1968 and are available for anyone aged 18 or older who is worried about his or her own or someone else's drinking. Community Alcohol Teams accept referrals from all professionals although most do not accept self referrals from patients. Services provided include assessment, community detoxification, home detoxification, counselling, group programmes and relapse prevention. In addition, some CATs offer complementary or alternative therapies such as auricular acupuncture for people who want to cut down or stop drinking.

Drug and alcohol liaison team

The Drug and Alcohol Liaison Team (DALT) offers a consultation/liaison service to nominated acute medial trusts for patients with substance misuse problems. The service provides advice, information, screening, fast track referrals, medical management, withdrawal and stabilization management, brief interventions, referral to Alcohol Liver Disease clinics, liaison work and referral on to specialist drug and alcohol services. The Drug and Alcohol Liaison Team also is responsible for contributing from a Tier 1 perspective (Models of Care) to the development of a strategy for the reduction of drug-related deaths.

Primary care and general practice

General practitioners are likely to encounter patients who misuse drugs and alcohol and/or display other addictive behaviours. Almost 40 per cent of all general practices are involved in the treatment of drug users – figures from the National Treatment Agency reveal a rise of 25 per cent in just five years (Pulse, 2008). Most doctors will provide some Tier 1 interventions (Models of Care, NTA 2006; 2007), even though they may mainly be providing interventions at other tiers. GPs providing enhanced services may run Tier 2 interventions within primary care, but, in some areas, there will also be a consultant in addiction psychiatry or another specialist involved (NTA, 2005). In order to meet the range of needs and demand for drug treatment in a locality, it is necessary to have a treatment system which involves a range of doctors, including GPs providing core and enhanced services, GPs with a special interest (GpwSIs), and addiction specialists (normally addiction psychiatrists) (NTA, 2005).

Doctors have a role in the provision of basic health care needs of substance misusers and their clinical management. They have a legal duty to notify the Addicts Index, Home Office, of contact with opioid and cocaine addicts and should report details of patients with any recent drug problem to the

Drug Misuse Database. The Drug Misuse Database provides data on new drug agency episodes (people presenting to services for problem drug misuse for the first time or for the first time for six months).

The involvement of general practitioners would not only provide general health care needs to substance misusers, within the context of their general practice but can also provide an effective response to patients with substance use problems or drug-related problems. Services that could be provided by general practitioners include smoking cessation clinics, health education regarding the use of alcohol, tobacco and other psychoactive substances, substitute prescribing, harm reduction and abstinence programmes. General practitioners have formal training in drug misuse as part of the Royal College of General Practitioners curriculum (Department of Health (England) and the devolved administrations, 2007).

Accident and emergency departments

Accident and Emergency (A&E) departments are considered to be the 'shop door' of the health service (Sbaih, 1993) and function with an open house policy. Drug misusers commonly attend accident and emergency (A&E) departments with problems such as accidental overdoses, abscesses and withdrawal effects (Cook et al., 1998). In addition, these departments offer important health care services for substance misusers suffering from the effects of acute toxic reactions such as hyperactive, aggressive or even violent, panic attacks, withdrawal symptoms from alcohol or drugs, deliberate self-harm and the physical complications of injecting drugs. It is suggested that A&E departments have a vital part to play, not only in the acute management but also in the prevention of drug-related deaths in the community (Ryan and Spronken, 2000). Appropriate referral to local substance misuse teams are sometimes the gateway for patients to come into contact with specialist drug and alcohol agencies. Individuals who attend A&E for substance misuse/mental health problems often have regular support from dual diagnosis liaison or drug and alcohol liaison staff.

Street agencies

Street Agencies or Advice and Counselling Services are especially found in large urban areas and are accessible to individuals and their families. They provide a 'user-friendly' link for those with substance use problems who are unwilling to attend statutory services for help or treatment. Street agencies have drop-in centres offering advice and help with practical problems, counselling and sometimes medical help. Some of them offer a needle and syringe scheme. No referral or appointment is necessary.

Self-help groups

Various self-help groups exist for those with drug, alcohol and non-pharmacological addictions, their families and significant others. Within the substance misuse field, the self-help groups include Alcoholics Anonymous (AA), Tranx (tranquillizers), Narcotics Anonymous (NA), Families Anonymous (FA), Al-Anon and Al-Ateen (alcohol) and Gambling Anonymous (GA).

Residential rehabilitation services

There are a number of centres throughout the United Kingdom who offer residential rehabilitation for those who cannot sustain a drug-free lifestyle. Most require that substance misusers are drug-free on admission and the programme varies between one and two year's expected length of stay. The therapeutic approach of the rehabilitation services include group work, social skills training, counselling and health maintenance. Some of the residential services are abstinence orientated and base their approach on the 'Twelve Steps' model of AA's programme of recovery. Other facilities focus on the spiritual dimension of substance misuse and are based on the Judeo-Christian tradition. The community-based facilities offer services which primarily focus on alcohol or drugs.

Residential rehabilitation (rehab) usually involves clients staying in a facility for weeks or months and provide a complete break from their current circumstances. There are several types of facilities including traditional rehabilitation units, with programmes to suit the needs of different service users. Different units have different approaches, for example therapeutic communities and the 12 Step programmes used by Alcoholics Anonymous and Narcotics Anonymous Crisis intervention units that help people in drug-related crisis. There are residential treatment programmes for pregnant women, people with liver problems and clients with coexisting psychiatric disorders. Some residential homes provide supported accommodation, where some clients go after rehabilitation. As with inpatient treatment, clients will generally access rehabilitation through community services. People entering rehabilitation will usually have gone through detoxification before entering.

Aftercare

Aftercare is support that is planned for when those with substance misuse leave structured treatment. The aim is to maintain the positive developments that the individuals have made in their treatment, and help them return to normal life. Examples include help with housing, education, employment, general health care and relapse prevention.

Private sector facilities

There has been a growth in the development of treatment and rehabilitation services for substance misusers in the private sector during the last few years. Private clinics offer a range of services and these facilities charge fees to the residents or their families. The treatment and rehabilitation programmes offered vary in length from a few weeks to several months and the therapeutic approaches are mainly based on the 'Minnesota Model'.

Principles of treatment interventions

Studies on the effectiveness of treatment interventions show that treatment can help those with addictive behaviours to stop using psychoactive substances, avoid relapse, and maintain their new lifestyle and behaviours. The key principles (NIDA, 2009) that should form the basis of any effective treatment programmes include:

- Substance misusers have multiple needs and the focus of intervention should not be on his/her substance misuse.
- No single treatment is appropriate for everyone.
- Treatment needs to be readily available.
- Remaining in treatment for an adequate period of time is critical.
- Counselling and other behavioural therapies are the most commonly used forms of substance misuse intervention.
- Medications are an important element of treatment for many patients, especially when combined with counselling and cognitive behavioural therapies.
- An individual's treatment and service plan must be assessed continually and modified as necessary to ensure that it meets his or her changing needs.
- Many substance misusers have coexisting psychiatric disorders.
- Medically assisted detoxification is only the first stage of addiction treatment.
- Intervention does not need to be voluntary to be effective.
- Substance misuse during treatment must be monitored continuously, as lapses during treatment do occur.
- Treatment programmes should assess patients for the presence of HIV/AIDS, hepatitis B and C, tuberculosis, and other infectious diseases as well as provide targeted risk-reduction counselling to help patients modify or change behaviours that place them at risk of contracting or spreading infectious diseases.

Aims and scope of pharmacological interventions

Pharmacotherapy plays a key role in the effective treatment of addictive behaviours combined with psychological and social interventions. A hierarchy of the goals of drug treatment has been identified in the UK (NTA, 2002): reduction of health, social and other problems directly related to drug misuse; reduction of harmful or risky behaviours associated with the misuse of drugs (e.g. sharing injecting equipment); reduction of health, social or other problems not directly attributable to drug misuse; attainment of controlled, non-dependent, or non-problematic, drug use; abstinence from main problem drugs; and abstinence from all drugs.

Alcohol, opiates and hypno-sedatives produce substantial physical withdrawal syndromes and pharmacological interventions are often needed to reduce withdrawal symptoms. Alcohol and hypno-sedative withdrawal are life-threatening and are associated with a significant mortality and morbidity rate without pharmacological interventions. For other addictive behaviours such as eating disorders, psychotropic medications such as selective serotonin reuptake inhibitors (SSRI) have also been shown to have some effectiveness in maintaining weight and also resolving some of the secondary symptoms such as mood and anxiety. Several medications have been studied as treatments for pathological gambling such as opioid antagonists, serotonin reuptake inhibitors and mood stabilizers. Emerging data from controlled clinical trials, however, suggest that pathological gamblers frequently respond to pharmacological intervention (Grant and Won Kim, 2006). For sexual addiction, antidepressants may be used in conjunction with psychological treatment for the treatment of depression.

The aims of pharmacological interventions are:

- To reduce harms associated with non-pharmacological addictive behaviours;
- To reduce harms associated with illicit psychoactive substances by prescribing a substitute opiate based medication (for example, methadone);
- To reduce withdrawal syndromes;
- To enable the maintenance of abstinence and the prevention of relapse;
- To prevent the complications of non-pharmacological addictive behaviours;
- To prevent complications from addictive substances. (For example, use of vitamins); and in the treatment of coexisting substance misuse and psychiatric disorders (Rassool, 2009).

The guidance for the pharmacological management of addictive substances among young people is covered comprehensively elsewhere (Department of Health, 2009). Effective pharmacological interventions involve prescribing a spectrum of medications but their roles depend on the stage of treatment and on the consequences of addictive substances. Pharmacological interventions are mainly used to help with different aspects of the treatment process: withdrawal and treatment. In withdrawal, medications are used to suppress or relieve withdrawal symptoms during detoxification. However, detoxification is not in itself the 'treatment' but is part of the journey of those with addictive behaviours in the treatment process. In the treatment phase, medications are used to maintain behavioural functions, to diminish cravings and to prevent relapse. Currently, there are medications available for opioids (heroin, morphine), tobacco (nicotine), and alcohol addiction and pharmacologists are developing others for treating stimulant (cocaine, methamphetamine) and cannabis (marijuana) addiction.

Principles of psychosocial interventions

The framework for delivering psychosocial interventions is based on the notion of an adequate assessment of health and social care needs. Key working is a basic delivery mechanism for a range of psychosocial components. It has been suggested that for the addicts who are help-seekers, the specific intervention delivered is important, but equally important are therapist characteristics, social stability, psychological morbidity and the occurrence of positive life events after treatment (Tober and Raistrick, 2007).

The effectiveness of a therapeutic alliance is crucial to the delivery of any treatment intervention and patient outcomes. The ability to engage a patient appropriately while demonstrating satisfactory levels of warmth and trust; adopt a personal style that is consistent with and meshes with that of the patient; adjust the nature of the intervention according to the potential of the client; deal with difficult emotions; and understand and work with a patient's emotional context including patient motivation (Roth and Pilling, 2007). A further principle is that goals of treatment should not be imposed on the service user but based on mutual agreement between the key worker and the service user and should be client directed.

Aims and scope of psychosocial interventions

The aims of psychosocial interventions are to: provide psychological support, enhance motivation, prevent relapse; help to address social problems (for example, family problems, housing and employment). Psychosocial interventions encompass a wide range of treatment strategies such as brief interventions, counselling, cognitive behavioural therapy, family therapy, social skills training, supportive work and complementary therapy. There is evidence to suggest that drug misuse treatment is effective in terms of reduced addiction to substances; improvements in personal and social functioning; reduced public health and safety risks; reduced criminal behaviour; and reduced longer-term health costs of problem drinkers (McLellan, 1997; Prendergast et al., 2002; NTA, 2006b; 2006c).

Transtheoretical stages of change model

The Transtheoretical Model (Prochaska et al., 1992; Prochaska and Velicer, 1997) is an integrative model of behaviour change (Figure 18.1). The Stages of Change Model evolved from research in smoking cessation but now has been applied to other addictive behaviours. The Transtheoretical Model construes change as a process involving progress through a series of six stages: pre-contemplation, contemplation, action, maintenance, termination or relapse.

In the precontemplation stage, the individuals have no insight into the problem or are unaware of the problem. Individuals may lack the awareness that life can be improved by a change in behaviour despite their high risk behaviour. In the contemplation stage, the individuals are seriously contemplating a change in behaviour. They are aware of the pros and the cons of behavioural change. Ambivalence develops as a result of the balance between the costs and benefits of changing. At the preparation stage, individuals are planning and making final adjustments before changing behaviour; to take action in the immediate future, usually measured as the next month. The preparation stage is viewed as a transition rather than a stable stage, with individuals intending progress to action in the next 30 days.

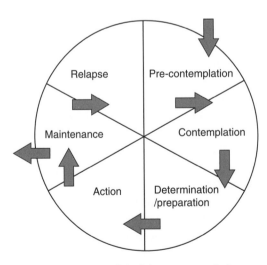

Figure 18.1 A model of the process of change
(Prochaska and DiClemente, 1986)

Action is the stage in which people have made specific overt changes in their lifestyles and behaviour. In this stage, individuals must attain adequate changes in reducing their high risk behaviours. This is a critical stage where there is the possibility of relapse. Maintenance – at this stage the individuals continue with desirable and acceptable actions and are working to prevent relapse and consolidate gains secured during the action phase. Maintainers are distinguishable from those in the action stage in that they report the highest levels of self-efficacy and are less frequently tempted to relapse (Prochaska and DiClemente, 1984). In the termination phase, the individuals have gained adequate self-efficacy to eliminate the risk of lapse or relapse. Their former lifestyles and behaviours are not longer perceived as desirable. Most of those with addictive behaviours experience relapse on the journey to permanent cessation or stable reduction of high risk behaviours.

This model of change is a circular rather than a linear model (see Figure 18.1). The individual may go through several cycles of contemplation, action, and relapse before either reaching maintenance, termination or exiting the system without remaining free from addictive behaviours. An individual enters and exits at any point and often recycles several times. The Stages of Change Model considers relapse to be normal. A relapsed individual may need to learn to anticipate high risk situations more effectively, control environmental cues and learn how to handle unexpected episodes of stress to reach the stage of termination.

Social interventions

The Social Interventions Model engages the interaction between the internal experience of the individual and networks and communities in which they live. However, there are many high risk factors such as poor housing, unemployment, and unaddressed special needs, which increase the likelihood of alcohol and drug misuse and other addictive behaviours. It is the cumulative effect of multiple risk factors that have a significant influence on the journey towards addictive behaviours. Social interventions which address several interrelated factors and build on the existing strengths of individuals and communities tend to be the most effective approaches. Substance misuse is closely linked with other risk factors for crime, such as heightened aggression and involvement with 'antisocial' groups, so this factor may be best addressed alongside other risk factors (Waller and Weiler, 1984).

The role of the family has been recognized as influencing the course of the addictive behaviour problem, improving substance-related outcomes for the user and also helping to reduce the negative effects of substance misuse problems on other family members (Copello et al., 2006). This model of interventions is based on advocacy by empowering and supporting the individual and the family social networks in developing strategies to cope with specific social problems and difficulties. There is an increasingly robust evidence base that supports both family-focused and social network-focused interventions and that family and social network approaches either match or improve outcomes when compared with individual interventions (Copello et al., 2006). Breaking the vicious circle of the social determinants and consequences of the harmful use of alcohol requires a combination of effective measures addressing social inequalities, alcohol availability and the context and patterns of alcohol use, as well as the availability of effective treatment for alcohol use disorders (Poznyak et al., 2005). This is also applicable to drug misuse.

Complementary therapies

Complementary therapies can be of great value for individuals with addictions to substances by increasing the options for care for this group of patients. There is evidence to suggest that alternative and complementary therapies are being used selectively as an adjunct to addiction treatment under the assumption that these therapies increase retention rates and otherwise contribute to treatment effectiveness (NASADAD, 2010). The advantages of using any of the complementary therapies are that they are more economical in comparison with expenses for drugs such as methadone (Rassool, 2009). There is no danger of therapeutic addiction. However, more research is needed to examine the safety and effectiveness of complementary therapies and adequate professional and legal regulations are of vital importance.

The best recognized form of acupuncture used in the field of addiction is auricular (ear) acupuncture. It has been used to treat most forms of addictive behaviours: cigarette smoking, alcoholism, methadone detoxification, detoxification of opiate, cocaine, crack cocaine, alcohol and tobacco addiction and preventing relapse. The evidence supporting acupuncture's effectiveness in detoxification treatment is largely anecdotal but it can be a complementary tool in the detoxification process. Aromatherapy involves the use of the organic essence of aromatic plants for healing the body, mind and spirit. The oils are obtained from the plants using distillation and solvent extraction. The combination of massage and aromatherapy can be of particular benefit to those who are addicted to psychoactive substances, allowing the client 'time out' from stress (McDonald and Rassool, 1997). There is no available literature on the use of aromatherapy in the addiction field. Reflexology is one of the many complementary treatments on offer to clients who present with addictive substance problems. The practitioner will work on the feet or hands, feeling for imbalance and energy blockage.

There are also herbal remedies that have been suggested to aid detoxification or withdrawal. Valerian has been suggested to improve sleep in people withdrawing from drugs like valium. Passion flower was effective when combined with clonidine in one small study, and St John's Wort may reduce alcohol craving (The Royal College of Psychiatrists, 2007). However, the evidence is limited. Kudzu or 'Japanese arroweed' flowers have a pleasant fragrance and have been used for many medical purposes including for menopausal and alcohol problems. It is envisaged that it may reduce anxiety caused by alcohol withdrawal. There is no clear evidence of its effectiveness in reducing alcohol use in heavy drinkers or its effect on craving. Iboga is a West African shrub producing ibogaine but causes hallucinations and has been used as a treatment for opiate addiction in the 1960s. However, it can have serious, life-threatening side effects. Until these safety concerns are clarified it cannot be recommended (The Royal College of Psychiatrists, 2007).

Summary of key points

- The changing nature and pattern of addictive behaviours and the emergence of eco-smart psychoactive substances require a flexible service provision and delivery in responding to the needs of the addicted person.
- Models of Care for Alcohol Misusers (MoCAM) identify four main categories of alcohol misusers who may benefit from some kind of intervention or treatment.
- The focus of service provisions and interventions including harm reduction approaches in reducing the risk of immediate death due to overdose and risks of morbidity and mortality due to blood-borne viruses and other infections.
- Studies on the effectiveness of treatment interventions show that treatment can help those with addictive behaviours to stop using psychoactive substances, avoid relapse, and maintain their new lifestyle and behaviours.
- Pharmacotherapy plays a key role in the effective treatment of addictive behaviours combined with psychological and social interventions.
- The framework for delivering psychosocial interventions is based on the notion of an adequate assessment of health and social care needs.
- The aims of psychosocial interventions are to: provide psychological support, enhance motivation, prevent relapse; help to address social problems (for example, family problems, housing and employment).
- The Social Interventions Model engages the interaction between the internal experience of the individual and networks and communities in which they live.

- Complementary therapies can be of great value in substance misuse services by increasing the options for care.
- Its most popular construct has been the Stages of Change, which reflects the temporal dimension of health behaviour change and involves emotions, cognitions, and behaviour.
- The Transtheoretical Model construes change as a process involving progress through a series of six stages: precontemplation, contemplation, action, maintenance, termination or relapse.

Reflective activity 18.1

- Identify four main categories of alcohol misuser who may benefit from some kind of intervention or treatment.
- List the various statutory, non-statutory and voluntary agencies in the provision and delivery of services for those with addiction problems.
- Discuss the principles of intervention strategies.
- What are the aims of pharmacological interventions?
- What are the principles of psychosocial interventions?
- Describe briefly one model of change that is applicable in understanding addictive behaviours.
- Discuss briefly the use of complementary therapies in addiction treatment.

References

Cook, S., Moeschler, O., Michaud, K. and Yersin, B. (1998) 'Acute Opiate Overdose: Characteristics of 190 Consecutive Cases', *Addiction* 93, 1559–65.

Copello, A.G., Templeton, l. and Velleman, R. (2006) 'Family Interventions for Drug and Alcohol Misuse: Is There a Best Practice?' *Current Opinion in Psychiatry* 19, 3, 271–76.

Department of Health (England) and the devolved administrations (2007) *Drug Misuse and Dependence: UK Guidelines on Clinical Management* (London: Department of Health (England), the Scottish Government, Welsh Assembly Government and Northern Ireland Executive).

Department of Health (2009) A *Guide to Good Practice in the Pharmacological Management of Substance Misuse Treatment of Young People* (London: Crown Copyright). www.dh.gov.uk/publications.

Grant, J.E. and Won Kim, S. (2006) 'Medication Management of Pathological Gambling', *Minnesota Medicine*, 89, 9, 44–48.

McDonald, L. and Rassool, G.H. (1997) *Complementary Therapies in Addiction Nursing Practice*, in Rassool, G.H. and Gafoor, M. (eds.), *Addiction Nursing: Perspectives on Professional and Clinical Practice* (Cheltenham: Nelson Thornes).

McLellan, A.T., Wood, G.E., Metzger, D.S., McKay, J. and Altermanv, A.I. (1997) 'Evaluating the Effectiveness of Addiction Treatments: Reasonable Expectations, Appropriate Comparisons', in Egerton, J.A., Fox, D.M. and Leshner, A.I. (eds.), *Treating Drug Abusers Effectively* (Oxford: Blackwell Publications).

NASADAD (2010) Traditional, Alternative, or Complementary Therapies in Addiction Treatment (Tatac) Report: National and State Profiles, http://www.nasadad.org/index.php?base_id 5 99, date accessed 12 March 2010.

National Treatment Agency (2002) *Models of Care for Adult Drug Misusers, Parts 1 and 2* (London: NTA Publications).

National Treatment Agency (2005) *Roles and Responsibilities of Doctors in the Provision of Treatment for Drug and Alcohol Misusers* (London: NTA Publications).

National Treatment Agency (2006a) *Models of Care for Adult Drug Misusers Updated* (London: NTA Publications).

National Treatment Agency (2006b) *Treating Drug Misuse Problems: Evidence of Effectiveness* (London: NTA Publications).

National Treatment Agency (2006c) *Review of the Effectiveness of Treatment for Alcohol Problems* (London: NTA Publications).

National Treatment Agency (2007) *Models of Care for Alcohol Misusers* (London: NTA Publications).

NIDA (2009) *Principles of Drug Addiction Treatment: A Research-Based Guide* (Bethesda, Maryland: National Institute on Drug Abuse, National Institutes of Health, US Department of Health and Human Services), NIH Publication No. 09–4180.

Poznyak, V., Saraceno, B. and Obot, I.S. (2005) 'Breaking the Vicious Circle of Determinants and Consequences of Alcohol Use', *Bulletin of the World Health Organization*, 83, 11, 801–80.

Prendergast, M.L., Podus, D., Chang, E. and Urada, D. (2002) 'The Effectiveness of Drug Abuse Treatment: a Meta Analysis of Comparison Group Studies', *Drug and Alcohol Dependence* 67, 1, 53–72.

Prochaska, J.O. and DiClemente, C.C. (1984) 'Self-change Processes, Self-efficacy and Decisional Balance Across Five Stages of Smoking Cessation', in Engstrom, P.F., Anderson, P.N. and Mortenson, L.E. (eds.), *Advances in Cancer Control – 1983* (New York: Alan R. Liss, Inc.).

Prochaska, J.O. and DiClemente, C.C. (1986) *Towards a comprehensive model of change*, in Miller, W.R. and Heather, N. (eds.), *Treating addictive behaviors: processes of change* (New York: Plenum).

Prochaska, J.O., DiClemente, C.C. and Norcross, J.C. (1992) 'In Search of How People Change', *American Psychologist* 47, 9, 1102–14.

Prochaska, J.O. and Velicer, W.K. (1997) 'The Trans-theoretical Model of Health Behaviour Change', *American Journal of Health Promotion* 12, 1, 38–48.

Pulse (2008) *GPs Take Growing Role in Drug Misuse Fight*, http://www.pulsetoday. co.uk/story.asp?storycode 5 4120114, date accessed 10 January 2010.

Rassool, G.H. (2009) *Alcohol and Drug Misuse: A Handbook for Students and Health Professionals* (Oxford: Routledge).

Roth, A.D. and Pilling, S. (2007) *The Competences Required to Deliver Effective Cognitive and Behavioural Therapy for People with Depression and with Anxiety Disorders* (London: Department of Health).

Ryan, J.M. and Spronken, I. (2000) 'Drug Related Deaths in the Community: A Preventive Role for Accident and Emergency Departments?' *Journal of Accident and Emergency Medicine,* 17, 4, 272–73.

Sbaih, L. (1993) 'Accident and Emergency Work', *Journal of Advanced Nursing* 18, 6, 957–62.

Task Force to Review Services for Drug Misusers (1996) *Report of an Independent Survey of Drug Treatment Services in England* (London: HMSO for the Department of Health).

The Royal College of Psychiatrists (2007) *Complementary and Alternative Medicines* (London: RCP) http://www.rcpsych.ac.uk/mentalhealthinfoforall/treatments/ complementarytherapy.aspx#add, date accessed 10 March 2010.

Tober, G. and Raistrick, D. (2007) 'Psychosocial Interventions', *Psychiatry,* 6, 1, 1–4.

Waller, I. and Weiler, D. (1984) *Crime Prevention Through Social Development* (Ottawa: Canadian Council on Social Development).

Index